Know Thy Roots

Know Thy Roots

Poornavad Way of Divine Life

DR T.P. DESHPANDE

An imprint of HarperCollins *Publishers*

First published in India by Harper Vantage 2025
An imprint of HarperCollins *Publishers*
HarperCollins *Publishers* India, 4th Floor, Tower A, Building No. 10,
DLF Cyber City, DLF Phase II, Gurugram, Haryana – 122002
www.harpercollins.co.in

2 4 6 8 10 9 7 5 3 1

Copyright © Dr T.P. Deshpande 2025

P-ISBN: 978-93-6989-211-2
E-ISBN: 978-93-6213-850-7

The views and opinions expressed in this book are the author's own and the facts are as reported by him, and the publishers are not in any way liable for the same.

Dr T.P. Deshpande asserts the moral right
to be identified as the author of this work.

All rights reserved. No part of this publication may be reproduced, stored in a retrieval system, or transmitted, in any form or by any means, electronic, mechanical, photocopying, recording or otherwise, without the prior permission of the publishers.

Without limiting the exclusive rights of any author, contributor or the publisher of this publication, any unauthorized use of this publication to train generative artificial intelligence (AI) technologies is expressly prohibited. HarperCollins also exercise their rights under Article 4(3) of the Digital Single Market Directive 2019/790 and expressly reserve this publication from the text and data-mining exception.

Typeset in 11.5/15.5 Minion Pro at
HarperCollins *Publishers* India

Printed and bound at
Thomson Press (India) Ltd

This book is produced from independently certified FSC® paper
to ensure responsible forest management.

HarperCollins Publishers, Macken House, 39/40 Mayor Street Upper,
Dublin 1, D01 C9W8, Ireland

*In memory of my wife, Dr Shobha Deshpande,
who accompanied me in all my academic and research activities.
And to my loving family—
Geeta, Hemant, Shampa, Tushar, Anand, Mandavi, Rajat, Riya, Trisha,
Ishita and Mahima*

Contents

Why Read This Book	ix
About the Cover Page	xi
Foreword I	xiii
Foreword II	xx
Foreword III	xxi
Introduction	xxiii
1. Guru: The Key to Transcendence	1
2. God as a Scientific Concept	5
3. India and Its Rich Heritage of Sanskrit and the Vedas	9
4. Jesus Christ: Scholar of Sanskrit and the Vedas, and the Impact of the Vedas on Buddhism	19
5. Jesus Christ's Questions Answered within Dr Parnerkar's Form-Relation Theory	25
6. Genome Chart of Poorna Purusha: Supreme Lord	28
7. Supreme Lord of the Universe: Poorna Purusha	33
8. Supreme Lord of the Corporate Universe	54

9. Maya: Nature of the Material World	62
10. Avidya: Knowledge of the Material Science	82
11. Parabrahman: Lord of the Infinite Universe	112
12. Vedanta Philosophy	120
13. Poornavad's and Vedic Science	123
14. Moksha: Liberation	143
15. Fear of Death	156
16. Aum: Powerful Mantra of Immortality	162
17. The Dream of a Universal Religion	169
18. Waves of Bliss	183
19. Divine Experiences in Worship	192
20. Mother	213
21. Some Closing Thoughts: On Literature, Life, Philosophy and Poornavad	216
Acknowledgements	229
Bibliography	231

Why Read This Book

1. To think about life in totality.
2. To think about mind and matter as one reality.
3. To learn the art of living life with discretion.
4. For total control over mind and how to act promptly.
5. To live life with a pleasant approach and to be intentional with your actions.
6. To decrease the fear of death from mind.
7. To show that philosophical and worldly life go hand-in-hand.
8. To live the invaluable span between birth and death with enthusiasm and a pro-conflict-management attitude.
9. To maintain the intensity of living life, and to celebrate every moment.
10. To undertake the penance of development of mind through gracefulness.
11. To synchronize the mind with the times.
12. To demonstrate good thoughts and deeds in tune with the times.
13. To learn why Poornavad is an ideal blend of knowledge, action, meditation and worship.
14. To face conflict squarely.
15. To convince learned, knowledgeable and philosophical thinkers about the truth of this modern interpretation of ancient Vedic literature.

16. To learn the six-faceted practice of:
    (i) Efficiency
    (ii) Planning
    (iii) Public opinion
    (iv) Public rapport
    (v) Awareness of time
    (vi) Worship and meditation
17. To gain motivation to subjugate vice and the dominance of thought.
18. To understand the importance of Aum.
19. To be blessed with the grace of the Supreme Lord.
20. To learn the contemplation of wisdom.
21. To learn the importance of worship and meditation for understanding the perception and the grace of God.

About the Cover Page

श्रीभगवानुवाच।
ऊर्ध्वमूलमधःशाखमश्वत्थं प्राहुरव्ययम्।
छन्दांसि यस्य पर्णानि यस्तं वेद स वेदवित्।।

shrī-bhagavān uvācha
ūrdhva-mūlam adhaḥ-śhākham aśhvatthaṁ prāhur avyayam
chhandānsi yasya parṇāni yas taṁ veda sa veda-vit
(Bhagavad Gita 15.1)

R OOTS UP and branches down: It indicates that although we think the roots of our thoughts are deep in the ground, in reality, the roots of our thoughts lie in the whole universe. It indicates that today's life is more controversial than what we think; reality is more adverse than the truth.

The Tree is the symbol of Knowledge and it indicates that Knowledge is beyond routine. The Vedas inspire us to think differently. Moreover, 'roots up and branches down' stipulates that for followers of the Vedic tradition, the fruits are within the reach of their hand. After the attainment of ultimate truth, one can get the fruits of this tree easily because of the downward nature of these branches. The whole universe is made up of thoughts, and reality is more beautiful than our imagination.

The reason for calling it Aswattha (the bodhi tree) is that it does not remain the same the next day, and we can always expect continuous change. In this world also, every moment, new jeevas (beings) take birth while others die. The form undergoes continuous growth. Therefore, it is called Aswattha, after the sacred tree, as trees change form with the seasons. Our biological and physical structure too changes form every moment; changes come and go and come again; it's an ongoing cycle of change. So, this is an endless process. Therefore, the Vedas have their own scientific reasoning behind every moment and are confident that life is also an endless process, indicating there is life after life.

The tree on the cover is the divine Vedic Aswattha Tree, under which sages of the Vedic tradition got the Supreme Knowledge and realization of Ultimate Truth and Reality. It is under the same tree that Lord Gautam Buddha realized the knowledge of Nirvana and in Buddhism, it is known as the Bodhi Tree.

Under the same tree, in 1948, Dr R.P. Parnerkar received the Supreme Knowledge of the doctrine of Form Relation (instead of causal relations) between the Lord and the World. He explained the doctrine of Poornavad with reference from Vedic hymns.

Foreword I

I HAVE GREAT pleasure in writing this foreword for the book, *Know Thy Roots*, by Dr T.P. Deshpande, which is the outcome of his lifelong research on the Philosophy of Poornavad founded by Dr Ramchandra Parnerkar Maharaj. The book in detail speaks about the importance of divine life as expounded in the Indian philosophical tradition and culture. Thus, the book explains the role of the Indian value system and heritage which has to be reinterpreted in the present-day world. The book also draws parallels between Indian and Western thinking and also different religious traditions of the world, showing the significance of Indian tradition, keeping Poornavad as the backdrop.

I am aware that both Dr Deshpande and late Dr Shobha Deshpande are committed to the philosophy of Poornavad, and consider it a way of life. Both of them followed Parnerkar's philosophy in their life and successfully spread the message of Poornavad philosophy. Like the countless number of devotees and followers of the Poornavad school of philosophy, Deshpande's life-long journey with Poornavad philosophy is exhibited in this excellent work. I congratulate him for this wonderful work, which is the synthesis of philosophy, literature, heritage, and human values. Deshpande's wide knowledge of Indian culture and values are exhibited throughout the book and this book definitely is a contribution to knowledge.

India being a great nation, consists of rich tradition of ethical values and cultural background, will always see the means and the end together. India is a country where there is a plurality of cultures. It always appreciates each and every culture whether it is small or big, giving each culture its due. Culture adapts itself to the situation. It considers the changes that are taking place outside. It is slow but steady. Culture unites men into one cultural group. Culture and tradition carry the values to the future generation and hence these values of it must be preserved.

It is necessary that we must re-examine our intellectual heritage and tradition in the light of our present situation. Tradition is always hermeneutical and accommodates new interpretation and understanding. This reconstruction means reconstructing the present categories of knowledge. Man's mode of being-in-the world helps a person to evaluate the tradition. It is not possible for a person simply to follow the tradition, but he has the right to evaluate the tradition. The world of historicity will have an impact on the tradition and it accepts evaluation and reinterpretation. This does not mean that we are revolting against traditions, but that we are interpreting them in the context of present historicity. The cultural world to which one belongs, allows a radical interpretation of the tradition. This sort of interpretation teaches a way of looking at the tradition afresh from a new perspective, which will suit for our present situation, and this explains how a particular person is placed in the surrounding world or tradition, though his physical world is supported by scientific and technological society. Every man is placed in a tradition or culture, which cannot be avoided.

Objectivity and intersubjectivity play important role in the cultural traditions of India. The Poornavad philosophy emphasizes the need for understanding the 'other'. There is always the place and acceptance of the other. In one of the programmes at Nanded during the celebrations of Poornavad, I could see a very large gathering, where there was an interpersonal understanding and a commitment among people since Parnerkar Maharaj has given them a new way of understanding 'life'. This perhaps is one of the reasons why large numbers of people were attracted to Poornavad and I could witness the love and affection the common man had for Ramchandra Parnerkar and [his son and successor] Vishnu

Maharaj Parnerkar. 'Dialogue' is a method which Parnerkar Maharaj has used in his philosophical discourses.

There is a benefit in this process of dialogue. In my dialogue with others, I take the responsibility for rational persuasion by which I try to understand and interact with others. In other words, in my dialogue with others, two things are taking place: (i) I persuade others; and (ii) I am also persuaded by others. Therefore, while dialoguing with others, I make certain claims and they become not only my claims but are claims made for the sake of others. In the life-world, it is the communicative action, which plays a significant role. Only in the context of life-world there is narrative presentation of events, which makes the self-understanding possible and acceptable. Here, one can think of Professor R. Sundara Rajan's (i) distantiating; and (ii) participatory modes of thinking. In the former, the object is held at a distance, there is a dissociation of the self from the object and the bond between them is replaced by a spectational mode of understanding, whereas in the latter there is a fellowship with the other. There is an interior or indwelling understanding of the object.[1] There is always 'a fellowship with other' that is practiced in the teachings of Parnerkar Maharaj. This is the uniqueness of Indian culture, tradition and philosophy.

In the Poornavad philosophy of life, understanding of culture is ever new and always creative. This must be done to preserve the culture to which we belong. Parnerkar Maharaj could do this very successfully, because what he has preached and practiced is simple and it could reach the common man. This was possible by participatory understanding of the tradition and culture. 'When people understand meanings by participating in a life-form, their participation can never be complete or total, ensuring unanimity in their understanding of the concerned cluster of meanings,' says Professor D.P. Chattopadhyaya.[2] This is also

---

1   Sundara Rajan, R. (1986), *Innovative Competence and Social Change*. Pune: Indian Quarterly Publications, University of Pune.
2   Chattopadhyaya, D.P. (1992), 'Reflections on Papers' in D.P. Chattopadhyaya, Lester Embree & J.N. Mohanty (eds.) *Phenomenology and Indian Philosophy*. New Delhi: Indian Council of Philosophical Research, p. 364.

supported by Professor Margaret Chatterjee who says as follows: 'The participation-understanding of a live tradition may be partial; it may show differences from the participant understanding of an earlier generation, but it would illustrate neither "distancing" nor fusion of horizons, but a continuity which would accommodate both change and encapsulation of the experience of earlier generations.'[3] Professor Kireet Joshi very rightly traces the cultural roots of India in Vedic tradition as follows:

> The earliest preoccupation of India, as expressed in the Veda, was the exploration of the Spirit in Matter and of Matter in Spirit; the intermediate preoccupation was with the seeking and experiment in a thousand ways of the soul's outermost and innermost experience marked by various conflicts and even exclusive affirmations and denials under an overarching tendency towards multi-sided development of the spiritual, ethical, intellectual, aesthetic, vital and physical parts of the being and some kind of synthesis.[4]

The book by Dr Deshpande is an attempt to understand the divine way of life as expounded in the philosophy of Poornavad. Some of the chapters are thought-provoking and innovative, explaining the special significance of Indian heritage and culture and tradition. While discussing the significance of the Vedanta school of thought, Dr Deshpande shows the significance of Sankara, Ramanuja, Madhva and other Acharyas. The uniqueness of the book is that it shows the importance of universal religion. I am happy that Dr Deshpande has explained the role of universal religion in the contemporary world. In

---

[3] Chatterjee, Margaret (1992), 'Towards a Hermeneutic of Centrality in Indian Art', in D.P. Chattopadhyaya, Lester Embree & J.N. Mohanty (eds.) *Phenomenology and Indian Philosophy*, p.337.

[4] Joshi, Kireet (1996), 'Significance of the Veda in Indian Religion and Spirituality', in *Science, Philosophy and Culture*, part-I, ed. D.P. Chattopadhyaya & Ravinder Kumar. New Delhi: PHISPC in association with ICPR, p. 175.

the philosophy of Swami Vivekananda and Dr S. Radhakrishnan, the concept of 'universal religion' has attained a special place. Keeping these great thinkers at the backdrop, Dr Deshpande is trying to argue how the Poornavad philosophy also seeks the establishment of universal religion, thus proving that Parnerkar Maharaj is a contemporary philosopher.

The title of the book, i.e., 'Know Thy Roots', is very interesting and it has lot of implications in present-day society. Dr Deshpande, by quoting the Bhagavad Gita (15.1), explains the importance of a description of a tree in which the 'roots are up and branches down'. The asvattha (peepul) tree, it is argued by Dr Deshpande, does not remain the same the next day as there is a continuous change. It does not remain the same till tomorrow. Dr Deshpande compares the tree with human beings who take birth and face death, and there is always a continuous growth in life. The Upanishads make use of this primordial symbol of the tree in order to convey the sense of rootedness of the entire universe, which includes both animate and inanimate. The *Katha Upanishad* (2.3.1) says: 'This is the beginningless asvattha tree that has its roots above and branches below. That (which is its root) is pure, i.e., Brahman, and it is immortal. On that (Brahman) are fixed all the worlds. None transcends that. This, verily, is that.' (Dr Deshpande says that it is necessary for us to trace the roots and our roots are our own tradition. A tree cannot exist without the root. A rootless tree will not be alive. The symbol of a tree suggests that a person should be rooted in the spiritual tradition which has shaped and sustained him.

Dr Deshpande is trying to show how there is a continuation of Indian tradition from the Vedic times up to the present. Great thinkers have taken care to preserve this tradition and it is passed from generation to generation. Dr Deshpande is of the view that Parnerkar Maharaj preserves the tradition and by giving a new interpretation to the ancient texts, he not only conveys the message available in our Indian tradition, but also gives a new interpretation which is necessary for human life. In the Western tradition, we use the term 'hermeneutics' to explain this.

In contemporary philosophy, hermeneutics plays an important role as the study of interpretation of scriptures. It teaches the rules regarding the way to handle and interpret the scriptures. In one way, hermeneutics is an attempt to mediate meaning expressed in one context to another.

Poornavad philosophy is a philosophy of values. According to Parnerkar Maharaj, values are nothing but reality, and not external to Being. Value and reality coincide in Brahman, which is the final value as well as the ultimate reality. The ontological status of this value of reality cannot be described in terms of predicates borrowed from the world of existence. The triad of values, *viz.*, Goodness, Beauty and Truth are important to human beings. Gadamer in his book, *Truth and Method*, tries to refound the notions of tradition and heritage to discover its real nature and foundation.[5] This revival of tradition is the most important aspect for Gadamer and also for Parnerkar Maharaj. According to Parnerkar Maharaj, one can understand the value and importance of tradition and heritage by living with other persons.

Parnerkar Maharaj, like Acharya Sankara, has a very high respect for tradition. In fact, he emphasizes the traditional way of looking at things and associates himself with the long line of Vedic seers, though 'distanciated' by time. But in insisting upon tradition, he does not forget that no generation can merely produce its ancestors. Both for Sankara and Parnerkar Maharaj, tradition is life and movement and perpetual reinterpretation. It must be remembered that the power of the Rishis, who intuited the Vedas and Upanishads, ought not be measured by our capabilities.

While discussing the philosophy of Poornavad which speaks of 'inclusiveness', Dr Deshpande examines different schools of Vedanta. His approaches to Sankara and Ramanuja are refreshing. Both Sankara and Ramanuja as great creative thinkers reinterpreted the philosophical ideas and themes according to the need of the age. Radhakrishnan, while writing about the age and background of Sankara, states that

---

5   Gadamer, Hans-Georg (2013), *Truth and Method*, New Delhi: Bloomsbury India Pvt. Ltd. First published in 1960 in German.

the age needed a religious genius who was unwilling to break with the past and yet was open to the good influences of the new creeds; one who could stretch the old moulds without breaking them and synthesize the warring sects on a broad basis of truth, which would have room for all men of all grades of intelligence and culture. Sankara, as a model and exemplar of tradition, always appreciated the values and importance of tradition and heritage. Similarly, Ramanuja in his interpretation of the *prasthāna-traya* (discussed below) adopts the phenomenological method, to use Western terminology. In the phenomenology of Ramanuja, the world is not unreal or illusory as in the case of Poornavad. This means the role of the world cannot be neglected. The world plays an important role in understanding the nature of Brahman. It is bhakti, which is practiced in empirical life that helps the individual self to understand the Supreme nature of Vishnu. Thus, the philosophy in Ramanuja is empirical in nature and by admitting the existence of plurality of selves, the 'everydayness' is purposeful and meaningful.

Ramanuja's philosophy is the philosophy of inclusiveness. The same thing can be said about the Poornavad Philosophy, because it includes everything and nothing exists outside. The fundamental doctrine of Poornavad is explained in the following maxim: 'Poornattva (All Completeness) only is the Absolute Pure Truth, Supreme God.' Parnerkar Maharaj, as the founder of Poornavad school of thought, by teaching practical Vedanta has given a new direction to humanity. The tradition of 'Poornavad', I am sure will reach the corners of the country and pave the way for the unity of mankind. I appreciate the effort of Dr Deshpande in this direction and with the blessings of Dr Ramachandra Parnerkar Maharaj and Dr Vishnu Ramachandra Parnerkar Maharaj, the message of 'Poornavad philosophy' will reach the entire globe to make it a perfect home for all.

Prof. S. Panneerselvam
Former Professor and Head, Department of Philosophy,
University of Madras, Chennai;
General Secretary, Indian Philosophical Congress

Foreword II

Dr PARNERKAR'S Form Relation theory of Poornavad introduced the Vedic system of science, which explains how the world is complete and autonomous in itself, and the vedic concept of God is environmental which worships the God in the form of Sun—The Solar; Agni—The Fire; Varuna—The Rain; Vayu—The Air, and Bhumi—The Planet Earth; to maintain the environmental balance, therefore, the book *Know Thy Roots* became a matter of investigation and research.

Dr Shailendra Deolankar,
Expert, External Affairs Policy of India;
Director of Higher Education, Maharashtra government

Foreword III

Although I am a scientist, I am always interested in the larger picture of life and living—the connection between the inner and outer world. I am also interested in creating links between the old and the new, the traditional and the modern, with an open mind. The creation of a Traditional Knowledge Digital Library after a battle with the US Patent Office on the wrong patent on turmeric that I fought is a classic example.

In that context, I view this book by Dr T. P. Deshpande as one that gives a unique and enlightened view of the world around us. This book is a scholarly treatment of the significance of Poornavad, which gives a holistic view of life with the study of the Vedas and Upanishads. It has a bigger message of harmonious living among members of society, which is much needed in the modern world today.

I want to congratulate Dr Deshpande for venturing into the scientific three-dimensional vision of the Vedas, which was introduced by the legendary Dr Ramchandra Maharaj Parnerkar. He beautifully articulates the applied dimensions of the Vedas in this this truly scholarly and insightful book—a wonderful gift to the society.

Raghunath Mashelkar,
FRS, Padma Vibhushan
Formerly: Director General, Council of Scientific & Industrial Research
Secretary, Department of Scientific & Industrial Research, Govt. of India
President, Indian National Science Academy; Chairman, National Innovation Foundation; President, Global Research Alliance; Member, Science Advisory Council to Prime Minister; National Research Professor

Introduction

For the first time in the history of philosophy, five-thousand years after the end of the Mahabharata War, an optimistic and scientific three-dimensional vision of the Vedas has been presented by Dr Parnerkar through his Form–Relation theory on the true nature of God, as part of the Poornavad doctrine. Among the many things that attract the human mind, are two great mysteries—one is the universe, and the other is energy which further motivates the universe. Our physical and psychological mindset is knowingly or unknowingly linked to this dynamic universe, which is the subject matter of modern physics, but is sometimes linked to Eastern mysticism too. This book sheds light on both realities, through the Poornavad Philosophy, a modern reinterpretation of the transitional vedic philosophy.

Poornavad philosophy discusses how to balance traditional Vedic teachings into our dynamic 21st century lives, to achieve harmonic and holistic existence. The techniques and teachings presented by the Poornavad philosophy, help one manifest their goals and desires through vedic traditions.

Western thinkers restricted the knowledge, by only accepting material evidence whereas vedic knowledge starts from trust, faith, intuition and mainly tacit knowledge and intuitional experiences. This is why they were debunked because it did not fit the evidence model of Western thinkers.

In line with this, some contemporary philosophy has become irrelevant today, and this has been a discussion point at several national and international seminars and conferences for a while now. But no efforts have been made to shape it or to make it relevant. Philosophy is the need of secular intellectuals across the world; philosophy that doesn't discriminate between the East and the West. The Vedas say that you should choose whatever is the best, no matter where it comes from.

आ नो भद्राः क्रतवो यन्तु विश्वतः

ā no bhadrāḥ kratavo yantu viśvataḥ
—*Rig Veda* 1.89.1

[Let the noble thoughts come from any side.]

In the 1960s and 70s, French philosopher Jacques Derrida along with Jürgen Habermas, German philosopher and social theorist started the deconstruction movement in Europe.[1] They proposed to show how the metaphysical definitions of 'being'—as such timeless self-identity of presence, which dominated Western philosophy from Plato, Aristotle to Marx, Hagel and to the present day—could ultimately be deconstructed. In deconstructing the pre-supposition of Western philosophy, Derrida offered a serious and constructive nomenclature. The movement then spread all over the world influencing world literature and philosophy.

Two decades before this, Dr Parnerkar had already started a deconstruction movement in India in 1948. Born into an orthodox priestly Brahman family, Dr Parnerkar went on to deconstruct Vedanta philosophy. The Vedas, though timeless, seemed to have become irrelevant in the modern perspective. He also studied different schools of thought—Dual, Un-Dual, Monism, the Vedas, the anti-Vedas; right from Bhagavad Gita, to Buddhism, Jainism, Charvak and many others.

---

1 Deconstruction, https://www.studysmarter.co.uk/explanations/english-literature/literary-criticism-and-theory/deconstruction/#:~:text=Deconstruction%20is%20a%20critical%20theory,underlying%20meanings%20in%20a%20text.

Interestingly, all mentioned the Vedas. After a thorough in-depth investigation, Dr Parnerkar came to the conclusion that everybody was right, but only partially; they stated the partial truth. All of them had applied the cause-and-effect theory to prove their doctrine. Dr Parnerkar also observed that while Eastern and Western scientists had accepted the world as 'effect', the Vedas did not. None of them could determine the cause with certitude and as such, each philosophy had to accept agnosticism. For instance, in reply to what is ignorance or Maya, Shree Shankaracharya replied it was beyond human intellect to explain. Is this not agnosticism? But Dr Parnerkar found no agnosticism in the Vedas.

Identifying cause and its effect is not all that difficult. But assuming the world as the 'effect' and going after its causality, will certainly lead to the same fate as that of the philosophies discussed hitherto. Any serious scholar of philosophy would have to definitely concede that none of the philosophies till date, having assumed the world as an 'effect', have been able to unravel its 'cause' somewhere or the other. Human intellect has had to surrender or espouse agnosticism, but why so? To this, Poornavad has just one reply: Treating "form" as "effect" sends you in the wrong direction. Therefore, no wonder that all further calculations went wrong because of this digression. In Dr. Parnekar's words, 'It is the error of intellect or the error in data.'[2]

The doctrine of Poornavad lays down the form relation of the Shiva-element, the Vishnu-element and the Vishwa-element with the Poorna Purusha—as forms that are parts of Him—as is contained in Vedas. And just as in the Vedas, Poornavad emphasizes equally the role of all the three 'means' i.e., knowledge, action and worship to attain one's goal. The Poornavad doctrine sets forth that none of these three means are inferior; neither can a single one alone serve the purpose. All three elements have a Form-Relation with the Poorna Purusha and such being the doctrine of Poornavad, nothing exists outside of Poorna Purusha. So, everything is in the Poorna Purusha. Of course, needless to say that each

---

2 Personal interview with the present successor of the school of Poornavad philosophy, Dr. V.R Parnerkar.

one of the three (Shiva, Vishnu and Vishwa) has complete non-duality with (i.e., is part of and not apart from) Poorna Purusha and therefore, it can be stated that Poornavad is a three-dimensional Vedic philosophy.

In an international conference hosted by the Council for Research in Values and Philosophy (RVP)in the United States (US), the Poornavad delegation was asked, 'How can you accommodate controversial theories like Gaudapadacharya's Ajatwad, Shankaracharya's Mayavad, Ramanuja's Vishisht Advaitvad, etc.?' The reply was, 'The whole universe along with our life too is full of controversy, controversy is a part of our life. Poornavad is parallel to modern physics, therefore, it accepts that every particle has an antiparticle, which is the nature of the universe. Controversy becomes a part of life.' Poornavad states that the 'Poorna' means the whole universe, the manifest and unmanifest, which contain these controversies like good and bad, bright and dark, beautiful and ugly, divine and devil, life and death, success and failure; everything comes under the Poorna—the whole Universe is controversial. Remember, the Virat Darshan of Purusha in the Gita.' Indeed His 'Vishwaroop' that Lord Krishna revealed to Arjuna, was nothing but the material representation of the universe.

The Form–Relation theory of the Poornavad doctrine is based on *Ishavasya Upanishad* and the *Rig Veda*. The preamble Sukta (hymn) of *Ishavasya Upanishad* states:

ॐ पूर्णमदः पूर्णमिदं पूर्णात्पूर्णमुदच्यते।
पूर्णस्य पूर्णमादाय पूर्णमेवावशिष्यते।।२१।।

oṁ pūrṇam adaḥ pūrṇam idaṁ pūrṇāt pūrṇam udacyate
pūrṇasya pūrṇam ādāya pūrṇam evāvaśiṣyate

[That is Whole, this is Whole; from the Whole, the Whole becomes manifest. From the Whole, when the Whole is negated, what remains is again the Whole.][3]

---

3 https://vedantastudents.com/wp-content/uploads/2018/10/08-Isavasya-Upanishad-Versewise.pdf.

Once we accept the world and universe are forms that are parts of (intrinsic to) the Poorna Purusha form, and not the effect of any external cause we realize that this is a case of the cause being the effect. The cause and the effect are not separate. This Form-Relation theory has parallels in modern physics. Dr Parnerkar is a scholar of Sanskrit and the Vedas, and has studied the modern sciences too. His Form-Relation theory is at the heart of the Poornavad doctrine based on the Vedas.

The world is Poorna, i.e., complete, entire, full, whole. Dr Parnerkar says that the entire world, the un-manifest universe, and the manifest material universe is One, and moreover these are inseparable interrelated entities as this world is three dimensional. The Vedas called this 'One', the 'Purusha', the personified form of the entire universe. Poornavad calls it the 'Poorna Purusha'.

There is a common human tendency to visualize everything, but how can you visualize the entire universe? Therefore, the Vedas personified the universe as Purusha. Every religion says that God is everywhere, but none have described him in a manner that can be visualized or imagined by everyone. If we refer to the 'Purusha Sukta' of the RigVeda, which describes and defines the concept of God in a scientific and secular way we understand why the RigVeda says Purusha is Poorna (see Chapter 6, 'Genome of Poorna Purusha: Supreme Lord'). As Chapter 6 will show, 'Poorna Purusha' is a concept that can be scientifically proven too.

The Purusha concept is related to 'vidya' (True Knowledge) and the God-Ishwar concept is related to avidya (knowledge of the material world). For the common man, an understanding of how to master the science of practical life is vital. In practical life, we look to the divine for our material needs and as a strong supporter in times of need. The Purusha concept is related to such 'vidya', i.e., one which provides us with such knowledge.

Another reference from the *Rig Veda* is:

सहस्रशीर्षा पुरुषः सहस्राक्षः सहस्रपात्।
स भूमिं विश्वतोवृत्वाऽत्यातिष्ठद्दशांगुलम्।।२।।

> sahasraśīrṣā puruṣaḥ sahasrākṣaḥ sahasrapāt
> sa bhūmiṃ viśvato vṛtvāty atiṣṭhad daśāṅgulam
> —*Rig Veda* 10.90.1
>
> [He who has thousand heads, thousand eyes, pervading the universe and the things and the knowledge therein, remains unfathomable. Such Purush is the God. We call him Ganapati, Shankar, Vishnu, the Supreme entity. Here in sanskrit, thousand (saharastra) means innumerous.][4]

Poornavad can be understood by understanding the *Rig-Vedic* system of science with its Sanskrit terminology, including word-concepts like 'idam' (literal meaning is 'this', but it refers to the manifested universe), and adah (literal meaning 'that', but it refers to the power experienced by the enlightened and evolved, which cannot be detected by material means). Naturally the nature of 'idam' and its relationship with 'adah' has become a subject of intense philosophical discussions, limiting ourselves to Eastern mysticism. We find that most of these philosophical discussions centre around the Upanishads and the Bhagavad Gita with occasional references to the Vedas.

It is often forgotten that the Vedas have never been literally understood, comprehensively and consistently. Hence, the references to the Vedas leave a lot of room for misrepresentation. One should be aware of the science of decoding the Vedas' Sanskrit hymns. This is the base for many philosophical interpretations. The interactive part of 'idam', the universe, is being studied by scientists, but science cannot say anything about 'adah' as it is non-material and non-interactive. Also, scientifically, modern understanding of the universe has yet to reach a point where we understand it completely or even to large extent. Our modern observations of the universe are limited and there are limitations to the experimentations. Therefore, it is not fair to make any comments from the modern scientific standpoint on 'idam'.

---

4 Poornavad, Dr. R.P Parnerkar.

However, Dr Parnerkar's Poornavad doctrine is consistent with the *Rig-Vedic* system of science and not modern science. Therefore, it can be said for Poornavad that no description of 'idam' can be complete without reference to 'adah', presenting a very pertinent question as to who created this universe; because in the interactive world something can be created only out of something.

The answer in the *Rig Veda* is that the interactive 'idam' or 'sat' (truth) was created out of non-interactive energy which the *Rig Veda* calls 'asat' (conscious). The 'sat' as well as the 'asat' are but different forms of the same entity called Purusha, which is the intuitional experience. Vedic research methodology relies on intuitional experiences while the Western research methodology relies on intellectual experiments, which has limitations as opposed to the field of intuitional experience which is wide and vast.

While quantum mechanical situations cannot be understood classically, it must be agreed that the Supreme Entity/Supreme Lord or 'adah' cannot be described, understood or put in mechanical terms. We can at best listen to the authority of the Vedas in the 'Purusha Sukta' from ancient scientists who were yet to discover the micro particle smaller than the neutrino, the God particle, the Higgs Boson.

पुरुषएवेदं सर्वं यद्भूतं यच्चभव्यम्।
उतामृतत्त्वस्येशानो यदन्नेनातिरोहति।।३।।

puruṣa evedaṃ sarvaṃ yad bhūtaṃ yac ca bhavyam
utāmṛtatvasyeśāno yad annenātirohati

—*Rig Veda* 10.90.2

[In this universe whatever has been created or can be created is all Purusha only. Purusha enters this world through anna (food) and still remains the same. By entering this universe, the Purusha is not divided. He is indivisible. In fact, all that exists is He only].[5]

---

5   Poornavad original text by Dr. R.P Parnerkar. English, second edition. 2017.

It may appear that the reference to 'anna' is meaningless. However, it is not so. 'Anna' or food is a suitable form of electromagnetic energy. This situation cannot be understood classically. (See the verses in Chapter 3 'Bhriguvalli' in the *Taittiriya Upanishad* that refer to '*anna vai Brahma*' i.e. 'Food is Brahman, Ultimate Reality').

Thus, the universe is not created by the Supreme Power but is 'Poorna' or Complete by the very nature of its creation. The *Ishavasya Upanishad* makes this *Rig-Vedic* concept amply clear. The universe is not needed for the existence of the Purusha, though the Purusha takes over the universe, in a unique way. Put in simple terms, if one imagines the removal of the universe, the Purusha remains unaffected. Scientifically speaking, the universe is complete in itself as there is nothing material beyond it. Thus, both idam/'this'/universe and adah/'that'/Supreme Lord are complete individually. We can think of the universe as another form of the adah. The universe can be likened to the ornamental form on the gold or to a wave on the sea.

The above suktas are parallel to with the Quantum Theory and Bootstrap Theory in modern physics. Dr David Bohm, who developed the mathematical theory of implicate order, wrote that quantum mechanics is widely accepted to be conceptually close to Eastern mysticism, which refers to the Vedas. The Vedas have their own system of science, of which mathematics is the backbone. Dr Bohm's theory speaks about the unbroken wholeness of the totality of existence as an undivided flowing movement without borders. This statement confirms Dr Parnerkar's Form–Relation Theory of the Poornavad doctrine.

Another scientist who went beyond quantum mechanics is Dr Geoffrey Chew. His bootstrap theory in physics propounds that nature is not an assemblage of individual entities but rather a dynamic web of interrelated events in which no part is more fundamental than any other part. This is parallel to the Poornavad doctrine's three elements: Shiva, Vishnu and Vishwa that are interrelated and inseparable. Each of the three carries equal importance and each is unparalleled.

The Doctrine of Poornavad

The main theme of this book elaborately deals with the significance of Poornavad, i.e., a complete holistic life with the study of the Vedas and Upanishads. The Poornavad philosophy teaches practical Vedanta and has significant relevance in the modern world. It also talks about members of society living harmoniously. The Poornavad philosophy does not reject the world, but recognizes its importance and shows how there should be a synthesis between theory and practice. The uniqueness of Poornavad is that it discusses how the Vedas and the Upanishads are relevant to our life. This makes Poornavad, practical Vedanta. Dr Parnerkar's contribution to contemporary Indian philosophy, has been great. He is among those important contemporary Indian philosophers who have reinterpreted the texts to suit the modern man.

The Poornavad philosophy can change individual and social life. In Poornavad, 'nothing exists outside'. Everything is included in it. It does not believe in a mere theoretical understanding of life, but gives a practical orientation to life. Man is said to be the combination of both matter and spirit. Dr Parnerkar states that we have discussed much on spirituality which is timeless today. In the philosophy of religion, material need becomes immaterial. Poornavad philosophy takes the human being to the higher plane of life, by maintaining the balance between knowledge, action and meditation, i.e., Upasana. This makes Poornavad philosophy more relevant to the twenty-first century by being a philosophical method that offers a guiding principle to life.

One of the great contributions made by Dr Parnerkar is his attempt to reinterpret the Vedas and Upanishads. This is the need of the hour and many contemporary thinkers like Swami Vivekananda, Sri Aurobindo, Tilak and many others have worked for the upliftment of man using reinterpretation as a mode of understanding the texts. No doubt, as a contemporary Indian Philosopher, Dr Parnerkar has also worked out a methodology in this direction, thus paving the way for liberation of the entire humanity. He is a synthesis of tradition and modernity. He is a great follower of the Indian tradition.

Dr Panneerselvam, General Secretary, Indian Philosophy Congress, says, "tradition is the finite unfolding of an infinite content, a history of finite actualization of an essentially inexhaustible, or infinite truth. To put the same in Gadamerian terms, it is 'inescapable facticity'. Every retelling of it is a renewal of the tradition. Our belongingness to tradition is our primordial ontological condition. Tradition is the locus of understanding. We are shaped by our past in various ways and this has a tremendous influence on our understanding. The past and the present are related and become a continuous process through tradition. In tradition, we think in our own concepts."[6]

Tradition is the tool which Dr Parnerkar applies for his understanding of the texts. Dr Parnerkar, although following the tradition since he comes in the great tradition of Sankara, Ramanuja and Madhva, deviates from Gaudapada or Sankara with regard to concepts like Maya or Ishwar. In this way one can say that Dr Parnerkar embraces modernity. Wherever necessary, he deviates from the orthodoxy to make the text more relevant to current humanity. His modern understanding of the Upanishads proves this. His methodology takes us to two further questions. They are: (i) What does the word 'modernity' mean?; (ii) Are tradition and modernity not irreconcilably opposed to each other? The answer is available in Dr Parnerkar's Poornavad.

The modern philosopher J.N. Mohanty says that if modernity means outright rejection of tradition, then of course, there is no promise of fruitful dialogue and mediation. There are two ways of understanding modernity. First, modernity consists in addressing oneself to what is contemporaneous. It is a contemporary ongoing dialogue. The second aspect is the idea of criticism. Tradition demands respect and continuity. Dr Parnerkar tries to understand modernity in this way. He addresses what is contemporaneous and also criticizes when the given interpretation by the predecessors is found unacceptable, thus making the tradition a living one.

---

6   'A Hermeneutical Reading of Indian Philosophy', Dr. S. Panneerselvam, Department of Philosophy, University of Madras, Chennai, www.vpmthane.org.

The Indian philosophical tradition is a commentarial tradition. Indian philosophical discourse has developed through the commentaries which are interpretational in nature. Following this, one can say that Dr Parnerkar, in his interpretation of the Vedas and Upanishads adopts the hermeneutic-analytical method. The *Prasthana Traya* is the source for Vedanta which rests on shruti, smriti, and tarka. Shruti refers to the hymns and verses from the Vedas and Upanishads. Smriti refers to the reinterpretation of those through further works, and tarka means logical reasoning or the Science of Logic. The Upanishads represent 'shrutiprasthana', the Bhagavad Gita represents 'smritiprasthana', and the *Brahmasutra* represents 'tarkaprasthana'. Prasthana Traya became the main source of Indian philosophical tradition. It has been narrated by Swami Yoganand in his *Autobiography of Yogi*.[7] The texts are connected with the commentaries or interpretation. The texts are expository and they are to be commented on. The role of interpreter starts here. The commentaries are as important as the texts. In fact, the commentaries do much more work than the texts, because sometimes the texts are not only brief, but also elliptical in nature. The interpreter, as a way of his commentary, explicitly analyses what the text says and interprets according to the need and the historical conditions. Thus, it is not a mere interpretation but an interpretation mingled with historicity.

It is inevitable for the interpreter or commentator to take into account his or her historical conditions and other factors. Thus, the text when it is written may have one goal or intention, but the commentator has to interpret the text taking into consideration various factors. Truthfully speaking, these factors which play a dominant role in interpretation are implicit in interpretation. The interpreter need not wait or search for historicity to operate on them, while interpreting a text. It is automatic. It is because historicity simply operates on while the interpreter simply exists in it. The interpreter not only understands the texts, but also presents them in a simplified way so that more people can have easy access to it. The text written by the author is not always

---

7   Marathi edition, 2019

elaborate and hence cannot pass the message to the reader; whereas the interpreter, who has a better understanding of the text, interprets and presents in a better way than that of the author. Thus the interpreter has a more important role to play than the author does. Here the author is transcended but not the text. In other words, the text becomes more meaningful in the hands of the interpreter.

As a great interpreter of Indian tradition, Dr Parnerkar explains the need for reinterpretation of the texts which is explained through the Poornavad philosophy. He reinterpreted the many Vedanta concepts like Parabrahman, Maya, Vidya, Avidya, Moksha and established the importance of Poorna.

The first chapter of the original text of Poornavad examines the philosophy of Poornavad in detail. It starts with the beginning of the first verse of the great book *Dnyaneshwari*.

ॐ नमोजी आद्या । वेद प्रतिपाद्या ।।
जय जय स्वसंवेद्या । आत्मरुपा ।।(अ. १)

Om namoji adya, Ved pratipadya
Jai Jai swasmvedya, Atmarupa

[I bow to the Primal, Supreme Being, whose existence is established by the Vedas. Victory, Victory to you, 'Om', self-sensitive Atman form.]

This verse pays obeisance to the Omkara. Like the Dnyaneshwari, Dr Parnerkar also offers his obeisance to the Omkara because it is Primordial and Primeval. The authority of expounding the Primeval form of Omkara lies with the Vedas. This Omkara is the Poorna Purusha's form. Dr Parnerkar explains how his philosophical and intellectual inquiry has been developed through the Vedas and the Upanishads. He states:[8]

---

8   'Heart to Heart', Poornavad, Parnerkar, 2017.

> My first acquaintance with philosophy was through the saint literature. With growing inquisitiveness, I turned to study the twelve *darshans* and the different schools of dualism, monism, etc. While studying with the best of my ability to comprehend, I realised that each one has relied on the *Shruti* to substantiate their argument and in the process created a diversity of opinions. Quite naturally, the foremost question that came to my mind was 'which one is the truth?' My intellect, or yours, may call it the logical reason, concluding that only one out of these must be the truth.

The above passage clearly shows how Dr Parnerkar has developed his philosophy of Poornavad on analysis and examination. This examination helped him to reach the truth namely the Supreme Truth can be revealed only by the study of the Vedas. Thus, he made a thorough study of the Vedas and Upanishads The result, he says, is quite contrary to what he had imagined earlier. He very rightly says: 'It was not that only one of them was right and the rest were not, but that everyone was right.'[9] The holistic approach of Dr. Parnerkar is something quite interesting and valuable to the entire humanity. He is of the view that different systems of philosophy explain the truth, but lack completeness and hence there was a need to develop a philosophy such as Poornavad, which is all-inclusive in nature.

Poornavad has neither disproved or proved any single ideology. It rejects the traditional method of refuting and maintaining a particular standard, but instead embraces all the methods which make it unique. Poornavad philosophy is based on the Vedas and rationalism, offering empirical proof of how each one can be right. Though each doctrine is right and unique, it is not seen from the holistic standpoint. On the other hand, Poornavad embraces a holistic view by the principle of 'all-inclusiveness'. He says that the different systems of Vedanta depend on the Vedas and the Upanishads. The question then arises: 'Why do they all give different interpretations. If the texts are the same then how do we

---

9   Ibid.

get different interpretations?' This question naturally arises in the mind of the common man. The answer is given by Dr. Parnerkar. He says that the philosophy of Poornavad transcends such partial and incomplete pictures of reality and takes into account the holistic approach to reality which many of the systems of philosophy have failed.

It is interesting to note that 'Poorna' includes both the animate and inanimate. This shows how Poornatva philosophy is concerned with the unconscious and inert also. We know that many of the systems of Indian and Western philosophical tradition deal only with the conscious beings. But the cosmos or universe consists of the inanimate as well. This is addressed by the philosophy of the Poornavad. The Poornatva of God pervades the entire animate and inanimate. He disproves the theory that the world is impermanent by quoting the Vedic hymn, '*annenaatirohat*' which means that the world is the Poorna Purusha's form and hence it is infinite and immortal.

In Dr Parnerkar's method of philosophy, we see three metaphysical categories namely, Brahman, the world, and the individual self. They play their vital role to accommodate the empirical and transcendental nature of the Supreme. His interpretation of the text is analytical in nature. The usual analogy gains a new interpretation in his hands. For example, while interpreting the Rig Vedic shloka, '*DwaSuparna...*' (1.164.20), Poornavad says that the Highest God is the tree and the two birds are intimate friends, single-souled, having only one wing each, inhabiting the same tree. Here, the word 'two birds' means the manifest world and unmanifest Brahman. The traditional definition or interpretation is that the tree is reckoned as the body and the two birds respectively as the being and the atman. This is rejected by Poornavad. The reason which Dr Parnerkar offers for this refutation is interesting. He says that the Sruti text, '*Ino Viswasya Bhuvanasya...*' suggests that this very tree was Ishwar. Dr Parnerkar says that just as man experiences different events, sorrows and happiness taking place in this world, he has the Brahman experience too in this world only. This means that Brahman is in the world and the world in Brahman. 'Since Brahman and the world are twin birds, when the world bird is visible the Brahman world is hidden behind, not visible and when Brahman bird is visible, the world bird is covered and is not visible,' says Dr Parnerkar. Therefore, there is no perception of the world during the Brahman experience and no Brahman experience when we are conscious of this world. Dr Parnerkar is very assertive in explaining his thesis that Poornavad is not mere Brahman experience. It emphasizes the need for understanding the Absolute Truth in all its completeness, the Poorna.

Poornavad advocates three paths: the religious rites involving prolonged penance and appropriate conduct, transcendental consciousness and the grace of Guru. After a thorough study of the Poorna Purusha, Dr Parnerkar examines the doctrine of Maya since Poorna Purusha's form cannot be determined without the definite knowledge of Maya. The concept of Maya, is an important theme in Shankaracharya's Vedanta philosophy. Vedanta philosophy says that the world is merely an unreal manifestation (vivarta) of Brahman. The Advaitins claim that all of Brahman's effects must ultimately be acknowledged as unreal before the individual self can be liberated. Furthermore, according to Sankara, adhyasa (superimposition) is the false superimposition of the characteristics of physical body (birth, death, skin color etc.) onto the atman, and also the false superimposition of the characteristics of Atman (sentiency, existence) onto the physical body. He uses the example of the luster of an oyster shell to be mistaken as silver, as superimposition of silver on the oyster shell. He equates this with Avidya.

Dr Parnerkar says that Shankara's understanding of the following verse, is incomplete. '*Yathaiva Bimbam Mrdayopliptam*',[10] meaning that just as a diamond ring enveloped in mud regains its dazzle after it is washed, similarly the embodied being, upon realizing the truth of atman, gains oneness and becomes sorrowless. Dr Parnerkar argues that the words 'adhyasa' (superimposition) or 'vivarta' (an apparent or illusory form), used in Vedanta, are not found in the Vedas and that Shankara has stretched his imagination too far to give this meaning. This

---

10 *Geeta*, Shankar Bhashya Bhavanuvad, Uday Kumthekar.

passage definitely shows that Dr Parnerkar is able to see the Shruti texts from a different perspective and is bold enough to show that Shankara's interpretation is unacceptable. By this detailed study of Shankara's Maya, Dr Parnerkar is able to explain that Vedas do not support Shankara's theory. The world, according to Dr Parnerkar is pervaded by Poorna Purusha, thus making the existence of world real and empirical in character. Further Dr Parnerkar argues that in Advaita, the negation of the 'particular' proves the non-duality with Brahman, i.e., they merge into the Brahman becoming one with it and losing their form and identity; but in Poorna Purusha, the non-duality of every entity stands proven with their respective particularity. The essential difference between Poornavad and the Advaita can be better understood within the context of non-duality.

The distinction between vidya and avidya is made by Dr Parnerkar to teach the philosophy of the Poornavad. In order to have the Poorna experience, he says nothing should be relinquished. Also, if you are relinquishing something, then that experience is not Poorna. Whether it is the world or Brahman or Ishwar, whatever you relinquish, it remains outside of Poorna thus making it incomplete and partial. Hence the Poorna does not ask us to either relinquish the material world or the spiritual world. Once something is relinquished from experience, then it is incomplete (*apoorna*). 'All completeness only is the Absolute, Pure, Truth, Supreme Lord,' says Dr Parnerkar. There are some beautiful insights given by him with regard to the distinction between avidya and vidya. He says that as long as avidya is not assimilated properly, the acquisition of vidya could possibly be dangerous. This is further supplemented by another interesting statement, which explains that without the knowledge of avidya, the knowledge of vidya is incomplete. By quoting the dialogue between Nachiketa and Yama, Dr Parnerkar says that Yama before imparting vidya to Nachiketa imparted avidya. Thus, by quoting the Katha as well as *Ishavasya Upanishad* and other texts, it is explained that one must know avidya in order to know vidya. For Dr Parnerkar, avidya means the knowledge of the material world.

The Poornavad philosophy is a complete philosophical discourse. It teaches the ultimate truth and the need for attaining it. It includes all the three means, namely, knowledge, karma and worship. It treats all the means on par with each other. All the three are essential and non-duality cannot be reached when one is singled out. It is because of the fact that all the three have relation with Poorna and nothing remains outside Poorna. In short, one can understand the doctrine of Poorna which is stated by Dr Parnerkar as follows: 'Poorna evolves from Poorna, Poorna taken from Poorna still remains Poorna, and Poorna merging with Poorna becomes Poorna.'[11]

The Absolute comes combined with the trinity—Vishwa, Vishnu, Shiva—all three in one form: Poorna Purusha. The Poorna Purusha includes:

1. Intellect (the knowledge of the self)
2. Divinity
3. Materiality

The knowledge of one, i.e., only intellectuality, only divinity or only materiality cannot be called Absolute Truth.

Finally, the simple logic: who was Lord Jesus before Christianity? Who was Lord Buddha before Buddhism? If we try to find the roots, the roots of Christianity lie in Buddhism and the roots of Buddhism lie in the Upanishads. In the words of Kersten Holger, the author of *Jesus Lived in India*, "It is a wonder how Christianity has consistently denied its connection with India? All roots go to the Vedas".[12] The scholars refer to the Upanishads in the name of the Vedas. Occasionally they refer to the Vedas.

The tradition of philosophy is still pessimistic because of the impact of Buddhism. The doctrine of Buddhism says, 'life is impermanent, sorrowful, full of suffering', which has a partial impact from the *Katha Upanishad*. In the dialogue between Nachiketa and Yama, Nachiketa says, 'Sarve dukkhim sarve dukkhim kshanikam kshanikam' [There

---

11 Poornavad, Parnerkar. English, second edition. 2017.
12 Holger, Kersten (2001), *Jesus Lived in India: His Unknown Life Before and After the Crucifixion*, New Delhi: Penguin Books India.

is sorrow everywhere and life is impermanent.]. But Yama advises Nachiketa to 'ask me for wealth, health, empire and all material prosperity.' It means, Nachiketa asks only about vidya. But Yama says without the knowledge of avidya, vidya becomes dangerous.

Lord Buddha only followed the path of vidya, which becomes the cause of sorrow and the frustration of impermanency. This is the negative approach of life. Misery and bliss are two essential phases and divinity in the intuitional sense is the third phase. Balancing the three phases well, is the only solution that will give peace and prosperity in life. Then we feel that 'God is in me and I am in God'.

Anand vai brahma or 'Bliss is God and God is Bliss'. The optimistic vision of the Vedas is the need of the day. Therefore, the contribution of Dr Parnerkar is outstanding in the history of philosophy and science, because for the first time his work explains the parallel between philosophy and science by explaining its interrelated and inseparable entity. Thus, all roots lead to the Vedas and the knowledge of the Vedas is both pragmatic and universal. The Poornavad philosophy too is pragmatic and optimistic.

By the grace and guidance of my Master, Dr Parnerkar, I have been able to complete this book. I bow before His Excellence.

Dr T.P. Deshpande
Manas, Uday Nagar, Nanded, Maharashtra
tpdeshpande1943@gmail.com

|| इदं नमम: ||

Founder of Poornavad, Dr. R. P. Parnerkar

My Divine Master, Dr. V. R. Parnerkar,
propagator, Poornavad school of thought

CHAPTER 1

Guru: The Key to Transcendence

गुरूर् ब्रह्मा गुरूर् विष्णु गुरूर् देवो महेश्वरः
गुरूः साक्षात्परंब्रह्म तस्मै श्रीगुरवे नमः

Gurur Brahma, Gurur Vishnu, Gurur Devo Maheshwara,
Guru Sakshat Parabrahma, Tasmai Shri Gurave Namah

[The guru is as Brahman: Creator of the Material World; the guru is as Vishnu: Ishwara, the Divine Power; the guru is as Maheshwara: the God of Spiritual Knowledge; and this trinity of God Parabrahma is Poorna Purusha: Lord of the Universe.]

POORNAVAD PHILOSOPHY starts with recognizing the importance of a Guru. In keeping with the deep regard that all followers of the Vedic tradition have for the guru and shishya (disciple) parampara (tradition), they pray to their guru before starting any task, ritual or on any special religious occasion, seeing the guru as the supreme authority on the Vedic and Vedanta tradition. It is believed that any person or group with such wholehearted faith in the divine authority of the guru attains success in the task, ritual, or the purpose behind the special religious occasion undertaken. The importance of the guru in the Indian tradition cannot be emphasized enough, words are not enough to define or describe the guru's station in the disciple's life. The guru's authority is said to be greater than that of God, as the guru leads the disciple to God. As the one to introduce the disciple to God, he represents the Poorna Purusha, as described in the Sanskrit verse above.

The history of this guru-disciple tradition goes back to pre-historical times, to the period dubbed as the Sat Yug, where the guru-disciple relationship was exemplified by Vishwamitra and Raja Harishchandra; the Treta Yug by Vashishtha and Lord Shri Ram; Dwapar Yug by Lord Shri Krishna and Arjuna; and Kali Yug by Ramakrishna and Vivekanand. In present times (a continuance of Kali Yug) the tradition continues with the founders of Poornavad philosophy, Ramchandra Parnerkar and Vishnu Maharaj Parnerkar, and from 1980 onwards with Vishnu Maharaj and Gunesh Parnerkar, the propagators of Poornavad philosophy. The guru increases the disciple's ability, efficiency and skill and nurtures him, just as Lord Shri Krishna left his kingdom to protect his disciple Arjuna in the Mahabharata War and guided him to success.

Among the godly, the yearning to know God becomes the only goal or one of the main goals in life as Divine Grace can bless one with a happy and prosperous life. But very few get such opportunities in life. Vedic tradition has it that one among a million gains the realization of God. This is wish is fulfilled by the grace and guidance of a true guru and is the culmination of a lengthy procedure which requires patience, curiosity, sincerity and devotion. The real, divine sadguru elevates you as high as you wish and you are expected to surrender wholeheartedly foregoing your ego, status, and rigidity etc. Throughout this process the guru remains an affectionate authority, providing the disciple parental shelter and guidance that safeguards his/her life.

The major problem of the twenty-first-century human being is the lack of trust, faith and patience. It is observed that the present generation is disturbed and distracted, an issue that is becoming more serious day-by day. It might be easy to conquer the world but it's very difficult to conquer and control the mind. The guru is one such person who can train you to control and command your mind and to turn it towards the divine way of life. His divine powers can work within you for your own good. The guru may look like a common man but possesses a divine quality which cannot be imagined by the common man. We should, therefore, treat the guru with utmost respect. It is the guru who helps us to find our roots (as we are not aware of our roots) as much as he raises us to meet the divine.

If the Supreme Lord and the guru were to stand before you at the same time, in such circumstances who would you bow down to first? Certainly, as the great saint Kabir said, it would be the guru. The guru not only introduces us to God but guides us and describes to us the infinite power of the Divine. Therefore, God also blesses the guru with His Grace.

God and guru are recognized or known by intuition and not by intellect. Finding one's true guru is a milestone in the Vedic tradition. He provides us an ideal which is useful to follow in our day-to-day practical life—for instance, how to behave with and speak to elders, youngsters and subordinates. The guru establishes the cosmos of discipline in our life and by explaining minutely, the shades and effects of the language he explains the hymns of the Vedas, and the Sutras of the Upanishads with their practical applications. Otherwise, the classical nature of these texts and the depth and complexities of Sanskrit grammar, can make it difficult for the common man to understand and interpret the Vedic hymns properly. It is for this reason that the Vedas have never been comprehensively understood and stand the risk of misinterpretation. In such circumstances the role of the guru is very important and this is the reason behind this ancient guru-disciple tradition still continuing in India and abroad.

We should worship our life as it is very precious, but this is becoming increasingly complicated with the many challenges we face. Therefore, the role of the guru in our life is absolutely essential as he has the power to mould our life after observing and judging the merits and demerits of our personality and that too without expecting any kind of monetary return, as the guru of the Vedic tradition does not run any professional agency of this nature. He is completing a God-gifted assignment to work for the welfare of needy people and in that spirit he helps us overcome and master our life's challenges.

The guru builds up our mindset in such a way that helps us realize God. Because awareness of God arises in us through the heart, mind and soul, the guru prepares our intellectual mind to accept the existence and the Grace of God. The guru explains that God is not just about undertaking religious practices, but is the need of the intellectual mind—and in such a way the guru confers upon us the moral courage to command our mind to stay steady on its path to God.

I bow before my guru, His Holiness Vishnu Maharaj Parnerkar, who is such an eminent and outstanding divine authority on the Vedas and Upanishads, who conducts several workshops on Vedic rituals that help unravel the essence and teachings of the Vedas, along with seminars on life-oriented subjects with relevant current topics. His disciples—who are doctors, engineers, professors, judges, political leaders, farmers, industrialists, information technology (IT) professionals, and homemakers—are able to, with the help of Guru Maharaj Parnerkar's guidance and grace, communicate with the infinite universe via means of intuitional power which can be developed and achieved through meditation. This is only possible under the guidance of such a guru, because it is a science and technique that is connected to the psychology (mind-emotion connect), anatomy (the internal and external structures of the human body) and physiology (the functions of these structures).

Parnerkar Maharaj is such a guru, who, through his philosophy and teachings, provides the key to unlocking transcendental life.

CHAPTER 2

God as a Scientific Concept

'GOD' IS a universal concept of global faith and contemplation is universally considered one of the gateway to the realization of God. Contemplation acknowledges that God is to be known by intuitional sense and not by intellect. The Vedas have described God, but the Vedant and Western thinkers comprehend God by way of metaphysics and spirituality. Though we accept God as being everywhere, we deny God's manifest form. God is both inanimate and animate, in other words God is present in a rock as much as in a plant or a human being.

Albert Einstein, for instance, had no faith in the traditional concept of God and religion but had faith in God in the form of the energy that permeated the entire worlds. The concept of 'Poorna Purusha' (the personified form of the Universe) in the philosophy of Poornavad, is parallel to Einstein's concept of God and religion when seen in reference to the Isha Upanishad.

ईशावास्य सर्वमिदं।

Ishavasya Sarvamidam

[God is everywhere in the entire world manifest and unmanifest, animate and inanimate][1]

---

1 Isa. I.

Carl Jung and Albert Einstein have been among those who have left the world a legacy through their works; a legacy that has advanced the search for the meaning of life and an understanding of the universe. Both Jung and Einstein made personal proclamations that their scientific inquiries had led them to conclude that God was indeed real but could not be measured or captured by any material means. India's spiritual heritage teaches us that right knowledge of God and devotion to Him are the means of salvation; these qualities (right knowledge and devotion) are in themselves aspects of the Divine. Bhrigu-Varuni Vidya in the Taittreya Upanishad explains the different manifestations of Brahman, 'The Divine'. Of those, Vidnyan ('Knowledge') is considered a manifestation of the Divine by equating Vidyanana Vai Brahmana ('Knowledge is the Divine').

Cosmic God

The one God is immanent and transcends the cosmic process. Some wise men speak of inherent nature, others likewise, of time (as the first cause), but it is the greatness of God in the world by which this Brahma wheel is made to turn. The cosmic process, if generally represented by a rotating wheel, is ever moving. This is the greatness of God that is the moving image of Eternity.

God is the Lord of Prosperity, having known Him as in one's own self, the immortal, the support of all. There is no action and no origin of God to be found. For God, there is no master in the world, no ruler, nor is there any mark of Him. He is the cause and effect of the world. He is the Lord of the Lords.

God is the eternal among the eternal, the intelligent among the intelligences. The only One, but as being immanent in His manifest creation, He is one among many. He is the One who grants desires. He is that cause which is to be apprehended by discrimination and discipline; only by knowing God is one freed from all fears. To create, preserve and dissolve is the power of God. He who is unconditional, an Absolute, cannot be regarded the cause of the world and Poornavad explains that God is neither the cause nor the effect, but is the form of the world which is cause and effect within Himself. The Poorna Purusha is the essence of two natures, Prakriti (female) and Purusha (male) that create the material world.

The realization of God can be attained by different means, by yogic practice, meditation and contemplation, by devotion (bhakti), by worship (upasana), by the grace of guru, the master, or by grace of God Himself. 'Never has any man been able to visualize God by means of sight, nor is it possible for one to realize Him either by the heart, or by the mind and imagination. It is only those who know this sublime truth that become immortal.' (S. 16 09)[2]

It is quite clear that God cannot be realized by words of mouth or the mind or by the eye. It is only those who know that God is, to them alone, and to none else, is God revealed. The nature of God realization is like the knowing of a 'fact'; you can never question it, or argue about it. If you know that God Is, then alone is God realized by you. The value of the fact can never be disturbed by any way. It is clear that neither sense nor thought enable us to realize God. Not the intellect but the intuition can lead us to the vision of God. The happiness of God realization can be apprehended by means of intellect, and the fact is that God is beyond all senses and mind. Even beyond the intellect and intuition. It is only when the whole moral being is purged of evil that one is able to realize the greatness of God. (S 17.b)[3]

A Description of God

The *Svetasvatara Upanishad* provides a description of God—He is just as oil is hidden in seeds or ghee in curd, just as water is hidden in springs or fire in the churning sticks, even so is the atman immanent in the body. Just as an extremely subtle film covers the surface of ghee,

---

2   From Svtasvatra Upanishad, the Taittiriya school of Yajurveda, which is theistic in character and identifies the concept of the Supreme Lord, the Brahman—The God. It is related to Samkhya also because God is manifest and unmanifest and the Divine Prakrit and Purusa.

3   Ibid.

even so does the Godhead, who is immanent in all beings, envelop the whole universe. By knowing Him alone is the human being released from all bounds.

The Western and Vedic concepts of God are not that different from each other. Western religious philosophy states that God is one, but accepts the principle of the Trinity (the Father, the Son and the Holy Spirit). The manifest and unmanifested universe is similarly expanded by Vedic Trimurty (Jeeva, Jagat, Jagdishwara). Jeeva (the Son of God), Jagat (the Holy Spirit) and Jagdishwar (God Himself).

CHAPTER 3

India and Its Rich Heritage of Sanskrit and the Vedas

India in the Eighteenth Century

THIS WAS an era when India was called the 'golden bird', so rich was it in natural, human and cultural resources. Though seen as bright, beautiful and prosperous, India was politically divided into hundreds of little nation-states—a weakness that the British and the French were able to capitalize on. Having made inroads into the country their ambition was to rule for a long time.

With a rich civilization dating back thousands of years, India was also known for its morals and values. These can be traced to the divine imprints of the teachings of the wisdom in the Vedas. India has never claimed that the wisdom of the Vedic tradition belongs solely to India. On the contrary, India believes that the knowledge and wisdom of the Vedas are universal property:

आ नो भद्रा क्रतवो यन्तु विश्वतः
ā no bhadrāḥ kratavo yantu viśvataḥ
—*Rig Veda* 1.89.1

[Let the noble thoughts come from any side.]

Colonial Conspiracy to Destroy India's Vedic

The British rulers could never tolerate a colonized country having such a prosperous civilization and they proposed to damage the very roots of this country. They did so by replacing the tradition of the Vedic gurukul system with their own English-based education system. They established a Sanskrit chair at Oxford University to ensure that Britishers learned Sanskrit, translated the Vedas and Upanishads, and then wrote commentaries and criticisms on them. These commentaries and criticisms, written with a prejudiced and biased mind, were nothing but misinterpretations—they stated that the Vedas were communal and discriminated between castes.

The idea behind such translations was that English-speaking Indians and the rest of the world would come to believe what the translations stated. Unfortunately, many so-called learned Indians were indeed convinced by these writings and the world also suffered a heavy loss as these did not bring out the scientific knowledge and wisdom in the Vedas.

Outstanding American historian Will Durant wrote an inspirational book in 1930, *The Case For India*.[1] This little-known gem has resurfaced and could still serve as a guide to India, a nation on the rise. Will Durant alludes to Indian civilization as the greatest known to man. His book reveals India's glorious heritage and philosophical underlay in a way that leaves no doubt that the point at which India is poised today is not just a historical accident. Durant refers to Indian civilization as the greatest known to man. His has a compelling style, which is objective and unbiased, with great attention to detail. His book highlights India's glorious heritage and philosophies, providing background and reasoning to India's rise and importance in today's world. In his masterly work.

In his masterly work, Will Durant wrote: 'I have the honor to agree with the British Government; I agree only for Home Rule.' He made a distinction between Englishmen and the British. He expressed

---

1   Durant, William. (2015). *The Case for India*, Mumbai: Strand Book Stall Publishers.

admiration for Englishmen and attributed the concept of liberty to them. However, he criticized the British for their imperialist actions. Durant emphasizes his prejudice in favor of liberty and aligns his views with the fine traditions of English liberalism. On his perspective of India, Durant highlighted India's vast territory and large population, positioning it as a significant global entity. He wrote:

> 'In the northern and more important half of India the people are predominantly of the same race as the Greeks, the Romans, and ourselves—i.e., "Indo-Europeans" or "Aryans"; that though their skin has been browned by the tireless sun, their features resemble ours, and are in general more regular and refined than those of the average European; that India was the mother-land of our race, and Sanskrit the mother of Europe's languages; that she was the mother of our philosophy, mother, through Arabs, of much of our mathematics, mother, through Buddha, of the ideals embodied in Christianity, mother, through village community, of self-government and democracy. Mother India is in many ways the mother of us all.' (Durant, 2015)

He pointed out archaeological evidence of advanced civilizations in India dating back to 3,500 B.C., noting the sophistication of their cities and industries.

Durant also discussed the influence of Indian civilization on other cultures, such as through the spread of mathematical and philosophical ideas via Arab intermediaries and the dissemination of Buddhist ideals that influenced Christianity. He praises India's rich literary and artistic heritage, from the Bhagavad-Gita to the works of poets like Sarojini Naidu and Rabindranath Tagore.

Moreover, Durant argued against the portrayal of India as a minor civilization, asserting its rightful place among the highest civilizations in history. He condemned the British conquest of India as the destruction of a vibrant and ancient culture by a profit-seeking trading company. Durant outlined the plunder and devastation inflicted upon India by the British, portraying it as an invasion and destruction of a high civilization.

Dr Sarvepalli Radhakrishnan states:[2]

> Whatever may be the truth about the racial affinities of the Indian and the European peoples, there is no doubt that Indo-European languages derive from a common source and illustrate a relationship of mind. In its vocabulary and inflexions Sanskrit presents a striking similarity to Greek and Latin. Sir William Jones, explained it by tracing them all to a common source. The Sanskrit language, he said in 1786, in an address to the Asiatic Society of Bengal, 'whatever be its antiquity, is of a wonderful structure; more perfect than the Greek, more copious than the Latin, and more exquisitely refined than either; yet bearing to both of them a stronger affinity, both in the roots of verbs, and in the forms of grammar, than could possibly have been produced by accident; so strong, indeed, that no philologer could examine them all without believing them to have sprung from some common source which perhaps no longer exists. There is a similar reason, though not quite so forcible, for surprising that both the different idiom, had the Sanskrit; and the old. Persian might be added to the same family.

Western theologians say that Sanskrit is a dead language, but they are under the wrong impression. Sanskrit is still a live language and is being taught from school to university level; it is still popular among students. The word 'Veda' stems from (vid) 'to know' and means knowledge; there is a bright future for Sanskrit at the academic level. There is a town in Karnataka named Mattur, Shimoga, where the language of communication is 100 per cent Sanskrit.

---

2 Radhakrishnan, Dr Sarvepalli (1967), *A Source book in Indian Philosophy*, Princeton, NJ: Princeton University Press.

Max Muller on the Vedas

In his work *Six Systems of Indian Philosophy* (1899), Muller wrote, 'We have no right to suppose that we have even a hundredth part of the religious and popular poetry that existed during the Vedic age', and he goes on to list the six systems:

1. Purva Mimansa
2. Samkhya
3. Yoga
4. Nyaya
5. Vaisheshik
6. Uttar Mimansa

He also states in another work[3]:

> 'The Veda has a two-fold interest: it belongs to the history of the world and to the history of India. In the history of the world, the Veda fills a gap which no literary work in any other language could fill. It carries us back to times of which we have no records anywhere, and gives us the very words of a generation of men, of whom otherwise we could form but the vaguest estimate by means of conjectures and inferences. As long as man continues to take an interest in the history of his race and as long as we collect in libraries and museums the relics of former ages, the first place in that long row of books which contains the records of the Aryan branch of mankind will belong forever to the Rig Veda.'

---

3 Mueller, Max (1860), *A History of Ancient Sanskrit Literature: So Far As it Illustrates the Primitive Religion of the Brahmans*, London. Williams and Norgate.

The Rig Veda, according to Ragozin, 'is, without the shadow of a doubt, the oldest book of the Aryan family of nations.'[4] As Maurice Winternitz observed[5]:

> If we wish to learn to understand the beginnings of our own culture, if we wish to understand the oldest Indo-European culture, we must go to India, where the oldest literature of an Indo-European people is preserved. For, whatever view we may adopt on the problem of the antiquity of Indian literature, we can safely say that the oldest monument of the literature of the Indians is at the same time the oldest monument of Indo-European literature which we possess.

Maurice Bloomfield noted that the Rig Veda was not only 'the most ancient literary monument of India', but also 'the most ancient literary document of the Indo-European peoples.'[6] Dr Nicol Macnicol noted: 'This literature is earlier than that of either Greece or Israel, and reveals a high level of civilization among those who found in it the expression of their worship.'[7] In his work, *Hindu Scriptures*, Dr Macnicol wrote:[8]

> Science is the knowledge of secondary causes, of the created details. Wisdom is the knowledge of primary causes. The

---

4 See p. 114 in Ragozin, Z.A. (1895), *Vedic India: As embodied Principally in the Rig Veda*, New York: G.P. Putnam's Sons; London: T. Fisher Unwin.
5 See page 6 in Winternitz, Maurice (1927), *A History of Indian Literature*, Volume 1, translated from German by Mrs S. Ketkar, Kolkata: University of Calcutta.
6 Bloomfield, Maurice (1908), *The Religion of the Veda: The Ancient Religion of India* (From Rig Veda to Upanishads), American Lectures on the History of Religions, Seventh Series (1906-1907). New York and London: G.P. Putnam's Sons.
7 Shinde, Vasant et al. (17 October 2019), 'An Ancient Harappan Genome Lacks Ancestry from Steppe Pastoralists or Iranian Farmers', Cell 179: 729–35, 2019 Elsevier Inc. https://doi.org/10.1016/j.cell.2019.08.048.
8 Ibid.: p 16.

Veda is not a single literary work like the Bhagavad-Gita or a collection of a number of books compiled at some particular time as the Tri-pitaka of the Buddhists or the Bible of the Christians, but a whole literature which arose in the course of centuries and was handed down from generation to generation through oral transmission. When no books were available memory was strong and tradition exact. To impress on the people the need for preserving this literature, the Veda was declared to be sacred knowledge or divine revelation. Its sanctity arose spontaneously owing to its age and the nature and value of its contents. It has since become the standard of thought and feeling for Indians.

The name Veda signifying wisdom suggests a genuine spirit of inquiry. The road by which the Vedic sages travelled was the road of those who seek to inquire and understand. The questions they investigate are of a philosophical character.

Destroying the Foundational Roots of Vedic Education, the British declared Sanskrit as illegal.[9] They also shut down all the gurukuls in the country. They were set on fire. The gurus teaching there were beaten up badly and put behind bars. Until 1850, India had 7,32,000 gurukuls and 7,50,000 villages. This means the access to gurukuls across the nation's villages was very high. These gurukuls were what we would today call institutes of higher education. They taught forty-eight subjects and were managed and run by the villagers themselves and not by any king. The education in gurukuls was free of cost.

Once the gurukuls were shut down or destroyed, English education was introduced and the first Convent school was opened in Calcutta and was called the Free School. Under the same rule, Calcutta University, Bombay University and Madras University were established.

---

9 Ibid.

The following subjects were taught in the gurukuls.

1.	Metallurgy	Agni Vidya	अग्नि विद्या
2.	Flight	Vayu Vidya	वायू विद्या
3.	Navigation	Jal Vidya	जल विद्या
4.	Space Science	Antrariksha Vidya	अंतरिक्ष विद्या
5.	Environment	Prithvi Vidya	पृथ्वी विद्या
6.	Solar Study	Surya Vidya	सूर्य विद्या
7.	Lunar Study	Chandra va Lokvidya	चंद्र व लोकविद्या
8.	Weather Forecast	Megh Vidya	मेघ विद्या
9.	Battery	Padartha Vidyut Vidya	पदार्थ विद्युत विद्या
10.	Solar Energy	Saur Urja Vidya	सौरऊर्जा विद्या
11.	Study of Day and Night	Din-Ratri Vidya	दिन-रात्री विद्या
12.	Space Research	Shrushti Vidya	सृषटी विद्या
13.	Astronomy	Khagol Vidya	खागोल विद्या
14.	Geography	Bhugol Vidya	भूगोल विद्या
15.	Time	Kaal Vidya	काल विद्या
16.	Geology Mining	Bhugarbha Vidya	भूगर्भ विद्या
17.	Gems and Metals	Ratna Va Dhatu Vidya	रत्न व धातू विद्या
18.	Gravity	Aakarshan Vidya	आकर्षण विद्या
19.	Solar Energy	Prakash Vidya	प्रकाश विद्या
20.	Communication	Taar Vidya	तारविद्या
21.	Plane	Viman Vidya	विमान विद्या
22.	Water Vessels	Jalyan Vidya	जलयान विद्या
23.	Arms & Ammunition	Agneya Astra Vidya	अग्नेय अस्त्र विद्या
24.	Zoology Botany	Jeeva-Jantu Vijnyan	जीव-जंतू विज्ञान
25.	Material Science	Yajna Vidya	यज्ञ विद्या
26.	Commerce	Vanijya Vidya	वाणिज्य विद्या
27.	Agriculture	Krishi Vidya	कृषी विद्या
28.	Animal Husbandry	Pashupalan Vidya	पशूपालन विद्या
29.	Bird Keeping	Pakshipalan Vidya	पक्षीपालन विद्या

30.	Animal Training	Pashu Prashikshan Vidya	पशू प्रशिक्षण विद्या
31.	Mechanics	Yan Yantrakar Vidya	यान यंत्राकार विद्या
32.	Vehicle Designing	Rathkar Vidya	रथकर विद्या
33.	Gems	Ratnakar Vidya	रत्नाकर विद्या
34.	Jewelry Designing	Suvarnakar Vidya	सुवर्णकार विद्या
35.	Textile	Vastrakar Vidya	वस्त्रकार विद्या
36.	Pottery	Kumbhar Vidya	कुंभार विद्या
37.	Metallurgy	Lohkar Vidya	लोहार विद्या
38.	Snake Science	Takshak	तक्षक
39.	Dying	Rangsaaj	रंगसाज
40.	Carpentry	Khatavkar	खाट्वाकर
41.	Logistics	Rajjukar Vidya	रज्जूकार विद्या
42.	Architect	Vastukar Vidya	वास्तूकार विद्या
43.	Cooking	Paak Vidya	पाक विद्या
44.	Driving	Sarathya Vidya	सारथ्य विद्या
45.	Water Management	Nadi Prabandhak Vidya	नाडी प्रबंधक विद्या
46.	Data Entry	Suchikaar Vidya	सूचीकार विद्या
47.	Animal Husbandry	Goshala Prabandhak	गोशाला प्रबंधक
48.	Horticulture	Udyanpaal	उद्यानपाल

Indian history starts with the Sindhu civilization, also called the Indus Valley/ Harappan/ or Saraswat civilization. This was a huge and prosperous urban civilization on the banks of the river Sindhu, with cities such as Mohenjodaro, Harappa, Kalibangan, Lothal, etc. It was believed that this civilization was spread across parts of modern-day Afghanistan, Balochistan, Sindh, Punjab, Rajasthan, Gujarat and Uttar Pradesh. The popular theory points to the origins of this civilization being around 3500 BCE. But recent findings indicate that this civilization might be much older than that, dating back to 6000 BCE, and also covering a larger part of the Indian subcontinent.

Hence, the language of the Sindhu civilization can be studied on the basis of Brahmi Language.

Findings Show Aryans Were Natives, Not Outsiders

The scientific journal *Cell* recently printed a paper titled 'An Ancient Harappan Genome Lacks Ancestry from Steppe Pastoralists or Iranian Farmers.'[10] The paper discussed the three-year-long study conducted by a team of Indian archeologists, and DNA experts from Harvard Medical School, on human skeletons found in an excavation in Rakhigarhi in Haryana. Their findings reveal that the Aryans were not outsiders, rather they were natives of India. It was also found that that they practiced agriculture and animal husbandry.

Study lead, archeologist Vasant Shinde concluded, 'Our research suggests that no DNA from central Asia has matched. This proves that there is no relation between the citizens of Rakhigarhi and citizens of central Asia.'[11]

Under British rule, the theory that the Aryans were outsiders and attackers became widespread. However, those who accepted Vedic religion were not outsiders or attackers. The segregation of Aryans and Dravidians did not exist. So, there was no war between them. All this is the imagination of the leftist historians.

Now the Indian Government has started to encourage and expand study and research in Sanskrit right from school level to college and university-level students taking interest in learning Sanskrit.

---

10 Shinde, Vasant et al. (17 October 2019), 'An Ancient Harappan Genome Lacks Ancestry from Steppe Pastoralists or Iranian Farmers', *Cell* 179: 729–35, 2019. Elsevier Inc. https://doi.org/10.1016/j.cell.2019.08.048.

11 Ibid.

CHAPTER 4

Jesus Christ: Scholar of Sanskrit and the Vedas, and the Impact of the Vedas on Buddhism

For thousands of years, many scholar-travelers have visited India to study its rich spiritual and cultural heritage; and Jesus Christ was one such noble visitor. Millennia later a poisonous, destructive communal spirit, spread by politicians subscribing to materialism and capitalism, has left India to deal with social polarity, social unrest and dissatisfaction. One place in particular, has caused concern across the world and, of course, in India—Kashmir. This is the same land where, as per some researchers and scholars such as Hazrat Mirza Ghulam Ahmad, Holger Kersten and Andreas Faber Kaiser, Jesus lies buried.[1]

---

1   The theory of Jesus' lost years (ages thirteen to thirty) are discussed in the following:
    (i)   An ancient reference regarding the lost years is found in Vol. IX of the *Bhavishya Puranas*;
    (ii) Notovich (1894), *The Unknown Life of Jesus Christ*;
    (iii) Prophet (1984), *Lost Years of Jesus: On the Discoveries of Notovitch, Abhedananda, Roerich, and Caspari*; and Prophet, (2019), *The Lost Years of Jesus: The Documentary Evidence*;
    (iv) Holger (2001), *Jesus Lived in India*.

Christ's work and his message for global human welfare and eternal peace and prosperity, is for those intellectuals in search of secularization in religion.

As an adolescent divine boy of thirteen, Jesus left his homeland secretly joining sages and traders and travelled to India by the ancient silk route via Persia, Afghanistan and Sindh. Upon reaching India he made his way to Jagannath Puri where he was welcomed by orthodox Brahmin priests. He lived with them for six years, learnt Sanskrit from them before studying the Vedas (with their linguistic phonology and philology with hailing pronunciations) as well the Samhitas, Aranyakas, Brahamanas, and Upanishads.

It was here that Jesus Christ experienced realization of the Ultimate Truth and Reality. However, he was to be disappointed when he asked the Brahmin priest who was his teacher why the sun must be worshipped as must be spirit of good and the spirit of evil. In his view this doctrine was false, for the sun has no power of its own. His teacher did not have enough knowledge of the Vedas to reply that it is powered solely through the will of the invisible creator, i.e., the Supreme Lord of Universe—the Poorna Purusha' of the Vedas. It is He who gave it birth and who has willed it to be the star to light the day, and to warn labour and the seed-time of man.

The problem lies with the orthodox authorities of every religion, who have not done a thorough study of the doctrine of their own religion and misguide and misinterpret the text to protect their own interests. This is the tragedy with every religion. The answer to the question raised by Jesus has been discussed in detail in the Chapter 'Maya'.

After his realization of the Ultimate Truth, Jesus also realized that the manner in which the priests disseminated the teachings of the Vedas was false. They disseminated knowledge only to the upper classes, the Brahmins and Kshatriyas, and discriminated against the lower classes, the Vaisyas and Sudras. Jesus again argued with his teacher about freely sharing this knowledge with the lower classes too, especially the Sudras. The priest was aghast and denied permission. However, Jesus, went ahead and shared his knowledge with all, including the Sudras.

The enraged priests hatched a secret plot to kill him, but one among his Sudra friends found out about the plot and told Jesus.

Jesus left Jagannath Puri that very night. From Puri he travelled northward, eventually reaching Ladakh. There he stayed for six years amongst the Buddhist monks. He learnt Pali, the sacred language of Buddhist Philosophy, and studied Buddhist Philosophy under the tutelage of the monks. However, he found that the Buddhist monks and lamas could not answer his questions on Buddhist philosophy. Disappointed, he finally left for home and returned to Jerusalem, where he carried out his divinely ordained mission.

The seeds of differentiation between God and His creation (i.e., the world) lie in the cause-and-effect theory present in almost all philosophy of religions. Right from Buddhism to Vedant, Christianity and Islam, all believe that God created this world. This implies that God and the world are two different entities. However, the doctrine of Poornavad elucidated by Dr Parnerkar's 'Form Relation Theory' or 'Swaroop Sambandha', states they are one universal form. There is no casual relation, i.e., one being the cause and the other being the effect, between the Lord and the world.

Jesus Christ rightly applied the same Form Relation Theory and realized that God is the one the Supreme Lord of Universe (See Chapter 7, 'Lord of Universe: Poorna Purusha'). Dr Parnerkar's Poornavad holds that Poorna Purusha, as described in Vedas, enlightened and powered the whole universe i.e., 'Poorna'—the complete and perfect.

Bhavishaya Puranas

In the Puranas, the ancient texts of Hindu mythology, there is a depiction of how Jesus came to India. As Kersten Holger mentions in his book in 2001, *Jesus Lived in India*, the ninth volume of the Puranas, the *Bhavishyat Maha-Purana* narrates that Shalivahana, the grandson of Vikramajit, came across a man in the mountains, who had a white body and wore white garments. The man introduced himself as 'Ishaputra [Sanskrit, 'Son of God'], born of a virgin, proclaimer of the teachings of the barbarians [Mleccha], which bear the truth,' as noted by Holger.

Holger then drew the conclusion that given the Sanskrit word Isha means Lord/ God and Masiha corresponds to the word 'Messiah', Isha-Masiha means 'the Lord, the Messiah'. The text in the Puranas also noted that the white-robed man called himself Isha-putra, meaning 'Son of God', and says that he was born of a virgin.

Given this narration in the *Bhavishyat Maha-Purana*, Holger concluded the person described had to be Jesus.

Centuries-old texts coupled with research on the philosophy of religion by international scholars, demonstrate the strong connection of Christianity with the Vedas and Upanishads.

The Roots of Buddhism in Upanishads

The study of the Upanishads also helps uncover the roots of Buddhism, especially as highlighted by Pratap Chandra.

> We find that the end of the Upanishadic era coincides with the dawn of Buddhism, suggesting an organic evolution between the two philosophies. The *Chhandogyab Upanishad's* description of the primordial state of Not-Being preceding Being, foreshadows concepts later proposed in Buddhist texts, particularly the idea of denial of existence and maintenance of a void. Sankaracharya's commentary on this passage, in stating that this refers to the doctrine of Buddhists, where they say 'sadbhava' existed by itself before the creation of anything, strengthens this correlation.
>
> Likewise, the *Katha Upanishad's* reflection on the nature of the soul upon death, where some claim that the soul lives, while others think it has ceased to exist, mirrors the Buddhist doctrine of 'anatmavada', denying the existence of a soul. Furthermore, the existential musings of Nachiketas echo Buddhist insights into the transient and unsatisfactory nature of material pleasures.
>
> Furthermore, the *Brihadaranyaka Upanishad's* call for renunciation in the face of worldly desires is quite similar to the lifestyle embraced in Buddhism and Jainism. Lastly, the discourse between Jaratkarava and Yajnavalkya in the Brihadaranyaka,

on karma, concluded that 'a man becomes holy by holy actions and sinful by sinful actions'. This moral principle of karma is seen strongly in Buddhism as well as in various other Indian philosophical systems.

In essence, though the discussion in Chandra's paper, we see that while Buddhism may manifest as a distinct philosophical tradition from the Upanishads, its principles, such as the negation of existence, denial of a permanent soul, renunciation, and karma, are all present within the Upanishads, highlighting an interconnection and shared lineage between the two traditions.

Difference between Dharma and Religion

Dharma and religion are two unique and separate concepts. Religion involves believing in and worshiping a supernatural power or powers that are thought to control human destiny. It's a structured system of faith and worship, with specific beliefs that may have limitations tied to certain groups or nations. On the other hand, Dharma, particularly in the Sanatan Vedic tradition, has a broader and deeper significance. It's derived from the root 'dhr', meaning to uphold or sustain. Dharma is seen as the norm that sustains the universe, encompassing religious rites and duties.

The *Chhandogya Upanishad* discusses various aspects of Dharma, including duties related to different stages of life, such as that of the householder, the hermit and the student. And when the *Taittiriya Upanishad* asks us to practice Dharma it refers to the duties of the stage of life to which we belong. For Buddhism, Dharma is one of the three jewels (Triratna) along with the Buddha and the Sangha (the community). It's considered essential for spiritual growth and sanctity, guiding individuals towards moral, material, and intellectual well-being.

For our understanding, we define Dharma as the duty of a human in connection to the four main goals of life (Dharma, Artha, Kama, and Moksha) and the four stages (Chaturthashrama), with the aim to ultimately nurture individuals towards spiritual excellence and sanctity.

The concept of Dharma has a lot of similarities with Buddhism and Christianity. In ancient India, rather than a concrete concept of 'Hindu' religion, there existed the Indian tradition, which has no concern with the present concept of different religions, and this tradition was known as Sanatan Dharma. And now, while several religions exist, we can find traces of the Sanatan Dharma.

CHAPTER 5

Jesus Christ's Questions Answered within Dr Parnerkar's Form-Relation Theory

As DISCUSSED in the previous chapter, after studying Sanskrit and the Vedas under a Vedic priest in Jagannath Puri and later in Varanasi, Jesus became a complete scholar of Sanskrit and the Vedas. Thereafter, he raised queries on points that he felt needed further clarification, with the priest who was his teacher. For instance, he wanted to know why he had been asked to offer water (arghya) to the sun and to worship Agni (fire). He also wanted to know why one should perform these rituals; who directed the sun to rise and shine; and who made Agni burn as heat and fire? The priest could not find answers that satisfied Jesus.

Regarding the Vedic hymns too, Jesus was sure that the Vedas did not state that the Shudras were not allowed to listen to or study the Vedas. He found that there was no hymn, no such order or any such reference in the Vedas. His teacher the priest, unable to accept that Jesus had dared to query him and, as he saw it, query the Vedas too, was angry enough to call a meeting of orthodox Vedant scholars. They concluded Jesus deserved the death sentence.

As mentioned in the previous chapter, Jesus was unaware that this death sentence had been passed. However, the Shudras had great goodwill for him and one of them informed him; Jesus left the city that same night. He made his way to Leh (in Ladakh) where he joined the Buddhist monks in a monastery.

These questions raised by Jesus find parallels in, and resonate with, Dr Parnerkar's Form-Relation doctrine of Poornavad. Interestingly, in 1948, Dr Parnerkar answered these very questions and more, posed by an august gathering of orthodox Vedant scholars in Banaras (Varanasi), during a viva-voce examination on the Form-Relation doctrine of Poornavad. The discussions were chaired by the Kashi Naresh (the king of Banaras) and the panelists included Sanskrit and Vedic scholars such as Pandit Madan Mohan Malviya, Pandit Gopinath Kavishwar and the scholar of 'Nyaya' philosophy Pandit Rajrajeshwar Shastri Dravid.

Before such scholars, and citing references from Vedic hymns and from *Isha Upanishad* and *Kena Upanishad*, Dr Parnerkar succeeded in proving to them that the Vedas did not discriminate between caste, gender, and religion. He also explained that the Vedic concept of Poorna Purusha, neglected by Vedant scholars, is the manifest form of the universe, and that the Poorna Purusha is the personification of the entire unmanifest and manifest universe and Shiva, Vishnu and Vishwa are His three forms.

When asked about why the priest could not give Jesus a satisfactory answer on who asked the sun to shine and fire to blaze, Dr Parnerkar replied it was due the priest's ignorance of the *Kena Upanishad*.

Knowledge of Brahman is the Ground of Superiority

Both Hinduism and Christianity describe God as perfect and as the source of all perfections. In the beginning of the *Isha Upanishad* it is stated, 'That is full; this is full. The full comes out of the full. Taking the full from the full the full itself remains.' Jesus Christ says, 'You therefore, must be perfect, as your heavenly Father is perfect.' It has been taken from the *Isha Upanishad* and this is the seed of Dr Parnerkar's doctrine of Poornavad.

ॐ पूर्णमदः पूर्णमिदं पूर्णात्पूर्णमुदच्यते ।
पूर्णस्य पूर्णमादाय पूर्णमेवावशिष्यते ॥[1]

Om pūrṇamadaḥ pūrṇamidaṃ pūrṇāt pūrṇamudacyate
pūrṇasya pūrṇamādāya pūrṇamevāvaśiṣyate

[Full [and complete] is 'that', full [and complete] is 'this'. Full comes out of the full. Taking the full from the full, the full itself remains. Om, peace, peace, peace.][2]

Christianity considers Christ as a divine incarnation, 'the Son of God'. In several passages of the Bible, he has been identified with God. Hinduism also has faith in the incarnation of God, but it differs from Christianity on certain issues. Firstly, Lord Vishnu assumes different forms during the various ages or yugs (Sat, Treta, Dwapar and Kali) and those embodied forms of Vishnu possess various degrees of the divinity and power of Vishnu. Secondly, the incarnation of God is considered to be God Himself and not a mediator between God and man.

Thus, the Christian view of divine incarnation as Christ does not seem very befitting. It is also rather inconsistent. Sometimes he is equated with God, but being a mediator he cannot be equal to God.

Hinduism believes that God manifests in three forms—as Brahma the Creator, Vishnu the Sustainer, and Shiva the Destroyer, of the universe—though His (God's) essential unity remains unaffected. It resembles the Christian Trinity—God the Father, God the Son and God the Holy Ghost, simultaneously. The Vedas too see these as the three divine agencies under the One Godhead, and identify this Godhead as the Poorna Purusha, says Dr Parnerkar.

---

1   Isha Upanishad, 1st.
2   Author's own translation.

CHAPTER 6

Genome Chart of Poorna Purusha: Supreme Lord

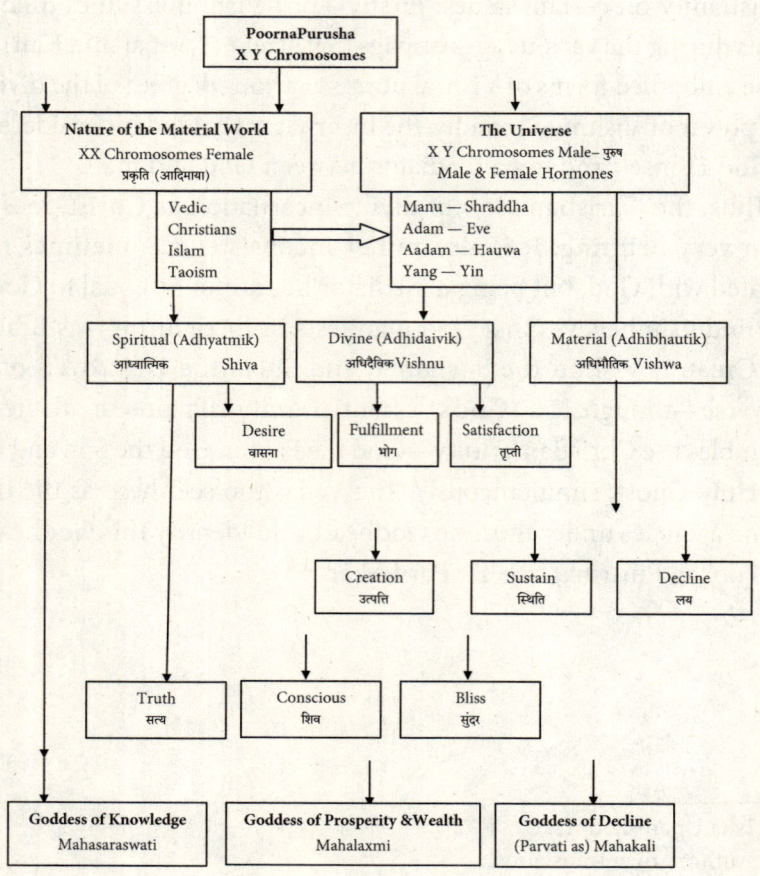

Lord Shiva in Ardhanareshwar avatar

Genome of Poorna Purusha: Supreme Lord

वागर्थाविव संपृक्तौ वागर्थप्रतिपत्तये।
जगतः पितरौ वन्दे, पार्वती-परमेश्वरौ।।

vāgarthāviva sampruktau vāgarthapratipattaye
jagataḥ pitarau vande pārvatīparameśvarau

> [I worship Prakruti and Purusha in the form of Parvati and Shiva i.e., Parmeshwar, the parent of the world, who (Purusha and Prakriti) are inseparable, just like a word and its meaning.][1]

The genome of the Supreme Lord of the Universe is the subject of cosmogony. Dr Parnerkar, in the Form-Relation theory of the doctrine of Poornavad has explained that Poornavad is the knowledge of the Vedas. Aeons ago a galaxy of great sages, called rishis, composed the hymns that constitute the Vedas. The vast ocean of knowledge (mundane, metaphysical, spiritual), contained in the Vedic hymns and its application, gave rise to the Vedic tradition known as Sanatan (eternal) Dharma which has nothing to do with the present concept of religion. In fact, Dharma does not mean religion, but rather a system to maintain moral values through which practitioners can attain enlightenment, and at a more mundane level can also attain material prosperity and lead a joy-filled life of natural ease.

As mentioned above, Sanatan means eternal. The Vedas divide time into four ages called yugs—Sat, Treta, Dwapar and Kali—that occur in succession, starting with Sat and ending with Kali, before starting again. The completion of twenty-eight cycles of the four yugs, makes up one kalpa. And at the end of each kalpa, the Vedas state that water levels rise covering most of the earth, causing a pralay (destruction and dissolution on a global scale). At the end of the pralay the Poorna Purusha, the Supreme Lord, alone remains and the next kalpa begins. Western scientists have accepted the concept of kalpas.[2]

The Sanskrit phrase '*Ekoham Bahusyam*' states that the Supreme Lord thought/willed 'I am One; let Me become Many' and so He did. Let us see how He multiplied Himself. The Poorna Purusha (Supreme Lord) has within Him the male procreative energy (the Purusha), and through this He manifests the feminine energy known as Prakriti.

---

1   Kalidasa's *Raghuvamsam*, 1; author's own translation
2   Fritjof Capra, *The Tao of Physics* (UK: HarperCollins, 2007).

Scientifically too, both males and females have forty-seven chromosomes each, in pairs. The twenty-third chromosomal pair in males is XY, but in females it is XX. Therefore, the female ovum (egg) only carries the XX (female) chromosome, while the male sperm can carry either X (female) or Y (male) chromosomes; which is why the gender of the child is determined solely by the father. In other words, only the Purusha or male aspect of the Poorna Purusha (the Supreme Lord) can create the female. Hence the Poorna Purusha, from within Himself, manifests both Purusha (male) and Prakriti (female).

In fact, the Vedas refer to the Poorna Purusha as 'Ardhanarishwara', which is a combination of three words: 'ardh' meaning half, 'nari' meaning female, and 'ishwara' meaning the Lord.[3] The Poorna Purusha has within Himself both Prakriti and Purusha, and once manifested they are personified as a divine couple in the form of Shiva and Parvati. Their harmony creates joy in the universe. The same personification also occurs with the first male and first female on earth: in Hinduism as Manu and Shraddha, in Christianity as Adam and Eve, in Islam as Aadam and Hauwa, and in Taoism as Yang and Yin.

Dr Parnerkar's doctrine of Poornavad also concurs with the Vedas with regard to the three Purusha energies—Shiva, Vishnu and Vishwa—manifested by the Poorna Purusha/Supreme Lord. Prakriti is present as the three female divine energies, and creates balance and harmony with the three Purusha male powers—Parvati with Shiva, Mahalaxmi with Vishnu, and Saraswati with Vishwa (see the chart).

Each of the three forms of the Poorna Purusha—Shiva, Vishnu, Vishwa—have three aspects of their own. Shiva's three aspects are truth, consciousness and bliss. Vishnu's aspects are desire, fulfillment and satisfaction; and Vishwa's three aspects are creation, sustenance and declination.

The Prakriti (female) counterparts of the Shiva, Vishnu, Vishwa trinity, are: Parvati in the form of Mahakali (Shiva's partner) bestowed

---

3   See: Raveesh, B.N. (2013), 'Ardhanareeshwara concept: Brain and psychiatry', *Indian Journal of Psychiatry*, January, no. 55 (Suppl. 2): S263-67. Doi:10.4103/0019-5545.105548

with the power of declination; Mahalaxmi (Vishnu's partner) bestowed with the power of wealth and prosperity; and Mahasaraswati (Vishwa's partner) bestowed with the power of creation. Each of the Purusha and Prakriti divine couples multiplies further in line with their divine purpose.

The Mathematics of this Genome

As per the doctrine of Poornavad: **1 + 1 = 3**. One male (Purusha) + one female (Prakriti) = (creates) a child (the world, the jeeva, i.e., life forms).

The Supreme Lord, Poorna Purusha, thus multiplies Himself into three entities and later this equation (3 x 3 = 9) is replicated multiple times into infinity. When the Poorna Purusha thought/willed *Ekam Bahusyam* (I am One, let Me be Many), He multiplied Himself into three (Purush, Prakriti and Jeeva) and thereon into infinity.

At the end of the very first kalpa, when the first ever twenty-eight cycles of the four yugs (Sat, Treta, Dwapar, and Kali) were over, water levels rose until they covered a major part of the earth, causing pralay, i.e., dissolution and destruction on a global scale. Sky above and water below. Sky and water are one, and the animate and inanimate are one reality. One and alone did Poorna Purusha remain, and once again began the cycle of creation through the setting in motion of the divine energies of Purusha and Prakriti.

This is the endless process that Poorna Purusha willed into motion at the very beginning, a process—sustained by the Poorna Purusha—that is ongoing and will continue into eternity and is hence known as eternal, Sanatan.

CHAPTER 7

Supreme Lord of the Universe: Poorna Purusha

'In vedas Poorna Purusha is the only Absolute Truth and Shiva-form, Vishnu-form and Vishwa (world)-form all three are His forms only' is the doctrinal statement of Poornavad by Dr Parnerkar. Thus these three have a form relation, rather than a casual relation, with Poorna Purusha as the sole cause.

Poornavad is consistent with Rig Vedic science. Understanding the concept of Poorna Purusha in the scientific way that the Rig Veda elucidates it—the same thread runs through all the mantras and suktas (hymns) in the Rig Veda—helps to establish Poornavad on a firmer footing, leading to its application in various fields in a holistic way.

Poornamadah, Poornamidam: Full and Complete Is That, Full and Complete Is This

Adi Shankarachraya closes his Introduction to the *Ishavasya Upanishad* with the following verse:

ओम पूर्णमदः पूर्णमिदं पूर्णात्पूर्णमुदच्यते
पूर्णस्य पूर्णमादाय पूर्णमेवावशिष्यते
ओम शांतीः शांतीः शांतीः

> Om pūrṇamadaḥ pūrṇamidaṃ pūrṇāt pūrṇamudacyate
> pūrṇasya pūrṇamādāya pūrṇamevāvaśiṣyate
>
> [Full [and complete] is 'that', full [and complete] is 'this'. Full comes out of the full. Taking the full from the full, the full itself remains. Om, peace, peace, peace.][1]

The 'that' and 'this' referred to in the verse above have attracted the human mind since centuries. Let's try and dissect them. 'This' or 'idam' is the visible universe. It is the material form of the universe and matter makes up a huge part of it. On the other hand, 'that' or 'adah' can be described as power and energy, which is correlated to the spiritual side of philosophy. Idam and adah, matter and energy.

For centuries together, people have only followed the spiritual side of philosophy without paying any attention to the applied side. The material side of the Vedas have been neglected. Poornavad philosophy brings to light both the spiritual and material aspects and personifies them as the Poorna Purusha.

The entire universe with unmanifest and manifest aspects is personified as the Poorna Purusha. It is a humanized concept of the universe. The Vedas personify the universe as Poorna Purusha as the authors of the Vedas wanted to visualize the universe. If man only focuses upon energy or the unmanifest, how do is he to understand the depth of the universe? To do so, the material, manifest form must be considered; we must accept that matter and energy are the two sides of the universe. No description of 'this/idam/manifest' (i.e., matter) can be complete without reference to 'that/adah/unmanifest'. The studies of this universe present a very pertinent question as to who created it, because in the interactive world something can be created only out of something else.

The Rig Veda refers to the interactive 'this/idam' as 'sat' and states that it was created out of the non-interactive energy called 'asat'. It is

---

[1] Author's own translation.

energy and matter that make up the entity called Poorna Purusha, the description of whom is found in the Rig Veda's Purusha Sukta hymn.

While quantum mechanical situations cannot be understood classically it must be agreed that 'that/adah/energy' cannot be described or understood if expressed in mathematical terms. We can, at best, listen to the authority of the Vedas. Verse 10.90.1 of the Purusha Sukta hymn in the Rig Veda describes the nature of adah and the relationship between adah and idam:

सहस्रशीर्षा पुरुषः सहस्राक्षः सहस्रपात्।
स भूमिं विश्वतोवृत्वाऽत्यातिष्ठद्दशांगुलम्॥

*Sahasra-śīrṣā Puruṣṣah Sahasra-ākṣsah Sahasra-Pāt
Sa Bhūmim Viśvato Vrtva-ātya[i]-ṭisṭthad-daśa-āṅgulam*

[He, who has a thousand heads, a thousand eyes, a thousand feet—here 'a thousand' signifies many, different, infinite, countless etc.; not a literal number—and pervades the earth and the universe on all sides, transcends the ten directions and even after assimilating such innumerable universes, remains unfathomable, He is That!][2]

There must be some special meaning to the shloka above, for it to be chosen from among thousands of Vedic hymns for dhyana. Dhyana can be explained as perceiving the ultimate reality through the mind's eye, whilst focusing on that which we constantly reflect upon, or wish to retain in our heart. Since this hymn is prescribed for dhyana, it must symbolize the true form of 'adah/that' on which we need to contemplate or focus whilst doing dhyana.

The purport of this verse is that though the One assimilates the many, innumerable, countless in Him, His Oneness remains unaffected; He is neither reduced nor expanded. Such Oneness has only one name, Poorna or Completeness. This is the Pure Truth, whether we call it

---

2 Author's own translation.

Ganapati, Shankar, Vishnu, the Supreme Lord or any other name. As stated in the Rig Veda's Purusha Sukta hymn (10.90.2):

पुरुषएवेदं सर्वं यद्भूतं यच्चभव्यम्।
उतामृतत्वस्येशानो यदन्नेनातिरोहति।।

Purussa ĕvedam Sarvam yad-Bhūtam yacca Bhavyam
ūta-āmrtatvasyeśāno yad-ānnena-āti-rohati

[In this universe whatever has been created or can be created, is all Purusha. He enters this world through anna (food) but still remains unchanged.]

The Purusha is not divided; He is indivisible. In fact, all that exists is only Him. It may appear that the reference to food is meaningless. However, it is not so, as food is a suitable form of electromagnetic energy. The Rig Veda has its own scientific system of knowledge.

Poorna means whole or complete, as the reference from the Rig Veda above explains. Thus, the universe is not created by the Supreme Power but is Poorna by the very nature of creation.

कोददर्श प्रथमं जायमान
[Who saw first, the creating of this world?][3]

—Rig Veda

The *Ishavasya Upanishad* makes this Rig Vedic concept clear—the universe is not needed for the existence of the Poorna Purusha. In other words, the absence of the universe does not reduce or take away from the Poorna Purusha in any way, i.e., the Poorna Purusha remains whole and complete. For its part, the universe is also complete in itself as there is nothing material beyond it. Thus, both 'this/idam/manifest universe' and 'that/adah/the non-material' are complete in themselves and we can think of the universe as another form of the 'that/adah'.

---

3   Author's own translation.

The universe can be likened to an ornamental form (of gold) or to an ornamental form etched (on gold) or to a wave (on the sea). As is obvious, the gold and the sea refer to the 'adah', i.e., the foundation from which the forms emerge and on which they rest. This is also what Poornavad holds true. In fact, Poornavad is a reinterpretation with Vedanta philosophy. Since the universe goes on following its rules, one is deceived into believing that nothing supports it and that it is independent of any other influence.

The Rig Vedic Science of Poornavad

The universe is in a constant state of agitation and the human mind is no different. It is because of this agitation that we perceive the world differently depending on our state of mind. This relative view gives us the status of an observer and the knowledge gained by us is Avidya (knowledge of the material world/universe). When the agitation stops completely, one experiences Vidya (the eternal Brahman).

The mind is not in a static state and is composed of more than one component. Normally, our mind is preoccupied by only materialistic considerations, and materialistic needs. This gives rise to Avidya. While Avidya is generally described as ignorance, it goes a bit further. Avidya is ignorance of our real/true self by only focusing on our material needs. Adiguru Shankaracharya said the Avidya leads to relative mind, where the mind is in a state of dilemma—to be or not to be.

To address this dilemma, Poornavad suggests looking beyond our materialistic preoccupations, calming our minds, and realizing the presence of two other important components, which Poornavad identifies as 'adhidaivik' and 'adhyatmik'. Adhidaivik means divine energy and it gives us empathy while adhyatmik means spiritual knowledge and gives us tranquility. Poornavad suggests that by realizing the presence of the other two components as well, we can free ourselves from the dilemma of self and recognize our true selves. This will lead to individual upliftment and social harmony.

Poornavad too holds that however materialistic and individualistic one may be, he should not forget that there are some more salient aspects to him. All one needs to do is to balance the materialist and individual aspects with these other aspects (adhidaivik that gives us empathy and adhyatmik that gives us tranquility). Basically, this is a matter of self-management in an expert Poornavad fashion. This is a continuous process of evolution leading to increased happiness and harmony. Finally, one attains an agitation-free state of mind. This state is nothing but Vidya and implies oneness with that Supreme Lord or Poorna Purusha.

Poornavad advises that even after achieving this state one must continue to undertake activities for the benefit of the world. Withdrawing from this world is tough and one requires guidance from the guru until this agitation-free state is achieved. The test of the agitation-free condition is that one is not influenced by Avidya (the material means, or relative perception).

Swaroopa Sambandha: The Meeting Point of the Fathomable and the Unfathomable

There are various terms in the Rig Veda that are interpretations of scientific realities—adhidaivik (relating to the divine) that represents antarikshya (relating to space) conditions; adhyatmik (relating to knowledge) that represents dyulokeeya (relating to heaven) conditions; and antarikshya and dyulokeeya conditions together represent space-time.

The concept of Poornavad states that the Lord, the world, and the individual soul are inseparable, interrelated and interact as one unit, i.e., the form (*Swaroopa sambandha*). And this theorem is contained in the Shruti hymn '*Vruksha iva stabdhoh*' or 'Still as a tree'.[4] A tree signifies oneness while its branches, roots, leaves, and flowers constitute its plurality. Likewise, even if there is diversity, or many'ness' in this Poorna Purusha-form Universe, He is One.

---

4   The Shruti or Shrutis refer to all those sacred scriptures that are 'heard', i.e., said to be directly received from the divine and written down by the sages. The Shrutis comprise the Vedas, Upanishads, Brahamanas, and Aranyakas.

Just as God begets man in this world, man also completes the circle by begetting God, only man appears to have begotten God with many forms and more qualities than what God gave to man: the creation of Gajanan, Shankar, Vishnu, Dattatreya are the examples.

Man's highest good is the knowledge of God. Although God creates good and evil men simultaneously in relation to times, the good have to progress for the existence and well-being of the human race by restricting the evil like weeds in a field. In the same way, though man created good and evil gods, the good gods, with the passage of time appear to have outlived the evil.

Science provided comforts to man but it also gave birth to the atom bomb and intercontinental ballistic missiles. Just as the United States along with other nations restricts and regulates the proliferation of harmful weapons in the larger interest and welfare of this universe; the sages of yore were required to control the evil powers in the divine field.

During a presentation on the Poornavad Philosophy in an international conference, someone asked 'How can you reconcile having controversial hypothesis like Ajatvad, Kevaladvait, and many others?' The reply was that the whole universe is also full of controversies that's why good and bad, divine and evil, black and white, strong and weak, life and death are also a part of the universal system. Unity in diversity and diversity in unity is the plan of nature.

Poorna Purusha: Do Forms Have Causative Relationships?

The universe being the Poorna Purusha's form, in each state—the material, spiritual and divine—it is He who causes manifestation at each stage of the circular cycle. Thus, water comes as rain from the clouds, evaporates as water from the earth to become a rain cloud again and rain upon the earth; the self-propagating cycle is complete. Similarly, parents beget a son or a daughter, the children marry others and beget children of their own, completing the cycle; a self-propagating circle-cycle. The Poorna Purusha is the sole cause of the manifestation of all these forms of itself. Therefore, neither is water or evaporation a cause, nor is the rain an effect; also therefore, neither is the father or mother a cause, nor is the son or daughter an effect (causal relation).

The wise should be aware that such 'form relations' exist between the old generation and the new (whether water or man). Since these forms of the Poorna Purusha are not themselves the primary cause that drives each circular cycle to completion, they cannot be said to have a causal relationship with each other. They are related to each other only through form and each form is driven by the same sole causative factor, the Poorna Purusha.

Summing up, it is not that first the Lord appeared and then the world or vice versa, both are simultaneous. All this is His form. And each and every thing and every process in this world transforms completing a cycle, evidencing completeness or Poornatva.

At this juncture, one may pose a question: that if God desired, He went into penance and created this world; then this world becomes God's doing and God becomes the doer. How can you then say that there is a Form-Relation between God and the world? Don't you see the doer God and His actions in the world distinctly? To which Dr Parnekar replies:

> This is a valid doubt of the reader. But even if it is the 'doing', it is none other than God's and God's alone. That Poorna Purusha, not as mere witness but possessing complete knowledge and having full control and authority over it. This is what I, like the seers, have to underline and have deliberately quoted Shruti hymns which arouse doubts about doctrine. Of course, I will clarify these doubts later. The world is real, real for the past, present and future and its ruler must be the one and only Poorna Purusha; there is no room for ignorance, Maya or illusion.
>
> In fact, Poornavad is not at all dogmatic. Howsoever, it may be, I will sing Its praise. It is however, quite natural for any being to be inquisitive about His form. And I am merely putting forth, before the learned authorities, His form which Vedas sing and my intellect is convinced about.

That the learned amongst you should also deliberate upon this is my humble request. You shouldn't be inflexible that whatever has come down traditionally is right. And all that which is new is totally wrong. My only request is you should deliberate upon it, test it, try it in real life and then only accept. I am sure that, if adopted in life this would show you the path to 'how to live life happily' and attain higher intellectual level during the process of living.

Poorna Purusha: Its Unfathomable Aspect and the World-Form

Poorna Purusha is Pure, Truth, Supreme Lord. Understanding time as past, present and future, man sought to realize and experience Poorna Purusha in relation to time and worked out that God was to be known as Anadi Anant (the Eternal), because He did not come into being in the past, He already existed; He would never come into being in the future, because He always Was, always Is, and always Will Be.

The Vedas describe the three forms of Poorna Purusha as Brahma, Vishnu and Shiva. All three together are Poorna Purusha. Man imagined Shiva in relation to the past (as the destroyer), Vishnu in relation to the present (as the preserver) and Brahma (as an agent of creation) in relation to the future. Even if man imagined these three independent forms of Poorna Purusha for his own convenience, it is important to remember these as three essential forms of Poorna.

The first of the six hymns of the Vishnu Sukta hymn written by Sage Deerghatama, touches on this. It states that Vishnu pervades all these worlds. He, as the trinity, has pervaded all these. A shloka from the *Taittiriya Upanishad* (2.6.6–8) connotes that the world has not emerged from Maya or ignorance; He deliberately created it with full knowledge.

सोऽकामयत । बहुस्याम् प्रजायेय इति । स तपोऽतप्यत।
स तपस्तप्त्वा इदम् सर्वमसृजत। यदिदं किंच।
तत्सृष्ट्वा तदेवानुप्राविशत् ।।

> *So'kamayata. bahusyam prajayeyeti. Sa tapo'tapyata.*
> *Sa tapastatva. Idagsarvamasrajata. yadidam kincha.*
> *Tatsrashtva. Tadevanupravishat. tadanu pravishya.*

[He desired to become many and be born. In order to achieve that, He went into penance and having completed His penance, He created this world. How did He create this world? He verily entered into it. That is, He acquired this form but prior to that He underwent Penance.][5]

Penance: The Role of Faith, Conviction, Certitude

Where the limit of knowledge ends, penance begins. Knowledge is acquired with the help of means, e.g., a book is a means, a guru's advice is a means, meditation is a means, dhyana, samadhi and chanting also fall under 'means'. Where there is not a single mean at hand, knowledge cannot be acquired. As knowledge unfolds the approach to achieve whatever we want, in a situation where no means are available we cannot acquire knowledge and we cannot get what we require. In such as case only penance can come to our rescue.

Discarding uncertainty: Penance has to be performed by the self alone; none other can serve as means by counselling us. Here, 'means fall short' and it is imperative to totally discard the 'uncertainty'. Nothing is impossible for God or Ishwara. If He desires He can grant us anything we want. Who educated the saints Dnyaneshwar, Tukaram, Kabir, and Meerabai? The answer is they became experts on Ishwara and an authority on the Vedas, without ever having received a formal education at any school or university.

Expecting results without a reason: The implicit faith that, 'our wish can be fulfilled', without any means, without any causal relation, firms up certitude. Penance is maintaining certitude even against odds, nurturing it, enriching it, refining it by making it true resolve. Here we have to come out of the conditioning of the causal relation. For instance,

---

5   Author's own translation.

there are examples of women past sixty, who attained menopause yet begot a child after penance. Only penance is the saviour.

There is a semblance between jeeva (animate creation) and Ishwara, in our lives too we see the jeeva getting things solely by penance, including by nurturing certitude—which normally would not have happened by causal relation. Penance, however, is contemplated only when knowledge is climaxed. It is also important to note that without efforts or endeavouring to acquire requisite knowledge, adopting the path of penance is detrimental.

Understanding Poorna Purusha's Penance and the Fallacy of Maya

Having desired to become many and in order to achieve it without the help of any means (because He didn't have any means) He underwent penance and created this world; it is not certainly the outcome of ignorance or Maya.

The real question is, out of what did He create this world? By what means? Certainly not from an illusion or any illusory means, because he had no means. He, following penance, consciously thought/willed it into existence, therefore there is no possibility of the world being an illusion or emerging from Maya. It is also absolutely wrong to call the world 'unreal' or 'an illusion'. On the contrary there are Shruti hymns that explain the impact of perceiving the Brahman as being unreal, e.g. *Taittraiya Upanishad* (2.6.1):

असन्नेव संभवति ।
असत ब्रह्मेति वेद्येत।।

Asannaeva sabhavati
Asad brahmoti vedhet

['One becometh as the Unexisting,
If he knows the Eternal as negation.'][6]

---

6 Meaning sourced from: upanishads.org.in/upanishads/7/2/6/1

The sixteenth and seventeenth shlokas of the sixth chapter of the *Svetasvatara Upanishad* assert that the world is real, that it is not the *doing* but is the *form* of Ishwara.

Shloka 6.16:

स्वविश्वकद्विश्व विदात्मयोनिर्ज्ञः कालकालोगुणीसर्वविद्यः।
प्रधानक्षेत्रज्ञ पतिर्गुणेशाः संसार मोक्षस्थिति बंध हेतुः।।

Shloka 6.17:

स तन्मयोह्यामृत ईशसंस्थो ज्ञः सर्वगो
भुवनस्यास्य गोप्ता।
य ईशेऽस्य जगतो नित्यमेवनान्योहेतुर्विद्यतेईशनाय ।।

[He is the Master of this world. Self-existent, Creator of Himself, i.e., form is the cause of everything. Knower, Creator of time, Possessor of many qualities. Aware of each and every happening, the Sustainer of manifest and unmanifest, the Purpose of transmigration, liberation, state and bondage; in short, such is That Complete Perfection, the Poorna Purusha.][7]

The foregoing meaning is indisputable, even then if world is 'activity'. The interpretation of 'Atmayoni' (*Sve.* 6.16) is that the form alone is the cause of that activity. This could probably trigger a controversy. We shall therefore examine the next verse (*Sve.* 6.17) which not only satisfies our doubt, but justifies our interpretation. Taking into consideration our interpretation, instead of causal relationship, it is the form relationship which emerges distinctly. However, instead of pondering over the issue, let us consider the verse (*Sve.* 6.17) which furnishes a clear understanding.

If instead of 'pervading the world', owing to 'tat' it is construed as pervading 'Brahman', then there is no justification for '*Hi Amrutaha*',

---

7 Author's own translation.

as this alone describes Him. Besides, the above description is 'world-specific' and 'tat' also depicts the same. It is therefore appropriate to infer as 'pervading the world', 'pervading the universe', etc. Such is He who pervades the world in Brahman-form and holds in Him the Devlokas (the worlds of gods) because it is through the eleven Rudras, twelve Adityas, eight Vasus, etc., that He regulates the functioning of this world. Aware of His own form He pervades everywhere, protects the three worlds.

It is said that the Poorna Purusha, who eternally controls the functioning of this world, has no purpose other than this in doing so. What should we understand from this? It is a contradiction here with the term 'Sakamayat' (meaning 'with purpose'). The purpose of this hymn is just that the world is 'real' and 'the Lord is its Master'.

Quite naturally we wonder as to why He created the world? And the answer is clear. No more importance can be attached to 'Sakamayat' except 'because He felt' like creating it. Likewise, the Vaishnavas, while admitting the reality of the world, assert the causal relationship and say that the Lord created this world for the welfare of devotees. When the doer is Ishwara and the activity is the world, it becomes imperative to spell out the purpose also. Then there is no recourse except to pledge that the purpose is 'His wish', and so on.

The Vedas have described three forms which are eternal, i.e. the Vishwa (world-form), the Vishnu-form, and the Shiva-form. Complemented by all these three is the fourth, the All-Completeness form, which is designated in the Vedas as 'Brahmanaspati' and which Poornavad identifies as the Poornatva (Completeness) of Poorna Purusha. Are the three forms poles apart from each other? Assuming such a situation let us see what the Shruti has to say on this: '*Samyuktam etat ksharam aksharam ch*', which means 'the destructible the manifested; and the indestructible the unmanifested, are inherently united'.[8]

---

8   From the *Svetasvatara Upanishad*.

Once the world is reckoned as His form then His expanse is like that of Poorna Purusha. Brahman is infinitely minute, beyond perception of the intellect, and it is very difficult to comprehend the Supreme Lord.

Even if among the great acharyas some advocated the path of knowledge, some prescribed the path of upasana (worship), some espoused the static consciousness and some the dynamic principle of preservation—the Vedas, prohibit espousing any one of the three aspects of Poorna Purusha singly.

People forgot all this and therefore, some started singing in praise of Ishwara with forms and attributes, while others construed as formless and without attributes and sang in His praise. Vedas however clearly say, '*andham tamah pravishyanti*' (*Yajur Veda*, 40.9), i.e., those who engage in the upasana of Avidya fall into darkness, and those engaged only in the upasana of Vidya fall deeper into darkness. But this is being practiced; it does not mean that the upasana of either of these two singly is prohibited.

The fruits of upasana are different, and therefore co-worship of both is prescribed. That hymn is: '*Vidyan cha vidyan cha*'. He who performs upasana of Vidya together with Avidya, overcomes death and the upasana of Vidya elevates him to immortality. Otherwise performing upasana of only Vidya or that of the formless and attributes leads to helplessly depending on fate till relinquishing the body. This frustration is a philosophical fallacy.

Ideally, for welfare during one's lifetime one must do the upsana of Brahman with attributes—the Lord Vishnu (avidya) who guarantees well-being; engage in worshiping vidya, which bestows immortality during lifetime. The injunction of the Vedas too is that till death, He who guarantees well-being and bestows immortality after death, the upasana of Poorna Purusha should be done alongside the upasana of vidya and avidya.

In the Bhagavad Gita, Lord Krishna espouses Swadharma—'Win after fighting, the entire kingdom on earth would be yours and heaven's gates would be opened for you'. Well-being during one's lifetime and emancipation after death are the fruits of collective upasana or co-worship of vidya and avidya, i.e., of Poorna Purusha.

Sapekshata Vision of the Vedas

We need to realize that as God desired and created this world, it has no place for action without longing for the fruit of that action. Every action has to be coupled with desire, with resolve. However, one should not think that there is a definite purpose 'for my life' and 'I must seek it, otherwise my life is a waste'.

God has no definite purpose in sustaining this world. It would be rather more relevant to find out what inspired early human beings to live, instead of wasting time in finding out the purpose of one's life. In short, each action should be guided by resolve but it shouldn't have a particular purpose. If at all there has to be a purpose in life, it should be to attain development of various facets and to derive happiness out of it. Because the being (jeeva) and the Lord (Ishwara) tend to develop innately. The world is not God's activity, it is His form. It could be enlightening for us to assess what is our share (atman and jeeva) in development, instead of evaluating a particular activity.

Furthermore, Ishwara created this world by undergoing penance. Whenever there is a desire and in order to fulfill that desire there are no means, one should resort to penance (The Rapport, Divine, 13-14).[9] Penance comprises persistence, restraint, strength, capacity and industriousness, having imbibed these, one must pray for God's grace. God also desired to be 'many' and fulfilled it by His industriousness. Doing something consistently is persistence and this leads to penance and one acquires strength. In day-to-day life also doing something consistently helps acquire strength and brings recognition. It should however be backed by desire and resolve. This persistence establishes a jeeva's perpetuity and increases his strength. Therefore, upasana should also be performed perpetually.

---

9 From Dr Parnerkar's Parichay book in Marathi. Translation to English, Dr Deshpande's, p.6.

In order to fulfill his desires, whatever activity the jeeva performs using his body and his mental power, his capability enhances with his strength. Therefore, instead of a variety of upasana for different problems, only one upasana is prescribed which is capable of making life happy. In this manner, while living life happily as per one's wishes, espousing Vedic Avidya one should keep deliberating upon Vidya, immortality, i.e., on true nature of soul and that of Brahman.

The Vedas also stress that the collective upasana of Avidya and Vidya tantamount to upasana of true nature of Poorna, i.e., Poorna Purusha. In this manner one attains both material prosperity and emancipation. He, who thus comprehends Poorna Purusha, attains Moksha.

Poorna Purusha's Siddhi Shakti

As a result of attaining siddhi during Poorna Purusha's upasana, the following things happen:
1. Direct experience of both the mutually heterogenous form characteristic and action, in the one and only Poorna Purusha.
2. Whatever form of Poorna Purusha the Sadhaka longs for, materializes with His grace and helps the Sadhaka live life with mastery.
3. Having direct perception that the Absolute, Pure, Truth, Supreme Lord, His Omniscience is dwelling in everyone's heart as the Atman-form Shiva Tattva.

In such manner, the Sadhaka has direct perception of the Form-Relation of Vishwa, Ishwara, Parabrahman with Poorna Purusha as a result of his upasana or siddhi. However, only Poorna Purusha's form siddhi does not mean Poorna Purusha's Poorna Siddhi.

The True and Definite Meaning of Maya

This chapter will only reach its fulfillment upon comprehending the true and definite meaning of Maya. For this, firstly we shall consider the meaning of another shloka from *Svetasvatara Upanishad* (3.1):

य एको जालवानीशत ईशनीभिः सर्वान् ल्लोकानीशत ईशनीभिः।
य एवैक उद्भवे संभवे च य एतद्विदुर अमृतास्ते भवन्ति।।

ya eko jalavan isata isanibhih sarvanllokan isata isanibhih
ya evaika udbhave sambhave cha ya etad vidur amrtaste bhavanti

[That Illusory, Peerless Poorna Purusha or the Highest God covers Himself with world-form cobweb (net) created out of His power, rules over all the world through His powers of rulership. He is verily alone, unaffected by the creation, sustenance and destruction. Those who know this become immortal. [10]

Here if cobweb (jaal, or net) is construed as Maya and the creator of Maya is a Jaalwan (weaver of nets) then we have to accept Ishwara is the cause and Maya is effect. As the spider creates many cobwebs from his body, this power of creating cobwebs becomes multiplied/plural. Like this spider who creates cobwebs, regulates and destroys those through his power; the Jaalwan Ishwara, it must be admitted, has the power to create Maya, regulate and destroy it.

The sadhaka meditating upon Ishwara or Poorna, upon closing his eyes, every moment whatever comes before him, that everything in a way is His form; He being verily there, the sadhaka's firm opinion nevertheless is that He is different and separate from what is visible. This is what is called the jaal (net) or Maya.

During meditation whatever appears before him is not That, and so the sadhaka brushes That aside. In fact, if the sadhaka takes whatever appears before him in meditation as Ishwara encouraging him, as though saying 'this is Ishwara', that would be a a positive approach and better and easier for dhyana. Sadly, even when he is closer to the Truth the sadhaka is not convinced, and *that* is Maya.

The point is: What is the root cause of the diversity seen in this world and the causal relationship creating illusion in man's mind?

---

10 Author's own translation.

1. Is it Ishwara who deliberately creates this illusion with a view to covering or hiding Himself?
2. Or is it because of His characteristic nature?
3. Or is it because of something different?

In short, if world is construed as activity then what is its 'cause'? In order to find an answer, if we assume for a while that this Vishwa is activity, then there is no other cause except Himself. This activity is not anybody else's except His, rather 'He Himself'.

It is important in this respect to examine shloka 6.5 from the *Svetasvatara Upanishad*. But prior to that it is important to discuss some points. In order to get acquainted with someone or to experience him, we observe his activities. Same method applies in day-to-day life.

A man's personality, knowledge, or strength are evaluated on the basis of his activities. Based on his activity even if it is possible to assess his capability, still to assess his total capability or strength is difficult. Even if we encounter him and he honestly acquaints us with all his qualities or qualifications, we are still not aware of whatever qualities or strengths he possesses and we are at a loss to make a fair assessment. Arising out of this, even if we have known someone's form, that is inadequate to tell us about the powers he possesses nor can we experience those. In order to get that knowledge or experience, we shall have to mingle with him, be one with him; this could be one method, even then we cannot evaluate his other powers of which many times he himself is unaware.

Just as this is true in case of people, so it is in respect of Vishwa, Ishwara and Parabrahman, i.e., Poorna Purusha. Merely being one with Brahman does not mean that all His powers residing as formless, attributeless can be comprehended. Similarly, even if Shiva is comprehended, it is difficult to comprehend Shiva's Shakti. At times, that Shakti could gulp Shiva. Man is not aware of his own powers and that is why the thrust of the Upanishads is on self-realization, God-realization and Brahman-realization.

The explanation of shloka 6.5 from the *Svetasvatara Upanishad* uncovers this truth:

That Original Purusha is the cause of entire activities of the five elements in the world. He is totally different from past, present, and the future. He transcends Time and hence is the present continuous or even though He is without the five vital forces and senses of cognition, He is clearly perceptible. Sages have known Him. We perform His upasana.[11]

In this shloka also, having said that He is the cause of everything, His non-duality with the world is indicated by 'Vishwaroopam'. He is world-form, first we perform His upasana who resides in our heart and having done His upasana, we comprehend Him. From this, it is clearly the description of Poorna Purusha and the sage is acquainting us with His powers is proven.

Lastly, we shall discuss a section from the *Svestasvatara Upanishad* that acquaints us with Poorna Purusha's powers and provides His comprehensive description. With this, we shall conclude the topic 'Poorna Purusha'.[12]

In the first shloka He is Ishwara of all the Ishwaras, and the sage says:[13]

'That Parbrahman, Poorna Purusha, Great Ishwara, Ishwara of Ishwaras, Great Ruler of Protectors, He is the Deity of all Deities and Protector of Protectors, is most befitting to be praised since He transcends the Parbrahman. We know the Self-Effulgent, Highest God Poorna Purusha'.

There are two forms of Poorna Purusha of which the transient world is one. He who is the doer, controls and is identified with this/idam/the manifest universe, the Vedas call venerate this divine manifestation as Lord Vishnu. Purusha's other form is unmanifest, and is venerated as

---

11 Author's own translation.
12 6th shloka, 7th stanza, *Principle Upanishads* by S. Radhakrishnan, under Svestasvatara Upanishad.
13 Ibid.

Parabrahman, the only witness. In the Vedas, He has names like Shiva, Shankar, etc.

The Hari-Har pair is well-known in the Puranas. (For well-being, Vishnu's upasana, and for direct perception of Parabrahman, Shiva's upasana is prescribed.) In short, the term Ishwara signifies this 'Hari-Har' and greater than Him who is Maheshwar or Great Ishwara is Poorna Purusha. He is the ruler of eight Vasus, eleven Rudras, twelve Adityas, Indira and Prajapati, who make up the thirty-three koti (cadres) of gods. The gods have their paraphernalia, attendants who are known as 'ganas' and their head is referred to as the 'pati', viz., Indra is the head of his 'marudganas',. He is also the (pati) master of all such masters (patis) and transcends the Parabrahman, He is the guardian of fourteen worlds who is immensely worshipped, to Him we know.

Thus speaks the sage in the shloka which implies that the sage had direct perception of Poorna Purusha. In the second, the sage says:[14]

> 'No activity is attributable to Him. He has no desire for any specific purpose or activity. He is not the cause of anything. There is nothing greater or higher than Him. We hear His unfathomable power which is beyond logic whose description we here as His knowledge, power and activity'.

This is His naturally manifesting innate equipoised state. In short, comprehension of Ishwara with reference to world's activities is not the true comprehension. Unless and until we comprehend His total capacity to work and his innate power, we cannot have complete comprehension of Ishwara. Whatever Ishwara does with a predetermined mind and the power behind it, even if it becomes comprehensible by becoming one with Him and about which Dharma, the Vedas, and science have provided important information; still whatever all happens on its own and quite naturally, without Ishwara's intervention or determination, is beyond human comprehension.

---

14 Ibid.

He, who is detached despite doing everything and learns to live in equipoised state, could perhaps due to that state have a little bit of comprehension. So long as man is not acquainted with this innate power of Ishwara, his awareness of God remains incomplete. In short, so long as the sadhaka does not truly comprehend '*Swabhaviki dnyan kriya*', it is difficult for him to comprehend Poorna Purusha.

In the third shloka: [15]

In the (Satya Loka) world of gods, none is His guardian, regulator and master. That from which He could be inferred there is no symbol at all. He is the purpose of all. He is the basis of organs and their deities. He has neither a creator nor a guardian. In short, this unborn perennial, absolutely free, self-existent, possessing dnyan, bal and kriya all-powerful Poorna Purusha has Form-Relation with Vishwa, Ishwara and Parabrahman. All these are His forms. From all these, it is unequivocally proved that Ishwara with Parabrahman locus is not the 'world-form-jugglery-indulging-Maya's' offspring. He is completely unfettered, self-existent, unborn. The witness, Ishwar and the world are His innate forms.

In all the three shlokas the subject of description is the Poorna Purusha. It is categorically elucidated that though heterogeneous, the world-form and the Brahman-form are His forms only. Even though He is All Completeness, we are taken over by the illusion that either He is with form and attributes or He is formless and without attributes and that is Maya; therefore, Shruti names Him as 'Jaalwan', and 'Mayin'. So that this illusion is dispelled, and Poorna Purusha's true form consistently retained in the mind, the seeker should contemplate on these three shlokas with an equipoised mind every day. It is believed that the seeker will gain complete and true comprehension of Poorna Purusha upon reflection and contemplation of the three shlokas above, and one must believe this with certitude.

---

15 *Principle Upanishads*, S. Radhakrishnan

CHAPTER 8

Supreme Lord of the Corporate Universe

THIS CHAPTER considers the applied dimension of the Vedic concept of Poorna Purusha. The Vedas are by nature secular and even professional. Lord Vishnu is the god of the Divine and Applied Sciences. The manifest form of God causes our material and monetary life to flourish. Dr Parnerkar introduced this optimistic dimensions of the Vedas, which are the subject matter of investigation in the twenty-first century as they meet the need of the era.

Contemporary philosophy is under the pessimistic impact of Buddhism, as stated earlier in the Preface. Buddhism denies the soul, the Vedas, and the existence of God. Despite denying the Vedas, Buddhist doctrine's assertion that 'life is impermanent, sorrowful and misery-filled' is taken from the *Katha Upanishad,* and reflects but a partial dimension of the Upanishads. Another side of the pessimistic approach of the Buddhist doctrine is 'Shunyavad' (void; non-existence). On the other hand, the Vedic concept of Poornavad is optimistic, as the Vedas have no concept of shunya (void or non-existence). On the contrary, what Buddhism calls 'Shunya', the Vedas call Poorna or complete.

The digit or the number that represents Shunya and Poorna is the same—zero. Again, Shunya takes the negative approach to zero using it to attribute to non-existence; whereas Poorna means complete, and takes the positive approach that sees zero as that which multiplies the figure to infinity. The placement of zeros behind any number increases the value of the original figure. This is the vision of the Vedas that creates an optimistic and positive approach towards looking at anything. Thinking or meditating upon a negative approach—that life is misery, life is sorrowful, life is impermanent—creates a negative feeling. Though it is true, it is not the whole picture. Why do you forget the bright side of life—that life is celebration, life is joyous and full of pleasure too? (see Chapter 18, 'Waves of Bliss')

The concept of the Divine as bliss was introduced in the 'Bhriguvalli' chapter—the dialogue between father and son, guru and disciple Varuni and Bhrigu—in the *Taittiriya Upanishad*. That father and son, Varuni and Bhrigu, can be said to have reincarnated in the form of Guru Dr R.P. Parnerkar and his son and disciple V.R. Parnerkar. Dr Ramchandra Parnerkar established the Form-Relation Theory of the Poornavad doctrine, expressing it in Sanskrit, and Dr V.R. Parnerkar has explained the doctrine of Poornavad in Marathi, Hindi and English. His book *Poornavad (Re-interpretation of Indian Philosophy)* published in 2016, introduces the reader to the optimistic, scientific professional and corporate vision of the Vedas that gave priority to material prosperity and monetary gain by the grace of the divine power of Lord Vishnu the god of prosperity and peace. He also explained the Divine Form of Lord Vishnu.

Well-known scientist of modern physics, Fritjof Capra, too experienced and realized the Form of the Dancing Shiva and shared his in an article 'The Dance of Shiva',[1] (also see Chapter 13, 'Poornavad Vision on Vedic Science'). The form and image of God is a scientific concept visualized in the Vedas. The purpose of referring to it here is to

---

1 Capra, Fritjof (1972), 'The Dance of Shiva: The Hindu View of Matter in Light of Modern Physics' in *Main Currents in Modern Thought*, Vol. 29.

guide you to trust the Vedic concepts, utilize the science of divinity and gain profit in your business—because the basic theory of any business, or of the corporate sector, is 'minimum effort maximum gain'. Poornavad advises you to take the maximum advantage of divinity and undertake an investigative project on the experience of intuitional power.

Lord of the Universe: Governance

How the Poorna Purusha, the Lord of the Universe governs and holds the entire universe is the ideal model to study. To understand the management skills of the Poorna Purusha you have to understand the Vedic concepts of Vidya/Avidya and especially, Maya. Maya is the network system created by Poorna Purusha that stops people from visiting or attaining realization of the Poorna Purusha, unless they are qualified to get through.

In corporate terms, Maya is the personal secretary who diverts non-serious visitors. To get past Maya to the Poorna Purusha you have to crack a code and it is a very difficult code to crack. The Poorna Purusha has six security circles known as Vyahrities, plus one final security circle. The six are: भू (Bhu), भूवः (Bhuva), ñd… (Swaha), महः (Maha), जनः (Jana), and तपः (Tapa). The seventh circle of security is closest to the Poorna Purusha and is known as: सत्य (Satya) where is the realm of transcendental peace and the overflow of Bliss. Experiencing this may excite you, which will increase your anxiety. If, during such a thrilling experience, you manage to remain cool you will realize the divine experience and you will be benefited beyond imagination.

The person who passes all the six security circles becomes eligible to attempt crossing this seventh circle. Once he crosses it, his work is done. There is no further need to ask or say anything before the Poorna Purusha, for He provides you all the comforts, luxuries and the higher status as you deserve, which allows you to be satisfied with whatever is the gain is- minimum or maximum. You will forget the greediness and anxiety of bitter competition in the corporate universe. All the poetic imaginations of the platonic world are also realities at this seventh layer of space.

Roger Penrose in his book *Road to Reality* discussed the concept of whether the Platonic mechanical world actually exists in a meaningful sense.² Many people, including philosophers, might regard such a statement as a complete fiction—a product merely of our unrestrained imaginations. Yet this viewpoint is indeed an immensely valuable one. The reference above supports the Vedic concept of Highest Heaven. That Poorna Purusha is productive in nature, is best expressed in the Sanskrit phrase: एकोहं बहुस्याम् (*Ekoham Bahusyam;* I am One, Let Me be Many). Poornavad says one alone can turn the tide; this is the corporate mantra: B+ (Be Positive).³

As mentioned in earlier chapters, Jesus Christ spent part of his adolescence in India gaining an education of Sanskrit and the Vedas. He was very curious to know about every aspect of Vedic hymns, so as to understand the complete Vedic concept of Ultimate Truth. As mentioned in previous chapters, Jesus asked his teacher, a priest, as to why the sun and fire (Agni) were worshipped as gods? On whose instructions did the sun rise and shine and by whose directions did the fire destroy anything? Were the sun and agni independent? Or more likely, there must be some invisible power behind it all, and he asked to learn about that Supreme Lord of the Universe. His guru, the priest, who was just a blind follower of orthodox rituals, did not know the answers.

We can see a parallel between Jesus Christ and Dr Parnerkar, who had the same curiosity to know the real authority behind the manifest universe. Himself a scholar of Sanskrit and the Vedas, Dr Parnerkar found the answer and introduced the Vedic concept of Poorna Purusha (see: Chapter 6, 'Genome of Poorna Purusha: the Supreme Lord'). Dr Parnerkar found that there was no higher authority than Poorna Purusha, and that the entire unmanifest universe and the manifest world was His form. He occupied the whole universe, yet remained above it.

---

2   Penrose, Roger (2006), *Road to Reality: A Complete Guide to the Laws of the Universe*. London: Vintage Books.
3   Robert Penrose, *Road to Reality* (US: Penguin Random House, 2007) p.12.

He governs the entire universe above ten times of the entire universe. As the *Rig Veda* (10.90) puts it: '*Atyatishthat Dashangulam.*'[4]

The Poorna Purusha governs the universe with the coordination of thirty-three types of ministerial gods.

Divine Administration: Different Types of Gods

Basically, there are three cadres that are known as the 'thirty-three Koti Devata'. In Sanskrit 'koti' means the cadre, like Class-I, Class-II, Class-III, etc., but all the gods have an equal status. You will find this reference in *Kena Upanishad*; gods like Surya, Agni, Varuna, Vayu—all work under one Supreme authority. These cadres include the: eleven Rudras, twelve Adityas, eight Vasus, and the two Ashwani Kumars.

The Eleven Rudras: 1. मनू (Manu) 2. मन्यू (Manyu) 3. महत् (Mahat) 4. शिव (Shiva) 5. ऋतूध्वज (Rutudhwaj) 6. महिनस (Mahinus) 7. उम्रतेजस (Umratejas) 8. काल (Kal) 9. वामदेव (Vamdeo) 10. भव (Bhava) 11. धृतध्वज (Dhrutdwaj).

The Twelve Adityas: Before writing about the twelve Adityas, I remember one of my meditational experiences which happened couple of years back when I was in deep meditation. I saw a group of suns on the horizon and before I could count them, I heard a voice in my ear, 'don't count, they are twelve'. I could not grasp the reference of that divine and transcendental event at that time, but today I understand the relevance of meditation about the twelve Adityas. They are: अंशुमन (Anshuman) 2. आर्यमन (Aaryaman), 3. इंद्र (Indra), 4. त्वष्टा (Tvashta), 5. धानू (Dhanu), 6. पर्जन्य (Parjanya), 7. पूषन (Pushan), 8. भग (Bhag), 9. मित्र (Mitra), 10. वरुण (Varun), 11. वैवस्वत (Vaivaswat), 12. विष्णू (Vishnu).

The Eight Vasus: आप (Aap), 2. ध्रुव (Dhruva) 3. सोम (Som), 4. धर (Dhar), 5. अनिल (Anil), 6. अनल (Anal), 7. प्रत्युष (Pratyush) 8. च्हास (Prahas).

The Two Ashwani Kumars: Dasra and Nastya.

These four cadres (kotis) comprising thirty-three devatas or gods govern the entire universe mathematically and mechanically using universal laws:

---

4 https://www.supremeknowledge.org/holy-vedas/rig-veda-mandal-10-sukt-90/.

Law of Gravity: The Supreme Power of the Lord of the Universe spans the entire universe and beyond.

Law of Action and Reaction: Every action has its reaction therefore be conscious before taking any action and step. Look before you leap. So that you will get positive action in return.

Law of Conservation of Energy: Dr Parnerkar's Poornavad also upholds the veracity of this law—that energy neither decreases nor increases, but remains constant. We can also refer to the Seed Sutra of the *Ishavasya Upanishad*: 'Om Poornamadaha, Poornamidam...', i.e., everything is within the Poorna (all complete, entire); He is the Cause and Effect in Himself. The Vedas state He is 'Purusha' and He is Poorna. Accept Him as the Supreme Power of the Universe; He alone is the Poorna Purusha and is the Supreme Lord of the Universe, which is His form.

Law of Quantum: In view of the quantum mechanism the entire unmanifest and manifest, animate and inanimate is an interrelated and inseparable unit, therefore, Dr Parnerkar's Poornavad doctrine says that the entire universe is the form of the one Supreme Energy of 'Brahma', the Purusha of the Vedas; this personification of the entire universe is called 'Brahmana' (see: 'Purusha Sukta' of the tenth mandal of the *Rig Veda*).

Dr Parnerkar says that the Vedas are parallel to modern physics, as the Vedas are the science of universal knowledge. Therefore, the Vedas are universal and belong to all. No one can claim this patent. The Vedas are the 'Dream Universal Dharma'.

The Poorna Purusha governs this universe through its scientific laws articulated in cosmogeny, cosmology, astrophysics, biology, psychology, anatomy, chemistry, bio-chemistry, nano-particle science; from micro to macro is the science of Poorna Purusha. Know Him and pray to Him. He is omniscient and omnipresent.

So let us come to the Supreme Lord of the Corporate Universe. How He is and where He is—as described in this chapter, when you surpass the six circles of security and succeed in breaching the seventh circle you reach the highest rank of space, the world of gods. You will realize the Supreme Lord of the Corporate Universe is Lord Ganesh with Riddhi-Siddhi smiling and welcoming you. Lord Ganesh is as bright as multi-trillion suns but still cool like a moon. Calm and quiet, always comfortable. There is no stress, no fear, everything is fair with him. He is the Lord of the Corporate Universe of Wisdom.

The Empire of Lord Ganesh

Under Him you will find many supernatural, unimaginable stars and planets with innovative intelligent superhuman cultures. You cannot imagine their beauty and talent. Bend and surrender before Lord Ganesh who is the Lord of Wisdom and can provide you anything that you wish and as you desire. My master is enlightened by Lord Ganesh, and has written a work in two parts, titled *Ganesh Purana,* that contains all information about Lord Ganesh. Both part I and II are neither fantasy nor fiction. They narrate how He is the Reality. He is only Ultimate Truth and the Ultimate Reality. A Road to the Supreme and Beautiful Reality.

Lord Ganesha possesses eight Siddhis: 1. अणिमा (Anima), 2. महिमा (Mahima), 3. गरिमा (Garima), 4. वसिता (Vasita), 5. लघिमा (Laghima), 6. इशिता (Ishita), 7. प्राप्ती (Prapti), 8. प्राकाम्या (Prakamya)[5]

Naturally questions then arise as to how and why we have not yet been able to realize the Road to Reality? Because we are under the impact of a pessimistic philosophy which denies the existence of the soul, and amps up the importance of Avidya whilst misinterpreting Maya. Maya, when correctly interpreted, has an important role in the corporate world as explained above. If you align with the Divine through belief, prayer and meditation Maya will support your endeavours by permitting only that to filter in which is best for your goals. In other words, Maya provides you the top security system that helps you to achieve your goals and targets.

This is the outstanding contribution of Dr Parnerkar's Poornavad doctrine which has introduced the scientific, optimistic and professional applied three-dimensional vision of the Vedas. The three dimensions

---

[5] Chapter 45 'Ganeshsatranam', *Ganesh Purana,* ed. V.R. Parnerkar, p.278.

of the Vedas can also be realized when you activate your third divine eye that is located between the eyebrows. The third eye can be activated by the grace of a divine Guru, such as my Master Dr Parnerkar. He is one such great Divine Authority who can activate your third eye. The third eye gives you three-dimensional vision of the material, spiritual and divine world.

Once that is done you can introspect your inner world where you can realize the Poorna Purusha's glory, prosperity and peace. Lord Shri Krishna showed Arjuna His Vishwaroopa (Universal Form) on the battlefield of Kurukshetra. The actual form of Poorna Purusha is so vast and bright that it is difficult to face Him, to see or comprehend Him without the presence or the grace of the Divine Guru.

Dr Parnerkar has shown the reality of such a divine form of God, the Poorna Purusha. But it is a very rare practice. Nobody can compel Him. If He feels the seeker is suitable and eligible, then He may oblige such a person. Therefore, it is better to increase your eligibility by way of worship and meditation or upasana under the guidance of a guru. But Poornavad stresses on the seeking God's grace rather than desiring to view the actual presence of His form before you.

CHAPTER 9

Maya: Nature of the Material World

WHENEVER WE hear the word 'Maya' many things come to our mind such as mystery, suspense, complications, some type of conspiracy, a little bit dramatic, harking after material gain, greed, doubt, secrecy, diplomacy, etc. Maya is tough to understand but once you understand it psychologically, then it becomes easy to comprehend and to unravel yourself from its web. That is when you will feel the fine-tuning in your life. Though depicted in the Vedas as tough and difficult to understand, when you observe and study the nature and utility of Maya, you will realize that Maya is a tremendous power of the material world that gives you all types of strengths in life and makes you prosperous and successful.

While the Kevaladvaitins[1] consider Maya as 'ignorance' and a 'hurdle' on the path to liberation or salvation, the Vedas accept Maya as the strength of the material world, which relates to creation, sustenance, and declination as linked to the three female deities, divine energies -Mahasaraswati, Mahalaxmi and Mahakali. Practically, Maya is useful and beneficial because of its nature: i.e., the material world. As the *Svetasvatara Upanishad* (4.1) states:

---

1 Followers of Shankaradvait school of thought.

मायां तुप्रकृतिं विद्यान्मायिनं तु महेश्वरम्।
तस्यावयवभूतैस्तुव्याप्तं सर्वमिदं जगत्।।

māyaṁ tu prakṛtiṁ vidyānmāyinaṁ ca maheśvaram
tasyāvayavabhūtaistu vyāptaṁ sarvamidaṁ jagat

[That which we call Maya is in fact Prakriti and Ishwara is its creator. As Ishwara is addressed as Maheshwar, the Great God, it would be appropriate to call Him Poorna Purusha (the All Complete).[2]

What is called Maya in the Vedas and Upanishads is created out of Poorna Purusha's or Ishwara's world-form; while as per the Advaitins, Maya creates the world, begets the world—what a difference! Vedanta philosophy says that the world is merely an unreal manifestation (vivarta) of Brahman. According to Sankara, adhyasa (superimposition) is the false superimposition of the characteristics of physical body (birth, death, skin color etc.) onto the atman, and also the false superimposition of the characteristics of Atman (sentiency, existence) onto the physical body Adhyasa (projection) or Vivarta (an apparent or illusory form) are not found anywhere in the Vedas. If we were to undertake a hair-splitting exercise and speculate on why 'vivarta' occurred to Shri Shankaracharya, we may come across a couple of shlokas, one of which is quoted below (*Svetasvatara Upanishad* 2.14)

यथैव बिम्बं मृदयोपलिप्तं तेजोमयं भ्राजते तत्सुधान्तम्।
तद्वाऽऽत्मतत्त्वं प्रसमीक्ष्य देही एकः कृतार्थो भवतेवीतशोकः।।

yathaiva bimbaṁ mṛdayopaliptaṁ tejomayaṁ bhrājate tatsudhāntam
tadvātmatattvaṁ prasamīkṣya dehī ekaḥ kṛtārtho bhavate vītaśokaḥ

[Just as a diamond ring enveloped in mud regains its dazzle after it is washed; likewise, the being upon realizing the truth of Atman separate from the gross body becomes divinely content and freed from all sources.]

---

2   Author's own translation

In this shloka from the *Svetasvatara Upanishad*, Shankaracharya believes the meaning of the word 'dazzling' is described as (being like) the superimposition of silver on the lustre of an oyster-shell. Projection (adhyasa) and an apparent or illusory form (vivarta) perhaps could be related to Shruti in this way. But how very remote and how much of a stretch of the imagination it is, the reader may decide for himself.

Well, in spite of this, Shruti does not reckon the world as having evolved from Maya or as unreal. On the contrary, Maya, which is the consequence of the world form, is dealt with in the Vedas. We shall, with the help of the shloka from the *Svetasvatara Upanishad* (2.10) critically examine it:[3]

यस्तूर्णनाभ इव तन्तुभिः प्रधानजैः स्वभावतो
देव एकः स्वमावृणोत्। स नो दधाद्ब्रह्माप्ययम्।।

[The only God, who like a spider, creates a web of multiplicity around Him in this world. May He bless us with the Brahman-Experience.]

One thing is clear from the shloka—at the very beginning of this 'Maya' chapter we said that Ishwara, Poorna Purusha, has enveloped Himself with the world-form. Why was this stated at the beginning? The object of this Maya chapter is to 'uncover' Him, to take away the mayic cover under which Ishwara is hidden, to see Him, to get acquainted with Him, to comprehend Him. To do so, we have adopted an analytical method. In the earlier chapter we deliberated upon the Poorna Purusha's form and its significance. Whatever 'Is', we covered 'It' with the doctrine of the Vishwa-form, Vishnu-form and Shiva-form of Poorna Purusha.

Those who have been blessed to see, as it were, the transcendental Poorna Purusha, gain the ability to discern the true nature of Maya as well. Thereafter, Maya cannot trouble such a person, as s/he can use Maya constructively, whilst seeing through it. Indeed, without His

---

3   https://www.esamskriti.com/e/Spirituality/Upanishads-Commentary/Svetasvatara-Upanishad-~-Chap-2-Invocation-to-Savitr-(The-Sun)-and-Practice-of-Yoga-3.aspx

Grace, to comprehend Maya is difficult. The Highest God Himself creates Maya—hence Shruti calls Him 'Mayin' (The creator, or master of Maya) The Advaitins, on the other hand, see Ishwara as 'maya's adjunct'.

Here again, it must be said that this Maya is evolved from the world. Because there is a clear mention in Sve 2.10 as '*Pradhanjai Swabhavtaha*' i.e., this is unborn and natural, therefore, this is the form. Owing to Prakriti (Primal Nature) and its diversity, man's view is obscured, leading him to treat the phenomenon as the causal relation—this is Maya. Though diversity is not due to Maya but diversity constantly keeps us busy with the worldly business, the day-to-day life, while the perception of the Divine form remains a distant possibility—this is Maya.

Therefore, by now we must have apprehended the Maya as contended by Advaitins and how it is unreal. It would be clearer still if we keep the following shloka from the *Svetasvatara Upanishad* (4.1) before us. which says, 'Maya means Prakriti':

मायां तुप्रकृतिं विद्यान्मयिनं तु महेश्वरम्।
तस्यावयवभूतैस्तुव्याप्तं सर्वमिदं जगत्।।

[That which we call Maya is in fact Prakriti and Ishwara is its creator. As Ishwara is addressed as Maheshwar, the Great God, it would be appropriate to call Him Poorna Purusha.]

Having called the world as Poorna Purusha's limb-form, the non-duality of the world with Poorna is highlighted. Similarly, it is said that: 'The world has not evolved from Maya, all the Prakriti of the world is Maya.'[4]

In this world, nine things—creation, sustenance and destruction; desire, enjoyment and fulfillment; the past, present and future—that are seen are verily called prakriti. In the same way the past, present and future and whatever sequence there is, viz., wind from sky, etc., are a part of prakriti. The seemingly visible casual relation leads us to think

---

4 Poornavad (2007 English edition), Dr Parnerkar, 4.10.

that there must be a causal relation between the world and Ishwara. This is the effect of the illusory prakriti and that is why she is called Maya. In short, as a result of what we see, i.e., the world, prakriti and the happenings therein, that which makes us feel that this is Ishwara's activity—this is Maya. But once Ishwara is reckoned as 'Mayin' it cannot be attributed to man's ignorance, rather it is providential.

What could be the root cause of this world-nature (jagat prakriti)? The authors of the *Svetasvatara Upanishad* (1.2) state:[5]

कालः स्वभावो नियतिर्यदृच्छा भूतानि योनिः पुरूष इति चिन्त्या।
संयोगएषां नत्वात्मभावदात्माऽप्यनीशः सुखदुःखहेतोः॥

kalah svabhavo niyatiryadrccha bhUtani yonih puruea iti cintyam samyoga eearh na tv'atmabhavad 'atma'py anisah sukhaduhkhahetoh

[The creation, sustenance and destruction, sunrise, sunset take place in consonance with time. Is that 'time' its cause? Or based on how a seed sprouts to grow into a tree, could therefore the inherent quality of each thing itself be the cause? Or are the pious or unpious the cause of the world? Or is it an accidental event? Or could the five elements, Purush or Jeevatma be the cause?

It is relevant to delve into this topic. In order to comprehend prakriti, it is essential to consider all these different causes. Just as 'to err is human', could 'man is mortal' also be taken as human nature? If any of these individually could not be the cause of the world, could all these put together be the cause? The sages realized that such questions could not be resolved merely by intellect or thought. To resolve those questions that could not be resolved by thought—or logic, such as the root cause of the world (jagat), nature (prakriti)—they adopted the path of dhyana. to reach for. Here the spiritual seeker should bear in mind that when a

---

5 https://www.esamskriti.com/e/Spirituality/Upanishads-Commentary/Svetasvatara-Upanishad-~-Chap-1Speculation-about-the-First-Cause-1.aspx

problem cannot be resolved by thought or logic, i.e., the intellect, there the path of dhyana has to be adopted.

With such dhyana, what sort of conclusive reply did the sages get? The authors of the *Upanishad* state: [6]

ते ध्यानयोगानुगता अपश्यन् देवात्मशक्तिं स्वगुणैर्निगूढाम्।
यः कारणानि निखिलानि तानि कालात्मयुक्तान्यधितिष्ठत्येकः।।

The meaning of this shloka needs to be looked into in detail: It states that the seers, with an equipoised mind, while in meditation, perceived 'Devatma Shakti', which is God's own Atmik power, as the cause of this world. They had the revelation of the incomprehensible, innate, Poorna Purusha form that the 'Devatma Shakti' had enveloped with her own qualities, from 'time', up to 'purusha' or jeevatma's thought-related all causes. The 'Devatma Shakti' was the fundamental seat, 'the master'; but what kind of Devatma Shakti was it? It was not as Samkhya Prakriti, such as 'Pradhan' and independent of Purusha, but rather was 'Atmabhoot', inherent in the Atman, embodied in Him, dependent on Him. Therefore, this was certainly not the Maya of Advaitins.

Devatma Shakti was described by the sages as '*Swagunairnigudham*', i.e., enveloped with her own qualities. This Devatma Shakti is Ishwara's very own inconceivable characteristic power and is the fundamental cause of Prakriti or the world. To say: 'She is the cause' or 'The world is His form' or 'The world is He', is the same. '*Swabhaviki dnyanbal kriyach*' the knowledge, power and activity innate in Poorna Purusha are called His Power. Therefore, there is no duality between Him and His power.

In short, the sages in their dhyana realized that the conclusive cause of the world and the prakriti is Ishwara's inconceivable innate 'knowledge-power-and-activity-form', i.e., Devatma Shakti or power. And Devatma Shakti is the seat of 'time', 'characteristic nature', etc. It

---

6   https://www.esamskriti.com/e/Spirituality/Upanishads-Commentary/Svetasvatara-Upanishad-~-Chap-1Speculation-about-the-First-Cause-1.aspx

therefore becomes clear that Ishwara's innate, characteristic Devatma Shakti means prakriti and prakriti is Maya.

With the utterance of '*ashtadha prakriti*' what occurs to us immediately is the 'five elements' and the 'trigunas' (the three qualities or gunas: sattva, rajas and tamas). But it is not correct to restrict the meaning this way. 'Time', 'characteristic nature', 'accidental destiny of Karma', etc., are also deliberated upon as the cause of the world. The cause of all these causes is His innate power, i.e., Prakriti, hence, He is the cause of all causes. By realizing that 'time' is inert while '"characteristic nature" is spirit', it becomes abundantly clear that sages in their dhyana ultimately envisioned and comprehended that the inert and the spirit have Form-Relation with Poorna Purusha. Therefore, the world is certainly not Maya's activity. If at all it is to be reckoned as activity, it is none other than the Ishwara's, the Poorna Purusha's.

From all the above, 'Maya' describes that power of Ishwara which creates illusion. The *Kena Upanishad's* deliberates who is the doer of worldly activity, and how is it done? The author of the *Kena Upanishad* in its first shloka (1.1) says:[7]

ॐ केनेषितं पतति प्रेषितं मनः केनप्राणः प्रथमः प्रैति युक्तः।
केनेषितां वाचमिमां वदन्तिचक्षुः श्रोत्रं क उ देवो युनक्ति॥

oṃ keneṣitaṃ patati preṣitaṃ manaḥ kena prāṇaḥ prathamaḥ praiti yuktaḥ
keneṣitāṃ vācamimāṃ vadanti cakṣuḥ śrotraṃ ka u devo yunakti

[By whose will does the mind proceed towards objects? On whose ordainment, does the breath first move? On whose desire, does speech be spoken? Who is the god that prompts verily the eyes and ears?]

Poornavad has come across several hymns on similar topics: has anyone seen the Animate Supreme Lord who looks after this Inanimate Universe

---

7 https://www.wisdomlib.org/hinduism/book/kena-upanishad-madhva-commentary/d/doc486065.html

being born? Or none? If yes, whither was this earth, its creatures, being, the soul and the blood prior to His birth? Did any learned one enquire about this?

Raising such questions, we were told that both have been simultaneous. The very same method seems to have been adopted in *Kena Upanishad*.

Who, in short, promotes both individual as well as worldly transactions? This is the question which has been raised in part-I of the *Kena Upanishad*. In reply, it begins with: 'who, by ears here is not heard but by whom all hearing itself comes to be energized; who by eyes here is not perceived but by whom does all the perception itself comes to be energized; who by breath breathed but by whom all the breathing here comes to be energized?'

That alone is Brahman. From the description above, it is clear that, the cause of total activity in the world is Brahman.

Further, in part-II of the *Kena Upanishad* the fruit of knowing Him is stated as '*amrutaha bhavanti*', i.e., knowing Him in all beings, wise men become immortal leaving this world. In part-II, it is also said that this Brahman verily won the battle for the gods and the gods were elated. '*Brahma ha devebhyovijigye*' means that the gods, under the spell of illusion, considered the Brahman's victory as their own. The power was blessed by Brahman, however the gods believed it be theirs. Here, the meaning of 'Brahman' should not be restricted to 'that which is experienced in the Turiya state' as put forward by Shankaracharya, but as That which is inclusive of Aparabrahman and Parabrahman, i.e., Vishwa, Vishnuroopa Apar and Shivaroopa Brahman. While the whole universe is regulated by this Brahman; the gods were under the illusion that they were regulating it. Man, also is under a similar illusion about his own powers; sometimes he underestimates it and at other times, overestimates. Man sometimes thinks of a task as quite easy, that he can do it in a jiffy but in reality, that doesn't happen. In short, neither men nor gods are able to have a correct idea of their power. Brahman emanates two kinds of power: one, illusory (called Maya), and the other sans illusion.

For example, man feels that he has legs therefore he can walk or he has eyes, so he can see. Fair enough, because of legs he can walk but he can't do so on water, he needs the support of hard ground underneath his feet and he forgets that this support he gets from Vishwa or the material world. Likewise, just being blessed with eyes does not enable him to see in dark. Eyes can see only in lamplight or sunlight. And he forgets that this light is imparted either by sun or by fire and thinks that he possesses the capacity to walk or to see. Because of this, he lands in a problem, causing embarrassment. In short, be it men or gods, both tend to forget that it is Brahman's power and wrongly consider it as their own. This illusion that 'it is their power' is the inherent quality of that Power and that is what is called Maya.

When the gods were elated owing to their false notion that that the power they exercised was theirs, He, having perceived their conceit, appeared before them to make them realize the reality. Him, they did not recognize. Who was this adorable Yaksha, they wondered? The *Kena Upanishad* (3.2) states:[8]

तद्धैषां विजज्ञौ तेभ्यो ह प्रादुर्बभूव तन्न व्याजानत किमिदं यक्षमिति॥
taddhaiṣāṃ vijajñau tebhyo ha prādurbabhūva tanna vyajānata kimidaṃ yakṣamiti

[That blade of grass was not able to be burnt by fire, agni; with all the strength, that blade of grass was not able to be blown by wind, vayu; when He was (thus) approached by Indra, He (Yaksha) disappeared from Him. Because of Uma, Indra was the earliest to know That Yaksha as Brahman therefore, verily Indra excels.][9]

In short, it is established that fire's ability to burn, wind's ability to blow etc.—what we call their characteristic or inherent nature—is verily that

---

8   https://www.wisdomlib.org/hinduism/book/kena-upanishad-madhva-commentary/d/doc486084.html
9   Author's own translation.

of the Brahman. Indra was imparted that divine or spiritual knowledge about Brahman by Uma thus: 'Athadhyatmam, Ityadhidaivatam'. And therefore, in the Kena Upanishad it is stated: 'Those who, viz. fire, wind, Indra, etc., are worshipped are not Brahman, know that He from Whom they get this power is Brahman.'

There is not an iota of Maya in the *Kena Upanishad* which solely discusses: 'who creates the worldly activity?' If in reality, the activity or the characteristic nature is because of Maya, then the ability of fire to burn, the ability of the wind to blow ought to be attributed to Maya. On the contrary, by referring to Brahman's divinity, the 'non-duality' of the trinity—Shiva, Vishnu and Vishwa being part of each other and of the Brahman (hence not dual, but One) including the spiritual and material aspects—is what is discussed in the *Kena Upanishad*. Therefore, the Brahman is Poorna Purusha.

If considering all these clearly, the Poorna Purusha has been referred to as Brahman, then why can't we infer Vyasa's Sutra: '*Athato Brahma Jidnyasa*' as referring to Poorna Purusha? Acharya Vyasa has glorified Brahman in the prologue in his commentary on these sutras by stating: 'it is for well-being into the Dharma' and for emancipation 'enquiry into the Brahman'. However, Acharya Vyasa begins his commentary by construing Brahman as only Parabrahman. Of the perception of Parabrahman for emancipation, which Acharya has imparted independently, the Upanishads say that such emancipation can be had by the wise from perception of the All Complete Purusha. From this point of view the Upanishads assert absolute non-dualism. If the comprehension that 'the activities of my organs are not mine' is adhyatma (knowledge), then to comprehend that 'that activity verily is Brahman's' is adhidaivik (divine).

We saw that 'time' and 'characteristic nature' are the qualities of the Devatma Shakti, the Power of Ishwara that is Prakriti and Prakriti means Maya. But that which the Kevaladvaitins expound as Maya is, despite intense efforts, not traceable in the Vedas. Rather, quite often, we find in the Upanishads that it is Ishwara alone who creates all this. For example, in one of the shlokas of *Svetasvatara Upanishad* (3.2) the sage says:[10]

एको हि रुद्रो न द्वितीयाय तस्थुर्य इमांल्लोकानीशत ईशनीभिः।
प्रत्यङ् जनांस्तिष्ठति संचुकोचान्तकाले संसृज्य विश्वा भुवनानि गोपाः।।

eko hi rudro na dvitīyāya tasthu-rya imāmllokānīśata īśanībhiḥ
pratyaṅ janāstiṣṭhati sañcukocāntakāle saṃsṛjya viśvā bhuvanāni
gopāḥ

[The Rudra alone, one without a second, who rules all the worlds with His many Powers. Regulates all worlds with His Highest Powers. Here it is the plural 'powers', therefore, singular 'Maya is inconceivable' just as, who dwells in all beings as omniscient, who destroys the world when the end comes, who creates the fourteen worlds in the Universe and nurtures them, He is the Rudra alone, one without a second.][11]

Of course, this condemns Maya. Therefore, the Ultimate Truth that Ishwara or Highest God (referred to in the verse above as Rudra) is alone is established. However, if Truth (which is alone with no second) and the world are juxtaposed, those would form causal change (Truth caused the world) and Truth also would be a kind of object like any other in this world. The principle is: that ('object') which is the cause of something must be the effect of something else (some other 'object'). The Kevaladvaitins call this world unreal, 'mithya', because: (i) the Truth is neither a cause nor an effect; and (ii) because they couldn't establish the relation between the world and the Truth.

While Kevaladvaitins have to accept the 'empirical form' of the world, and whereas the Truth, Parabrahman cannot be cause of this world, and according to the principle stated earlier, there cannot be an activity without its preceding cause, therefore, 'Maya' is the cause of this

---

10 https://www.esamskriti.com/e/Spirituality/Upanishads-Commentary/Svetasvatara-Upanishad-~-Chap-3-The-Highest-Reality-1.aspx
11 Author's own translation.

world. And if Maya is the cause, it has necessarily to be the activity of something else and that something else is 'Ignorance'.

As per the chain of causation, Ishwara is reckoned as the cause of the world and perforce, we have to accept that Ishwara too is the activity/effect of some other cause. That is why Shankaracharya expounded that Ishwara was Maya's activity and Ishwara created the world. He attributed Maya's creation to Ignorance, i.e. Maya was deemed the activity of Ignorance, Ishwara was Maya's activity, and the world was Ishwara's activity. Having said so they proceeded further: the cause of Ignorance was projection (adhyasa) and transformation (vivarta) and the cause of both of these was beyond human intellect. Thus, not being able to establish any kind of relation between Truth and the world, Shankaracharya called the world 'unreal'.

Ajatvad, emphasizing on the term 'mithya' or illusion, contends: 'From mithya is evolved mithya only', hence where is the question of a separate cause when there is no activity/effect. And relying on this contention, the Ajatvadis vindicate themselves from the cause-effect enquiry. Just based on the principle that Absolute Truth cannot be the cause of anything, to reckon the world is 'unreal' and espouse the 'no cause' the Ajatvad view is not correct.

The Poorna has a form-relationship with the world and the Parabrahman therefore: (i) the world need not be reckoned as unreal; (ii) nor is Truth the cause of Highest God. Thus, without a logical fallacy, 'the reality' of the world remains unaffected and it does not contradict our empirical experience.

But while discussing the Form-Relation (*swaroopa sambhadha*) point of view, quite naturally two doubts arise in our mind. Firstly, as above in many other shlokas and hymns also, because of the verbs 'samsrujya' (regulate), 'jayate' (to arise), 'sanchukoch' (construe), 'jayamanas' (born), it only proves the world as Lord's activity. Secondly, from the Shruti hymns—that Vaishanavacharya relied upon to prove the existence of this world and indicate it to be the Lord's activity in one way other the other—how did he resolve issues arising from the Parinamvada (the Theory of Evolution postulated by him?

The reply to this is, we observe the world-nature, the activities in the world as cause-effect phenomenon. As creation and destruction is perpetually taking place in the world as reflected from the trinity—the Creator, Sustainer and Destroyer. Shruti describes the Lord as the doer and the incomprehensible world as His activity. For example, we see the tide when the moon appears in the sky, then we say that the tide is due to the moon or the moon brings the tide, and therefore determine the moon as the doer. In fact, the moon which is far away from the ocean cannot do anything. And owing to such occurrences, the world-nature is called Maya. But Shruti cautions man to keep away from such illusion. So also, none other is responsible for the power of Ishwara or for nature. Creating illusion, Ishwara Himself has been called the 'Mayin' which is affirmed in the Bhagavad Gita as '*Daiviheshyam Gunamayi Mamamaya Duratya*' (It is very difficult to overcome my divine energy Maya, consisting of the three modes of nature, translation by the author) and indeed it is very difficult to overcome it.

Even according to our mindset when we say that 'time' and 'characteristic nature' are attributes of divine power, it is important to bear in mind that those attributes do not evolve from divine power but are verily its forms. As a man gets older, for instance, he tends to become more irritable, in other words the inherent nature of anything will manifest automatically, without provocation or cause; hence the inherent nature is a form of divine power (Devatma Shakti) and not its creation. Similarly, it is important to bear in mind that the world is Ishwar-Shakti's form and not its creation.

Hence in day-to-day life also the spiritual seeker while praying, rather than saying 'Oh God please do this for me', should beseech God (in tune with reality): 'Oh God, please let this task attain fulfillment quite naturally in the normal course.' This kind of prayer guards the seeker against demerits like false pride and lack of faith. Otherwise, false pride on fulfilment or losing faith in case of failure and naturally breeding a feeling that: 'God did not favour me even in such a little task.' Therefore, it is important to bear in mind too that 'Nature is the form of His innate Power', that 'time' and 'characteristic nature' are also a form of nature, and the world is the form of 'time' and 'characteristic/inherent nature'. If we don't, then there is a definite possibility of getting stuck in the cause-effect chain. At the same time, it is also important to remember that ever after, pervading the world by His Ishwar-form He transcends it in ten directions. We must bear in mind that the world is the limb-form of Ishwara and therefore not complete. When I put my hand on my chest and claim that: 'I am so and so', then the chest does not mean I. Similarly, Ishwara pervades not just the world, He transcends it and this should never be forgotten.

Upon realzing the reasoning behind and better understanding of this cause-effect Maya, we infer that both the Ajatvad and logically unacceptable Parinamvad (the theory of evolution) indulge in controversies. Even though there is no cause-effect state that we observe in nature, between Truth-form Poorna Purusha and Vishwa, we still feel that is Maya. Of course, it is mithya, a myth, an illusion. The cause-effect relation that we feel as in the shloka '*Mayantu Prakritim Vidyat*' (Maya is the nature of the material world. Shvetashvatara Upanishad, chapter 4, verse 10) between Ishwara and Vishwa, is false, illusory. This is established and then what is left is the Form-Relation between Vishwa and Poorna Purusha. Although, Shruti clearly lays down that nature should be called Maya, still the nature-maya is different from the nature that the Samkhya envisage, and the Maya that Vedantins envisage.

Summing up: (i) that which Shruti asks to be reckoned as Maya; and (ii) Samkhya's nature, and (iii) Vedanta's Maya—all three are quite often reckoned by a single term 'Maya'. It is therefore, imperative for us to get summarize these three.

Nature as per the Samkhya

First of all, Samkhya, instead of only one, postulates two Ultimate Realities—Purush and Prakriti (nature)—while deliberating on Vishwa. Of the two, the world evolved from Prakriti. Hence Prakriti was the unmanifest cause of this manifest world. Here the question is that Prakriti cannot be perceived by any of the organs of the body, since she is called unmanifest. Thus what is the proof that Prakriti exists?

Samkhya's reply to this question is:

By examining many manifest things, inference proves that even if their fundamental form is not perceivable, those do exist in minute forms. Because nothing evolves from Shunya or nothingness. This is what is meant by the Gita shloka (2.16): '*Nasato Vidyate Bhavaha*' (Nature of Prakriti and the Maya is fathomable). Therefore, whether the cause is known or not known, activity proves the existence of cause. Whereas, the world as an activity is manifest and is seen, its cause even if un-manifest must exist and that is what we call as Prakriti.[12]

The Naiyyayikas [The Naiyayikas (the Nyāya scholars) accepted four valid means (pramaṇa) of obtaining valid knowledge (prameya), perception (pratyakṣa), inference (anumāna), comparison (upamāna), and. word/testimony of reliable sources (śabda)] treat the atom as the cause and it is not perceptible to the organs, hence unmanifest. But as each atom is independent and innumerable, there is a possibility of some gap (space) even if very minute, between two atoms. How do we explain such a gap? Therefore, the atom cannot be the cause of this world. Samkhya therefore, postulates that, Prakriti or nature does not consist of the independent atoms but it is all pervasive, continuous and formless. But a doubt arises whether Prakriti, the cause of this world, could evolve into a variety of things in the world which are innumerable and diverse from each other. Therefore, the question is: is Prakriti oneness (unity) or manyness (plurality)? Chemistry talks of 92 to 120 elements, on these, Samkhya's reply is that if the diversity we see in the world were classified we would observe that it consisted of three constituents or gunas: sattva, rajas, tamas. Before the manifestation of the objective world, the three gunas are in a state of perfect balance, equipoised. When this condition of equilibrium is disturbed, the phenomenal world begins to make its appearance.

---

12 Maya chapter, Poornavad, Parnerkar

When these three constituents are in equilibrium, what triggers their action, the manifestation of which is the world form? To this, the pandits or the learned reply that the agitation of the three gunas is an inherent quality of nature. Samkhya considers Prakriti as the primary matter which, though inanimate, conducts the world's activity independently. And that the agitation of the three gunas occurs especially in Purusha's presence. The sattva's quality is knowledge, that of tamas is ignorance and of rajas the force impetus. These gunas are never apart. Each and every entity in this world is a combination of these three gunas. The prominence of one or the other of these three constituents accounts for diversity and the variety in this world. Samkhya also considers Prakriti eternal, like Purusha. Kapil Muni propounded the Samkhya Shastra (Kapil's Samkhya was non-dual however, there is a view prevalent that Ishwarkrishan's Karika is dualist). Samkhaya is dual and undual. It accepts both Theist/Atheist, Manifest/Unmanifest, Dhyana/Bhakti. Therefore, Samkhya is secular. What is called dual and undual are but two sides of one coin. This is Vedic Samkhya, as per Dr Parnerkar.

While acquainting oneself with Samkhya's Prakriti it would be appropriate to acquaint oneself also with Satkaryavad (the doctrine of pre-existence effect). We shall briefly consider what it is. What is non-existent can never be brought into existence. According to Samkhya the elemental qualities of any effect are necessarily present in the cause already, even if minutely. This is the doctrine of pre-existence effect. It is therefore, hoped that the concept of eternal, indestructible and independent formless Prakriti of Samkhya must be sufficiently clear.

Thus far, we discussed Prakriti in which time and characteristic nature are inherent and we call it Maya. We shall see the difference between this and Samkhya Prakriti.

1. Samkhya reckons that Purush and Prakriti are eternal and independent elements and inert. World is Truth and its cause—Prakriti (with its three qualities of Sattva, Rajas and Tamas)—also is Truth. This limits Prakriti, and it ceases to have any relation with Purusha. Whereas our reckoning of Prakriti/nature states

that being of the nature of 'time' and inherent/characteristic nature (inert and spirit) and being Ishwara's innate power, it proves to be Poorna's power and its Form-Relation with Poorna Purusha prevails. Therefore, the Ved Samkhya's have to superimpose Poorna or Poornatva on it (in respect of creation of world), which is not the case in Poornavad.

2. Samkhya is not able to properly explain as to what causes the disturbance to the equilibrium the gunas (Satva, Rajas, Tamas) which evolves the world. Poornavad points out that as the time and inherent/characteristic nature-form power, Prakriti, is constantly dwelling in Ishwara, the Ishwara's own form 'world' perennially exists.
3. Samkhya has to accept the three gunas or qualities, viz. knowledge, inclination, and ignorance, and therefore they have to accept ignorance as an entity, which Poornavad does not
4. Samkhya calls Atmatattva and Parabrahman as Purusha, we too call it Poorna Purusha. But Samkhya's Purusha has no control because Samkhya's Prakriti independently takes care of the worldly-activity. Samkhya's Purusha cannot be called All-Powerful Master, Ishwara or Highest God. Poorna Purusha, however, is Master and Highest God.

Thus, having apprehended the difference between the Samkhya's Prakriti and Poorna Purusha's Power placed in time and inherent/characteristic nature or world nature or Maya, we now turn to summarize Vedantins' Maya.

The Vedantins' Maya

Samkhya treats its Prakriti as independent for her activity. Advaitins, however, consider their Maya as incapable of independent activity. The following verse in the Uttar Mimamsa states:

तुच्छाऽ निर्वचनीय च वास्तवीचेत्यसौ त्रिधा।
ज्ञेया माया त्रिभिर्बोधैः श्रौत यौक्तिक लौकिकैः।।

[That which Shruti calls as Tuccha, the Uttar Mimamsa calls it an accessory, Yukti and the Advaitin's as inexplicable, Anirvachaniya.][13]

As such, it is known by different names and like Prakriti has several names, viz. 'Tuccha' (non existant), 'Anirvachaniya' (that which cannot be described), 'Satasat Vilakshan' (Netither sat or asat, neither real or unreal), etc. Samkhya treats the world as real and reckons the cosmic substance Gunmayi Prakriti or Truth as its cause. But the Advaitins regard this world as unreal and attribute it to Maya, i.e., Ignorance and consider it to have evolved from Ignorance. The cause of untruth cannot be Truth, consequently Ignorance is unreal. Let us first see what is false?

False means unreal, i.e., when we say the world is unreal it means that it is false, it does not exist. Both Ajatvadis and Mayavadis say so, but there is a difference between these two. When Ajatvadis contend that this world is false, they mean it doesn't exist, it never did. For example, Samarth says, '*Aga je zalechi nahi ….*' (What are you asking about, that which never was). The reason for saying false, instead of the 'world never was', is when you say it 'never was', it indicates non-existence. This non-existence is basically of four kinds: (i) Pragbhava (non-existence); (ii) Pradhvansabhava (destruction); (iii) Sthanabhava (negation of space). All these kinds of non-existence are space-time relative. Therefore, non-existence is related to space and time whereas in the concept of 'mithya' (illusion, false), there is dissolution of time and space. Hence, the Ajatvadis in order to convey that there is no world, use the term false.

But when the Advaitins, Mayavadis call the world as 'mithya, that is in accordance with 'Bhrammulamidam Jagat' (evolved from illusion), not evolved in reality. In their concept of mithya, non-existence also attracts 'mithyatva' (falsehood). In Vedanta Shastra by reckoning this world as (vishayatvat mithya) empirically false, very existence has been defied. The Advaitins do not accept any other authority except that of Atman and Parabrahman.

---

13 Author's own translation.

Just as the existence is experienced only in 'I', it is not so in the object-form. If the objects had existence, they would have made that awareness of existence known. The object's inert name-form or the world does not render their existence known, rather 'I' by virtue of its existence experiences them. Therefore, objects have no existence, they are an illusion. Such definite knowledge of Maya is illusion. Maya is established through the theory of projection (adhyasavad) or transformation (vivarta).

As the Advaitin-Mayavadis reckon the detached, unchangeable, non-doer, eternal, pure, intellect Parabrahman or the Atmatattva as the only Truth, the evolution of world from it is an impossibility. But because it is empirically experienced, in order to regulate it, something like Maya, lodged in Parabrahman, has to be construed. If at all Maya is to be accepted, it has to compulsorily possess sattva, rajas, and tamas, the three gunas, i.e., it should be 'trigunatmak' for properly regulating good and bad, bondage and salvation in this world. Therefore, the Mayavadi's Maya is trigunatmika. In short, because the world is called empirically false, even if the world or Maya has no authority, Maya has Parabrahman's authority. So, it is important to remember that there is no authority 'of Maya' but there is authority 'to Maya'. The reader would have discerned the vast difference between the Samkhya's Prakriti and Vedantin's Maya.

1. Samkhya admits existence of the world. As such, their Gunmayi (with its three gunas Sattva, Rajas and Tamas) Maya, nature (prakriti) has existence. Whereas, the Vedantins' Maya has neither existence nor authority.
2. As Samkhya considers Purusha and Prakriti to be independent, it is dualist philosophy (i.e., they do not consider these parts of the One). Prakriti or nature of its own free will can bring about union with Purusha, but it can as well detach. Therefore, man cannot independently seek or gain liberation. The locus of Vedantin's Maya being Parabrahman and That being Truth, Maya cannot be called unreal as also real. It is *Sat-Asat-Vilakshan*, real-unreal-inconceivable. Therefore, man is able to attain liberation.

3. Samkhya's prakriti/nature is trigunatmak, Vedantin's Maya is also trigunatmak but is illusory.
4. In Veda, Maya has no authority, it is the nature of Prakriti; Prakriti is independent whereas Maya is dependent.
5. Because of all these, it cannot be said that Samkhya's prakriti and Vedantins' Maya are the same. Likewise, readers would find from what we discussed above about '*Mayantu prakritim vidyat*', [Maya is the nature of the material world] both of these are totally different than the time-inherent/characteristic nature-form-Maya. Here we are quite acquainted with all the three 'Maya'.

CHAPTER 10

Avidya: Knowledge of the Material Science

For thousands of years, philosophers have had a singular topic of discussion—spirituality, i.e., truth, consciousness, beauty, non-violence. Therefore, it is a wonder why the scholars of philosophy could not discuss philosophy beyond Buddhism. It is not a very difficult task to take a look at the multi-dimensional Vedic philosophy which gives you the wider, optimistic and scientific vision. Modern thinkers discuss the partial truth of universal knowledge. Dr Parnerkar expresses astonishment over this negligence on the part of scholars of philosophy and further says that it is great ignorance to say Avidya is ignorance.

If we look into the history of Buddhist philosophy—which relies on the doctrine that life is misery, life is sorrowful, life is impermanent—and ask why it is so, what is the reason behind it? The Buddha says it is because of Avidya or ignorance that we suffer in this sorrowful life. Dr Parnerkar, through references from Vedas, makes it clear that 'Avidya' (as per Poornavad) is not ignorance but is knowledge of the material world, which is the applied dimension of 'Vidya' (the Eternal, Impartible, Mute, Brahman). Hence, as per Poornavad, Gautam Buddha followed only Vidya, and neglected Avidya by declaring it as ignorance. Though Buddha denied the Vedas, he followed partial Vedic philosophy. But with references from *Katha Upanishad*, Dr Parnerkar shows that the knowledge of only Vidya or only Avidya will throw you into the dark, it is the correlation between Vidya-Avidya that makes the man complete, perfect.

This chapter is important in regard to further understanding the concept of Poorna Purusha and Maya discussed in earlier chapters—the chapters in this book are thus all linked to each other. As discussed earlier, Dr Parnerkar's Form-Relation Theory in his doctrine of Poornavad is parallel to Derrida's movement of Deconstruction to keep the European identity, which started from the sixth decade of the twentieth century. The movement then spread all over the world. The intellectual members of this movement suggest deconstruction of the timeless concepts of orthodox philosophy right from Plato, Aristotle, Marx, Hegel onward. But two decades before Derrida's Deconstruction Movement, Dr Parnerkar had started the same movement alone in 1948, deconstructing the orthodox Vedanta concepts like Parabrahman, Maya, Avidya and Moksha and established the Form-Relation between the Lord and the world by explaining the Vedic concept of 'Poorna Purusha' which has been neglected by Vedic philosophers. The period of Vedanta philosophy starts from the end of the Mahabharata war, but the available history of philosophy indicates Vedanta began from the Buddhist era as the impact of the Upanishads is found on Buddhism.

Though the historians of philosophy are yet to consider Buddhism under Vedanta; the roots of Buddhism lie in the Upanishads, therefore Buddhism lies within the fold of Vedanta. Due to the misinterpretations of Avidya by Vedanta philosophy the world has borne heavy losses, as those unfamiliar with Sanskrit have been denied access to a treasure-house of knowledge and wisdom. Before Gautama attained Nirvana, his guru was Alarkolam, a Samkhya scholar and Buddha chose a part of the Samkhya philosophy (one of the six darshanas or philosophies found in the Vedas). Samkhya is secular in nature and accepts God as being both form and formless. Equating 'Avidya' with ignorance,

Buddhism deemed it as the cause of misery, sorrow and impermanency of life. Samkhya is and. As mentioned above, Dr Parnerkar says that in the Vedas, Avidya means the knowledge of the material world. When we are living twenty-four hours in this material world, how can it be neglected, set aside as ignorance?

Vidya: Knowledge of the Parabrahman

Vidya means knowledge of the infinite universe which is known as the Parabrahman. Vidya is the knowledge of the eternal time and space concept of the Vedas, and Vidya is to be achieved by penance. After a thorough study of Vidya and Avidya, Dr Parnerkar suggests that three Vedas—*Rig Veda* for Vidya or higher (para) knowledge, the *Yajur Veda* for Avidya or applied material knowledge (which is highly essential for dealing with day-to-day practical life), and the *Sama Veda* for upasana, worship—are inseparable, correlated with each other and taken together are more advisable for use in our practical life.

Dr Parnerkar differs from the partial vision of Shankara, who advocated only the perusal of the divine infinite and neglected the study of the material world (Avidya) as described in the Vedas, deeming the latter as 'ignorance'. Here Shankara was parallel to the Buddha, who also neglected Avidya and said it was ignorance. In fact, the scholars of Vedic literature are aware that the Brahmanas, Upanishads, Brahmasutras, etc., have originated from the Vedic-hymnal text. Therefore, it is imperative to ascribe utmost importance to the Vedas. An aspect of truth from the Vedas—self-realization, or Brahman-experience—is contended in the Upanishads. It is absolutely improper to reckon only that much as important and belittle the Vedas, which expound the 'spiritual' together with 'the material' and 'the divine'. Any deliberation that begins with the Vedas is ever appropriate. However, if the beginning is from the Upanishads or the Bhagavad Gita, there is always the possibility of any deliberation turning out to be lopsided or one-sided. Scholars have begun to realize that the cracks appearing in the Hindu way of life have occurred due to the decline in reverence toward the Vedas and the epics such as the Ramayana and the Mahabharata. The Vedic way of thinking has lagged behind, causing considerable damage. It may not be possible to avert the danger of an illusion taking firm root that the Upanishads, etc., *soot* (sutra or sudra) literature is reckoned as higher (para) Vidya and the Vedic-hymnal literature as lower (apara) Vidya. The wise should reckon the Vedas which impart spiritual and divine knowledge as Paravidya. Therefore, the 'bhautik' or (material) is all Aparavidya. One should not even let such a thought touch the mind that hymnal literature is Aparavidya, while the Upanishads and *soot* literature are Paravidya.

That which affords knowledge of the material i.e adhibhautik plane, if gained with effort, may be Paravidya (higher knowledge). When such knowledge is not gained with effort, but is gained only because it is easily comprehensible with growing age, it is called Apara (lower) Vidya. That which imparts the knowledge of spiritual and divine is always Paravidya or higher Vidya. The learned should always remember this. Two shlokas—one from *Mundaka Upanishad* (1.2.8) and the other from *Katha Upanishad* (1.2.5)—are almost identical, but for the difference one word in the second line of each ('*janghanyamansh*' in *Mundaka Upanishad*, and '*dandramyamanah*' in *Katha Upanishad*). Both these shlokas must always be borne in mind. The shloka from *Mundaka Upanishad* (1.2.3) states:

अविद्यायामन्तरे वर्तमानाः स्वयं धीराः पण्डितं मन्यमानाः।
जङ्घन्यमानाः परियन्ति मूढा अन्धेनैव नीयमाना यथान्धाः॥

avidyāyāmantare vartamānāḥ svayaṁ dhīrāḥ paṇḍitaṁ manyamānāḥ
jaṅghanyamānāḥ pariyanti mūḍhā andhenaiva nīyamānā yathāndhāḥ

[Those who, with their worldly knowledge alone, (being content with Avidya or Apara) conduct themselves and their business in life, consider themselves as intelligent and enlightened and also being recognized by people: this illusion takes them round and round following crooked courses, just like the blind led by the blind.]

The shloka in *Katha Upanishad* (1.2.5) states:

अविद्यायामन्तरे वर्तमानाः स्वयं धीराः पण्डितं मन्यमानाः।
दन्द्रम्यमाणाः परियन्ति मूढा अन्धेनैव नीयमाना यथान्धाः॥

avidyāyāmantare vartamānāḥ svayaṃ dhīrāḥ paṇḍitaṃ manyamānāḥ dandramyamāṇāḥ pariyanti mūḍhā andhenaiva nīyamānā yathāndhāḥ

['Living in the middle of ignorance and regarding themselves as intelligent and learned, the ignorant go round and round, in many crooked ways, like the blind led by the blind.'][1]

Samarth Ramadas also states in his *Dasbodha*:

जेकाप्रापंचिक जन।जयासि नहीआत्मज्ञान।
जेकेवळअज्ञान।त्यांचीलक्षणे॥

(मराठी दासबोध ग्रंथ)

The householder, without the knowledge of atman which is ignorance, for sure is a fool. Here also the Samarth clearly mentions that he who is without the knowledge of Vidya and leads his life only on the strength of Avidya is a fool. The next shloka from the *Mundaka Upanishad* (1.2.9) depicts this tendency:

अविद्यायं बहुधा वर्तमाना वयं कृतार्था इत्यभिमन्यन्ति बालाः।
यत्कर्मिणो न प्रवेदयन्ति रागात्तेनातुराः क्षीणलोकाश्च्यवन्ते॥

avidyāyaṃ bahudhā vartamānā vayaṃ kṛtārthā ityabhimanyanti bālāḥ yatkarmiṇo na pravedayanti rāgāttenāturāḥ kṣīṇalokāścyavante

[Continuing diversely in the midst of ignorance, the unenlightened take pride in having attained the fullest achievement. Since, the men

---

1   https://www.wisdomlib.org/hinduism/book/katha-upanishad-shankara-bhashya/d/doc145182.html

engaged in karma obsessed by attachment forget Him and become afflicted with sorrow and are deprived of heaven upon the exhaustion of the results of their karma.]²

Multiple verses in multiple texts show us the folly of abandoning Vidya for Avidya, or Avidya for Vidya—neither option brings good results, hence a balance must be found. *Ishavasya Upanishad* points out, in the second half of verse 9,³ that those who espouse only the higher Paravidya and abandon the search for lower Avidya or Apara that gives us knowledge of the Adhibhautik (the material)—they go deep into darkness.

The two shlokas (1.2.8 and 1.2.9) cited earlier from the *Mundaka Upanishad*, show us that those who are only after lower Aparavidya, and abandon the higher Paravidya i.e., the adhidaivik and adhyatmik, end up in darkness. Looking at these outcomes, it is clear that the Vedas simply espouse the co-worship of Para and Apara vidyas. The Shruti texts do not say that Apara, the lower, is erased by Para, the higher Vidya; or that the higher (Para) and be erased by the lower (Apara). By following just one path, leaves the other undeveloped in the seeker's life. Hence, following only one leads the seeker into darkness.

This also amply proves that our interpretation of the meaning of Vidya-Avidya and Para-Apara is not a mere figment of our imagination. We have taken the entire shloka 'Ksharantum avidya...'⁴ for consideration and there it is clearly stated that, 'Xar vishva' means Avidya and 'amrut' means Vidya. Since both adhyatma and adhidaivat are included in Paravidya, it is clear that knowledge and devotion are part of it and it is also proven that karma or action has pre-dominance in Avidya or Aparavidya. Therefore, the knowledge or Vidya acquired from worship and that acquired from karma are referred to, at some

---

2   Author's own translation.
3   https://www.wisdomlib.org/hinduism/book/ishavasya-bhashya-by-sitarama/d/doc145026.html
4   *Poornavad* (2017), Parnerkar, p.38-39.

places, independently as three Vidyas. For instance, the following shloka from *Sre* 5.1 states:

अयमुद्गाता स एष सर्वस्यै त्रयी विद्यायाआत्मैष उ
एवास्यात्मैतदात्मा भवति य एवं वेद।।

[The Brahmin or Rutvik who skillfully braids the *Rig Veda*, *Yajur Veda* and *Sama Veda* in the sacrificial fire should be reckoned as the Atman of these three vidyas.][5]

The *Rig Veda* means knowledge, *Yajur Veda* means karma and *Sama Veda* means worship and devotion. At many places in the Vedas, life is reckoned as a *yajna* (sacrificial fire). Hence, he who intertwines these three types of knowledge skillfully in the sacrificial fire (of life), is really wise and erudite. The *Kaushitaki Upanishad*, therefore, rather than prescribing the worship of any one of the three, insist on employing all three Vidyas for Yajna. Here, a synthesis of the three Vidyas is not suggested, rather that all the three should be employed to live a fruitful life. The Vedas clearly state that the worship of the Poorna Purusha is by way of such an Anushthana or religious rite.

In gist, Vidya is basically complete and one. Its material form (adhibhautik)—learned or acquired with ease as one grows in age—was earlier called ignorance (Avidya), and its divine, transcendent, spiritual (adhidaivik and adhyatmik) forms were regarded as Vidya. But with changing times and development and progress, the subject matters that fell under these three classifications (adhibhautik, adhidaivik and adhyatmik) were felt to be inadequate. Particularly due the huge development in the field of material knowledge, the ease of its acquisition with growing age also ceased; its acquisition had become difficult and required penance and endeavour. As a result, knowledge of the material world (archery, weaponry, music etc.) began to be included in the category of higher knowledge or Vidya.

---

5 Author's own translation.

Therefore, instead of dividing knowledge into two branches—Avidya (knowledge of the material world) and Vidya (divine, transcendent, spiritual knowledge)—it became a popular tradition to divide knowledge under Aparavidya and Paravidya. With this new division, knowledge of the material world, whether easily acquirable or with penance and effort, was included under Aparavidya and the knowledge of Ishwara and atman was included under Paravidya. In short, Aparavidya meant the knowledge of the manifest world, whereas Paravidya meant the knowledge of the unmanifest and intangible. This new classification gained popularity.

The adhidaivik (knowledge of the divine) also began to develop, and with the spread of Bhagavat Dharma and path of devotion, the knowledge of unmanifest, i.e., Paravidya was further divided into two parts: (i) the worship of Ishwara and the deities as an independent adhidaivik or divine aspect; and (ii) self-realization and experience of the Supreme (Parabrahman), the only spiritual aspect, as a separate aspect. Hence, with emergence of the means—karma, devotion/worship, and knowledge, which found predominant application—the concept of the three Vidyas, i.e., Yajur, Sama, and Rig, also emerged.

While such knowledge and complete form of Vidya was developing and progressing on the one hand, on the other it was as though a wave of reaction was gripping society. Study, deliberation on a particular subject or a form of Vidya was progressing in a focused manner to the extent that each subject or form of Vidya—self-realization; God-realization; knowledge of material science—was claimed as the complete form of knowledge, and attainment in any one of the three was considered the be all and end all by its followers. The belief that progress on any one path (rather than a balanced approach that included all three paths) would make a person happy, had taken deep root in peoples' minds.

This led to an emphasis on the either knowledge, or devotion or action and their respective ends, singly or in isolation. Everyone seemed to have forgotten that all three were but a form of that divine complete Vidya and were not complete in themselves. In order to have complete knowledge, it is even today imperative to study all three—adhibhautik, adhyatmik and adhidaivik—simultaneously and only when this is done, the co-worship of these three Vidyas can lead to true comprehension of the Poorna Purusha, the reality of the whole world, and make the practitioner happy.

The Vedas have always advocated complete knowledge and therefore appear to have emphasized from the beginning the worship of all three Vidyas—adhibhautik, adhyatmik, adhidaivik—without which it is not possible to benefit from the All Completeness. Today the Western nations are suffering the fruits of worshipping only Avidya, the material realm, and it needs no mention as to what level India has reached in its slide downwards by espousing only Paravidya and devotion.

As natural and easy it is to acquire material knowledge, i.e., Avidya, it is just as difficult to acquire Vidya with efforts and penance.

There is a shloka (5.14.6) in the *Brihadaranyaka Upanishad* which tells of the mutual relation between the three Vidyas and the three quarters of the Gayatri:[6]

स य इमांस्त्रींल्लोकान्पूर्णान्प्रतिगृण्हीयात्सोस्या एतत्।
प्रथमं पदमाप्नुयादथ यावयीतं त्रयी विद्या यस्तावत्प्रति गृण्हीयात्।।

sa ya imāṃstrīmllokānpūrṇānpratigṛhṇīyāt so'syā etat prathamaṃ padamāpnuyāt atha yāvatīyaṃ trayī vidyā yastāvatprati gṛhṇīyāt

This verse can be explained as: He who is the recipient of the complete three quarters of the Gayatri's Bhu, Bhuva, Swaha lokas (worlds) would attain the first quarter of the Gayatri. There are two quarters of Vidya, of which second is adhidaivat and the third is mentioned as '*yavadivitam pranihi*'. Therefore, the being, the intellect and the mind are considered under adhyatma as one, the witness Parabrahman Supreme Lord is mentioned independently as Turiya (the essential nature Shiva, witness Atman or Parabrahman) and it is further categorically stated that it is a state not attainable by any of the three quarters. Rather it is not, necessarily, mentioned independently each

---

6 https://www.wisdomlib.org/hinduism/book/the-brihadaranyaka-upanishad/d/doc122201.html

time in Vidya. Sometimes however, it is split as 'Trai [or three] Vidya[s]' or 'Tripada' (three quarters). In the *Brihadaranyaka Upanishad,* also like the *Ishavasya,* the worship of only vidya is said to be worse than the worship of only Avidya (the material world). The *Brihadaranyaka Upanishad* (4.4.10) states:[7]

अन्धं तमः प्रविशन्ति येऽविद्यामुपासते।
ततो भूय इव ते तमो य उ विद्यायारतः॥

andham tamaḥ praviśanti ye'vidyāmupāsate
tato bhūya iva te tamo ya u vidyāyāṃ ratāḥ

[Those who worship Avidya fall into darkness but those engaged only in Vidya's worship fall deeper into darkness.][8]

Just as only worship of Vidya is prohibited in the *Brihadaranyaka Upanishad,* stating that Vidya alone shouldn't be worshipped; in another shloka the Upanishad praises Vidya and recommends its worship. It, therefore, appears to be advocating co-worship of Avidya and Vidya, whilst asking to refrain from worshipping any one alone. The relation between Vidya and adhyatma is well known, however, there is a shloka from the *Brihadaranyaka Upanishad* (4.16) clearly underscoring the relation of vidya with adhidaivat and the deities. Let us see that shloka:

यस्मादर्वाक्संवत्सरोऽहोभिः परिवर्तते।
तद्देवा ज्योतिषां ज्योतिरायुर्होपासतेऽमृतम्॥

yasmādarvāksaṃvatsaro'hobhiḥ parivartate
taddevā jyotiṣāṃ jyotirāyurhopāsate'mṛtam

[Below which the year with its days rotates, upon that immortal Light of all lights the gods meditate as longevity.]

---

7 https://www.wisdomlib.org/hinduism/book/the-brihadaranyaka-upanishad/d/doc122058.html.
8 Author's own translation.

In the above shloka, three worlds are mentioned, those of men, manes and gods respectively. These can be attained through son, sacrifice and Vidya. Of the three, the world of gods being superior, it is said that Vidya is praised. Of course, the worlds of men and manes are included in Avidya. Many a time, Avidya is also referred to as karma or sacrifice. Because accomplishment of the world of gods is said to be with Vidya, its sphere is limited to adhidaivat.

We shall now consider a shloka in the *Katha Upanishad* (2.3.18) in which Vidya connotes adhyatma so that it would be clear that Vidya encompasses both the spheres, the adhyatma as well as adhidaivat:

मृत्युप्रोक्तान्नचिकेतोऽथ लब्ध्वा विद्यामेतां योगविधिं च कृत्स्नम्।
ब्रह्मप्राप्तो विरजोऽभूद्विमृत्युरन्योऽप्येवं यो विदध्यात्ममेव॥

[In this manner, having acquired the teachings from the Lord of Death with complete Yogic rituals, Nachiketa transcended Dharma (virtue), Adharma (vice) and Death and attained the Brahman-form, emancipation. As such, whosoever acquired the vital knowledge of Adhyatma as did Nachiketa, attains Brahman form like him.]

In the shloka, the first reference is to Vidya and then to Adhyatma. And from the discussion so far, it is evident that only two vidyas have been referred to—Avidya (the material or adhibhautik); Vidya (knowledge or adhyatma, and that related to the spirit or adhidaivik). Man does not take the moral from Nachiketa's story—he asked for Vidya instead of Avidya, in delusion bragging that Avidya was worth abandoning and must be abandoned. Therefore, because the co-worship of Avidya and Vidya never happens, instead of desired fruits, the outcome is adverse feelings.

The Vedantins had to perforce separate the divine aspect, i.e., the knowledge about the Ishwara and the deities and Vidya because their objective was to establish Brahman as the Absolute Truth. Same way, God being Omniscient and the being as ignorant, both had to be set apart, both could not be brought under Avidya. And they had necessarily to differentiate God's Maya and being's Avidya. But those who would comprehend true import of Vidya and Avidya from the Upanishads would know that there is no difference between God's Maya and being's Avidya.

On the contrary, since Avidya means the knowledge of world-form 'material', adhibhautik; and as discussed earlier in the Maya chapter, it is proven that the characteristic nature of the world (Vishwaprakriti) the Vedmaya emerges from the Vishwa. Therefore, because Maya evolves from avidya there is not even an iota in the Vedas to support the stand of the Vedantins: 'God's Maya and being's Avidya'. Maya falls under Avidya only. Similarly, there is a shloka in the *Svetasvatara Upanishad* (5.1) to show that Avidya is not of the being but it certainly is of God:

द्वे अक्षरे ब्रह्मपरेत्वनन्ते विद्याविद्ये निहिते यत्र गूढे।
क्षरं त्वविद्याह्यमृतं तु विद्या विद्याविद्येईशते यस्तुसोऽन्यः।।

dve akṣare brahmapare tv anante vidyāvidye nihite yatra gūḍhe
kṣaraṃ tv avidyā hy amṛtaṃ tu vidyā vidyāvidye īśate yas tu so 'nyaḥ

[Impermanent is (spiritual unintelligence), ignorance–Avidya
and permanent is (spiritual intelligence) knowledge–Vidya. But
both of these are permanent. He in Whom, the unintelligence and
intelligence dwell and Who regulates these, is apart from these, the
Supreme Spirit, Poorna Purusha is Infinite and Mystic.][9]

It only means that being (the jeeva) does not regulate Avidya. Had Avidya evolved from jeeva or being (as the Advaitins say), its regulator ought to have been the jeeva, the being. In which case man could have erased Avidya and attained moksha by achieving Vidya. The verse above clearly mentions this is not the case, it is Ishwara or God who regulates (but is apart from) Avidya and Vidya. This proves that both Vidya and Avidya are of God. It is therefore, not imperative to erase, or cause

---

9 https://www.esamskriti.com/e/Spirituality/Upanishads-Commentary/Svetasvatara-Upanishad-~-Chap-5-The-One-Immanent-God-1.aspx.

erasure of, Avidya. Also, as we saw above, Vidya does not erase or cause erasure of Avidya. Non-Vedic literature, however, construes the adverse effect on a man due to lack of Vidya as Avidya. In this light it could be said that Avidya is of the being (the jeeva). This understanding most certainly cannot be construed as being in line with that Avidya which is expounded in the Vedas. It is indeed reprehensible to assign for each word, the terminology which in fact contradicts the Vedas and to use these very words to show the reliance on Shruti.

A closer study reveals a vast difference between the views of Vedic and other literature. Isn't it therefore, quite surprising that though we call ourselves the followers of Vedic religion, how very contradictory are the impressions (conditioning) we have been subjected to! Vidya comprises two dimensions or categories (Vidya and Avidya) and that is the main assertion of the Vedas. However, as the Poorna Purusha's very form is adhibhautik (the world), adhidaivik (Vishnu) and adhyatmik (Shiva), two categories of knowledge or Vidya and sometimes even three are indicated for its comprehension. As Avidya is quite natural and effortless, man cannot get rid of it, there is not much described on it in the Vedas. But that which needs a lot of effort, which cannot be acquired without penance and the Grace of God, and that it should not remain so incomprehensible, i.e., Vidya—the Vedas have dealt with it predominantly and at length.

A considerable portion of the Vedas is made up of hymns, i.e., adhidaivik Vidya. Therefore, adhyatmik Vidya appears to have a secondary position as reflected by the literary elaboration. However, as regard to their importance, all the three categories of Vidya are on par and the Vedas do not discriminate between them. Sacrifice (karma), knowledge (gyan) and upasana (worship) all three are important in life. One is poor without the other. It is not just the Brahma Vidya which bestows both 'the power to curse and valour to fight'. The 'terror of malediction' is adhidaivik, the 'power of arms' is sacrifice (karma) i.e., Avidya, and the peace and power of self is adhyatmik. All powers without the power of self (i.e. self-confidence) are worthless; we also find that any one, singly, is of no use. For living a meaningful life, all three vidyas are equally needed. We shall now see a few shlokas referring to Vidya in the sense of adhyatma. *Kena Upanishad* (2.4), for instance, states:

प्रतिबोध विदितं मतममृतत्वं हि विन्दते।
आत्मना विन्दते वीर्यं विद्यया विन्दतेऽमृतम्॥

pratibodha viditaṃ matamamṛtatvaṃ hi vindate
ātmanā vindate vīryaṃ vidyayā vindate'mṛtam

[The shloka may be translated as follows—every time the knowledge that Acharyas have imparted to us in a different manner, our comprehension of it has helped us learn about our immortality. By the self is obtained the power and by wisdom is gained immortality. Immortality means the three vidyas—Avidya, Atmavidya (the knowledge of self as aforesaid, and due to which is obtained the power), and Devavidya (knowledge of God). Further, '*Atmana vindate veeryam*' is Adhyatmavidya (knowledge of spirit), and '*vidyaya vindate amrutam*' is the knowledge of very form of God, thus both are described very clearly.][10]

However, the commentary differs from our interpretation. To dispel any doubt about the interpretation or translation above, let us consider the following shloka in *Prashna Upanishad* (1.10):

अथोत्तरेण तपसा ब्रह्मचर्येण श्रद्धया विद्ययात्मानमन्विष्यादित्यमभिजयन्ते।
एतद्वै प्राणानामायतनमेतदमृतमभयमेतत्।
परायणमेतस्मान्न पुनरावर्तन्त इत्येष निरोधस्तदेष श्लोकः॥

athottareṇa tapasā brahmacaryeṇa śraddhayā vidyayātmānamanviṣyā
dityamabhijayante|
etadvai prāṇānāmāyatanametadamṛtamabhayametat|
parāyaṇametasmānna punarāvartanta ityeṣa nirodhastadeṣa ślokaḥ||

---

10 Author's own translation.

[Having elaborated upon the worship of fire, the Vishwaroopa, possessor of all forms (being embodied in the universe), world of the moon, the path of the manes, the portion of food and Southern Course (the impermanent path, Avidya, xar), now dwells upon the Northern Course (the path of permanent immortality, the Vidya, Axar). The control of the senses and meditation, consistent penance, by practicing brahmacharya (celibacy) with faith and vidya (here vidya should be construed as shlokas in praise of the Sun) contemplating the Sun in the seat of Atman, the seeker (meditator) attains the Sun.][11]

In the latter part of the shloka, it is repeated as '*Etad Amrut Pratrayam*'. Here, the shloka refers to adhidaivik as amrut (elixir) which is divine. Hence, equating adhidaivik with the divine. The term 'Vidya' appearing in Shruti signifies both adhyatmik as well as adhidaivik knowledge. It is, therefore, incorrect to accept a one-sided interpretation.

In the *Prashna Upanishad* (6.8), Sage Pippalad has imparted knowledge to his six disciples. Upon the conclusion of his discourse, the disciples have made offerings saluting him with their heads bowed in obeisance and reverence, and said:

ते तमर्चयन्तस्त्वं हि नः पिता योऽस्माकमविद्यायाः परं पारं तारयसीति।
नमः परमऋषिभ्यो नमः परमऋषिभ्यः॥

te tamarcayantastvaṃ hi naḥ pitā yo'smākamavidyāyāḥ paraṃ pāraṃ
tārayasīti namaḥ paramarṣibhyo namaḥ paramarṣibhyaḥ

[You indeed are our father who ferried us across to the other shore of knowledge (vidya). Obeisance to thee O great seer.] [12]

Thus, filled with great joy, the disciples paid their respects by repeatedly offering their salutes. It is made abundantly clear that the sage has ferried

---

11 Author's own translation.
12 Author's own translation.

them from Avidya to Vidya. Here the reference is to two banks of the river, one bank being Avidya and the other, Vidya. Like the two banks of river, there is a natural need for both in the river of life. The manifest Avidya and the unmanifest, distant, invisible Vidya are the two banks and the river of life flows between these two. He alone, who has made the difficult crossing from the bank of Avidya (i.e., the bank of worldly life) to the far bank of Vidya, is evolved in true sense. The summum bonum of the shloka is that 'his life is indeed contented.'

The purpose of taking the above shloka for deliberation is that the bank opposite to or across from Avidya is Vidya. Merely, worldly knowledge can never lead to comprehension of God's form. Therefore, thanks to such knowledge imparted by Sage Pippalad, his six disciples referred to the other bank of Avidya as Vidya. Therefore, Vidya does not negate Avidya, but exists alongside as the other bank of the river of life. In the following shloka from the *Mundaka Upanishad* (1.2.13), there is not even a passing reference to Avidya:

तस्मै स विद्वानुपसन्नाय सम्यक्प्रशान्तचित्ताय शमान्विताय।
येनाक्षरं पुरुषं वेद सत्यं प्रोवाच तां तत्त्वतो ब्रह्मविद्याम्॥ १३ ॥

tasmai sa vidvānupasannāya samyakpraśāntacittāya śamānvitāya
yenākṣaraṃ puruṣaṃ veda satyaṃ provāca tāṃ tattvato
brahmavidyām

[To him should be unequivocally imparted Brahmavidya as prescribed in the shastras, who approaches with humility, settled mind and self-restraint which would enable him to comprehend that eternal Poorna Purusha transmitted through the Truth (Satyam), the seventh Vyahriti.][13]

Similarly, since vidya means Brahmavidya which clearly provides perception of Poorna Purusha, the philosophy of Poorna Purusha is verily called Brahmavidya. Brahmavidya so clearly being the Vidya

---

13 Author's own translation.

relating to Poorna Purusha and the Vedas referring to Poorna Purusha as Brahman, what was the object in shrinking the scope of the Vyasa Sutra's '*Athato brahama jidnyasa*' [Now is the time to inquire about the Absolute Truth] to just '*jidnyasa*' or enquire into 'witness Brahman' (which is just one form of Poorna Purusha the Shivaroopa), instead of enquiry into Poorna Purusha? The interpretation of hymns like *Janmadhyasya Yataha* (Brahman is the origin of this world; Brahma Sutra 1.2) are quite in harmony when construed as Poorna Purusha. And when the meaning of the term 'Brahman' is construed as Poorna Purusha, the prologue-form of the shloka in the *Mundaka Upanishad* describing Brahmavidya as '*Sa Brahmavidyam* ….', the refuge of all the Vidyas makes sense. Otherwise, how can the Vidya relating to 'Turiya Parbrahman' become the refuge of all Vidyas? And once everything except 'witness' is negated, wherefrom do the other Vidyas come? Therefore, when it is construed as: that which acquaints us with the very form of Poorna Purusha is Brahma Vidya, then all 'Vidyas' would comprise Avidya and Vidya. Or to classify further, it would encompass all the Vidyas relating to adhibhautik, adhyatmik and adhidaivik, etc. are enshrined in Brahman, Poorna Purusha. And then only it would truly be: Once you know Brahman you know everything. Mere Brahman-experience cannot take you beyond comprehension of only the witness Brahman.

The second chapter of this book 'God as a Scientific Concept', on the Poorna Purusha attempted to shed light on the Poorna Purusha's form using the path of knowledge (logic). Chapter three 'India and its Rich Heritage of Sanskrit and the Vedas', looked into the fallacy in the doctrine of 'Brahman is the only Truth, the world is unreal'. It discussed how the world is not Maya's action or creation, it is Maya that evolves from the characteristic nature of the world. Therefore, Ishwara is not evolved from Maya. He is not Maya-evolute; because it is He who assumed the world form; Maya evolved from the world.

In the same way the jeeva or the being is not Avidya-evolute, on the contrary Avidya dwells in him and he has the capacity to acquire Vidya. Had the jeeva been, as the Vedantins contend, evolved from

Avidya he would never have had the capacity to assimilate Vidya. It is therefore, more appropriate to say that Avidya and Vidya both dwell in the jeeva. And that Vidya does not erase Avidya. A little while ago we saw that Ishwara mimicked the world, meaning the world is His. Vidya, Avidya and the Traividya (the Trinity) are enshrined in Him. God being Omniscient, that all Vidyas are enshrined in Him does not need any proof. This cannot be said about the Vedantins' concept of the Parabrahman.

Fallacies in the Vedantin Concept of the Parabrahman

The Vedantins' concept of the Parabrahman cannot be said to incude both Vidya and Avidya, since the Vedantins hold that the Parabrahman means Pure Truth, the Parabrahma's nature cannot be partly pure and partly impure. Since to stretch the concept to make it All Complete or Poorna, the Vedantins had to reconcile with the existence of Avidya by finding a place for it. To do this, the Vedantins took recourse to the concept of the 'impure Brahman' and 'Pure Brahman'; contending that there is an illusion of Parabrahman in the 'impure Brahman' that can deceive, however the real Parabrahma is just Pure Truth no illusion. Hence, the all pure Vedantin Parbrahman had no room for Avidya.

For the Vedantins it became imperative to erase Avidya. This they did by concluding that as Vidya helped one attain the Parabrahman or witness-Brahman state, it (Vidya) did so by erasing Avidya. However, we saw earlier that even after attaining the Parabrahman-state, Shri Shankaracharya established four monasteries and composed melodious praises to the deities—these actions or karmas happened with the help of adhibhautik (Avidya) and adhidaivik (Vidya) knowledge, confirming that Vidya does not annihilate Avidya but can work alongside it.

The Vedas decree the co-worship of Vidya and Avidya and this is the real path. Owing to this, there is no self-deception, unlike that of the Vedantins who erroneously conclude that Vidya has annihilated Avidya. The Vedas confirm the import of Brahman as Poorna Purusha, but the Vedantins construe it as only as Parabrahman. In the Vedantin view the Brahman and Parabrahman being reckoned as one and the same, the

Vedic and Upanishadic hymns and shlokas relating to Brahman were employed for Parabrahman. When it did not fit, a lot of exercise was undertaken to make sure it did. As Parabrahaman is one of the forms of Poorna or Brahman, no one noticed this error. And this having continued over a very long period of time, this fault cannot be attributed to the propounds of the original Parabrahman doctrine.

Besides, when the Vedantins popularized the direct experience of Parabrahman through the path of dhyana-knowledge, they popularized the attainment of just one form of the Poorna Purusha. Thanks to their diligent efforts, the path of experiencing the All-Complete form of Poorna Purusha lagged behind. The mistaken belief that attaining the Brahman was the same as attaining the Poorna Purusha, gained ground in public mind.

The first to assail the Vedantin philosophy were the Vaishanavacharyas, who were filled with anger because the divine or adhidaivik form of God-experience or Ishwara was lost sight of in the Vedantin approach. But they also made the mistake of accepting the causal relation between the world and the Lord. They reckoned only the divine, the adhidaivik was the whole truth. As a result, they did not advocate the Vedic path that would allow one to attain the Poorna Purusha.

In the sixth chapter on 'Genome of Poorna Purusha: Supreme Lord' we saw how the Parabrahman experience through dhyana of Omkar's 'quarters' can be attained by the path of knowledge. We learnt, through words, how to go to the dream state from wakefulness and to deep slumber from the dream state. Instead of this process, now we see here how the reverse process, i.e., attaining Turiya from wakefulness through the equipoise state, can help us attain not only Parabrahman form or atman realization but the experience of complete form of Poorna Purusha as laid down in the Vedas. That is to say: Parabrahman, Ishwara and the world can be experienced simultaneously. The students of Poornavad ought to bear this in mind. Ultimately, this being a circular phenomenon, people feel it may be easier to go clockwise instead of anti-clockwise to reach the ultimate destination. The seeker should remember that by following the clockwise route, all aspects of Poorna are comprehensible or manifest, while by the reverse or anticlockwise, i.e., from deep slumber to Turiya only one aspect—the Parabrahman-experience—is attained.

The Poorna is Attained in Action

By the circular (cyclic) path, since man proceeds from wakefulness to Poorna state, he can adopt any of the three Vidyas, viz., knowledge, action or worship, to attain Poorna. However, if he chooses to go straight from slumber to Turiya he has to abandon karma, i.e., action. Action is required to gain knowledge and also for worship. Therefore, to transcend wakefulness and attain the Poorna state nothing needs to be relinquished. And history bears witness to the fact that Poorna is attained during action. Arjuna had the vision of Lord's Universal Form on the battlefield. There, the Lord had said that the form that He showed Arjuna was difficult even for Great God (Mahesh) to see, because the vision of this form was not possible during the Samadhi state. The Lord also said that the Virat form that He had displayed to Mother Yashoda in his open mouth was very much an action as she had asked Him to open His mouth and show her what He had eaten.

The Poorna's experience is during action in the life, there is no need to build monasteries, dhyan-mandirs. It is imperative to build homes and perform actions with good sense in one's own home as a householder. The Grace of God and God-Experience is felt there only and gradually His other forms and ultimately the complete form is experienced. It is important, therefore, to understand Vidya, Avidya and to employ those as the means. We have to employ Vidya and Avidya as the means of Poorna Purusha experience. And we should study from this point of view. Applying Vidya and Avidya as the means in life implies living life with good sense. While doing so, continue to experience all aspects of material life and satisfy doubts, about Poorna Purusha's forms with the help of Vidya relating to knowledge acquired through logic. In this manner, all doubts being cleared, the faith in Poorna Purusha would automatically take root and lead to the Poorna Purusha experience. Just as at the end of the road lies the destination, so is the Poorna Purusha-experience and with it vanishes the difference between Vidya and Avidya. The worldly life itself feels like spirituality nay, it truly turns into it, because the Vedas reckon Poorna Purusha's comprehension as Brahman-knowledge.

The *Mundaka Upanishad* (2.1.10) states:

पुरुष एवेदं विश्वं कर्म तपो ब्रह्म परामृतम् ।
एतद्यो वेद निहितं गुहायां सोऽविद्याग्रन्थिं विकिरतीह सोम्य ॥

puruṣa evedaṁ viśvaṁ karma tapo brahma parāmṛtam |
etadyo veda nihitaṁ guhāyāṁ so'vidyāgranthiṁ vikiratīha somya

[Penance, action, ultimate nectar-form Brahman and the world, all these is He the Ultimate Purusha, Supreme Personality Poorna Purusha. He who comprehends the intimate Supreme Personality abiding deep in the heart's cave, unties the knots of Avidya in this very life.][14]

This shloka appears elsewhere also in this treatise. Here it is clearly mentioned that Brahman means Poorna Purusha. As stated earlier, He unties the knots of Avidya, i.e., the adverse effect of Avidya due to lack of Vidya, viz., self-pride, belittling others, conceit, denying God's existence. Even if it is agreed for a while that existence-truth-bliss is Vidya, then faith, feeling and love etc. qualities that exist in a householder's life are Avidya. But such a description of Avidya does not occur. Atheism, ill-will, etc., however, seem to be described as Avidya. According to Vedantins, without comprehension of form everything else is Avidya. This, however, is not so in the *Manusmriti*. In the same way, Shruti does not imply that Brahmavidya is Parabrahman. At some places even if it is like Vidya, the Parabrahaman is said to be the form of Poorna Purusha or Brahman only.

Mundaka Upanishad (1.1.3) states Poorna Purusha Vidya is verily Brahmavidya and its order of succession also is mentioned:

---

14 Author's own translation.

शौनको ह वै महाशालोऽङ्गिरसं विधिवदुपसन्नः पप्रच्छ।
कस्मिन्नु भगवो विज्ञाते सर्वमिदं विज्ञातं भवतीति ।

śaunako ha vai mahāśālo'ṅgirasaṃ vidhivadupasannaḥ papraccha |
kasminnu bhagavo vijñāte sarvamidaṃ vijñātaṃ bhavatīti ||

[Brahma was the first among the gods to manifest Himself. The knowledge of Brahman that Brahma imparted to Atharva, Atharva transmitted to Angira in days of yore. Angira passed it on to Satyawah of the line of Bharadwaj. He of the line of Bharadwaj handed down to Angirasa this knowledge.][15]

Therefore, considering the above tradition of succession, readers would be convinced that Poornavad is not a creation of my imagination but that the entire Vedic philosophy speaks Poornavad. It is not that only this Upanishad supports Poornavad but that other Upanishads also expound only Poornavad. Dealing with only the fourth phase in a householder's life—the ascetic phase or Sannyasa Ashram—even the *Jabala Upanishad* supports Poornavad. We have interpreted the unmanifest as the Atman, whereas the Kevaladvaitins construe the unmanifest Brahman as the cause of Prakriti or unmanifest Maya. From the following shloka, the correctness of our interpretation yet again proved:

अथ हैनमात्रिः पप्रच्छ याज्ञवल्क्यं य एषोऽनन्तोऽव्यक्त
आत्मा तं कथमहं विजानीयामिती।।
स होवाच याज्ञवल्क्यः सोऽविमुक्त उपास्यो य
एषोऽनन्तोऽव्यक्त आत्मासोऽविमुक्ते प्रतिष्ठित इति।।

atha hainamatriḥ papracchayājñavalkyaṃ ya eṣo'nanto'vyakta ātmā
taṃ kathamahaṃ vijānīyāmiti|

---

15 Author's own translation.

sa hovāca yājñavalkyaḥ so'vimukta upāsyo ya eṣo'nanto'vyakta ātmā so'vimukte pratiṣṭhita iti||

[Atri, Brahma's son sought to know from Sage Yajnawalkya as to how could the Unmanifest Atman be known. Yajnawalkya replied that the confined Atman, the being, whose object of worship was That Infinite Unmanifest Atman, i.e., enshrined in the confined Atman with adjunct. (Here the questioner has used the term 'unmanifest' and so did Yajnawalkya while satisfying the doubt.) He pointed out that 'It was established in the being (the confined Atman) and its comprehension was through knowledge and penance hence it was referred to as the unmanifest'.][16]

We too have interpreted it in the same manner. The Advaitins admit that the Vidya required to comprehend Atman is verily Parabrahman-related Brahmavidya. There is a shloka in the *Taittriya Upanishad* (Brg. 6) relating to Bhargavi and Varuni Vidya:

सैषा भार्गवीवारुणी विद्या।परमेव्योमन्प्रतिष्ठिता।
सः य एवम् वेद प्रतितिष्ठति ।।

(Tai. Brg. 6)

[Sage Bhrigu having performed penance (Tapa), learnt that food is Brahman. But food is subject to production, therefore, how could it be Brahman? He approached his father Varuna with this doubt. Varuna told him if he was earnest enough to comprehend Brahman, he should perform penance, because penance also is Brahman.
So Bhrigu again went into penance and having performed it he realized that mind is Brahman. But on reflection he discovered that, mind is dependent on senses of cognition so how can it be called Brahman? Having known that, he again approached his father Varuna requesting him to teach him 'Brahman'. Varuna again told him that he should desire to know Brahman by penance because penance

---

16 Author's own translation.

also is Brahman. So Bhrigu again went into penance and having performed it, he realized penance is Brahman. But the acquisition of that knowledge was not without effort, therefore, it was not correct to call it Brahman. Therefore, yet again he went to his father, then also Varuna told him to perform penance. Having performed penance, he realized that Bliss is Brahma.][17]

This is the knowledge learnt by Bhrigu through penance, therefore it is called Bhargavi Vidya and because it was taught by Varuna hence Varuni Vidya. This knowledge is established in the Poorna Purusha, i.e., it acquaints one with the Poorna Purusha. Similar to Bhrigu, whoever establishes this learning through this Vidya and settles in the Poorna Purusha, comprehends His very form and realizes one's own non-duality with Him. If this Brahmavidya is restricted only to 'Anando Brahmeti Vyajanat' [Bliss is Brahma] then it is the Brahmavidya pertaining to Parabrahman.

Here what is to be noted is, that after penance when Bhrigu realized food as Brahman, Varuna did not say that it was wrong. But Bhrigu himself had a doubt, 'how could this be Brahman?' Thereupon, Varuni told him to do penance but did not tell him that he was wrong. Later, realizing that 'Prana is Brahman' also he had a doubt. This only means that by virtue of penance Bhrigu comprehended one after the other, the forms of the Poorna Purusha and at the same time realized that those were not the complete forms of Poorna. Upon reaching 'Bliss is Brahman' his doubt was dispelled, because by then he had had comprehension of all the forms of Poorna Purusha. He realized that he attained complete knowledge and became very happy.

Nowhere it is mentioned that as a result of achieving the 'Bliss is Brahman' state, he felt that the earlier knowledge was wrong; or that the 'Bliss is Brahman' state had wiped out all the earlier knowledge. Disregarding this the Vedantins take only 'Bliss-Brahman' as true and contend that this is the 'Parabrahmavidya' or 'Brahmavidya'; but that

---

17 Author's own translation.

is not the original scriptural view. Had it been so '*Annavanannado bhavati*'—he who performs worship of 'Anna Brahman' shall flourish as a fortunate person blessed with cattle, wealth, etc.—such fruition would never have been told of this Vidya. And there would not have been the teaching: '*Annamunividyat*'. Therefore, it is proven that this Vidya affords perception of Poorna's form and not mere 'Parbrahmavidya'.

The shloka from the (Tai Brg 6) states:

स याश्रयं पुरुषे। यश्चासावादित्ये। स एकः ॥

[That Highest Atman which dwells in this Purusha or man dwells in Sun too; that is to say that Poorna Purusha is intimate to man as well as the Sun. In short, there is non-duality of Poorna Purusha with man and the Sun. But the Kevaladvaitin interpretation would be 'non-duality of man and Sun's Atman'].

The point of difference between the Vedantins and Poornavad is that the Vedantins reckon only Parabrahman as the Absolute Truth, while Poornavad also includes adhibhautik and adhidaivik in Poorna. the Vedantins don't do so therefore, the world turns out to be unreal. To call the world unreal, as the Vedantins do, implies the regulator of this world 'Ishwara' is also unreal, then what is the fate of hymnal literature in the Vedas?

The Samhitas and the Upanishads are in hymnal form. Assuming that the subject of the Vidyas is restricted only to that, it does not mean that it deals only with the Turiya Parabrahman. Isolating only a few hymns from heaps of hymns, for exposition, and discarding the rest as meaningless is like digging the mountain to retrieve mouse. Then what is the difference between those Western pundits who reckon the Vedas as the literature of shepherds, and us?

Parabrahman has also been called Poorna or Complete in the Vedas and the doctrine of Poornavad brings out the true importance of the Vedic hymns. No hymn is treated as fanciful or as having imaginative reasoning. There is a distinct possibility, owing to the philosophy of the Kevaladvaitins, of the divorce between philosophy and the Vedas, which does not happen in case of Poornavad. From this, too, the readers can very well speculate which Absolute Truth has been dealt with in the Vedas. We have considered the Vedic import as well as the Vedantin interpretation of terms like Maya, Prakriti, Vidya, Avidya and readers must have noticed as to how totally adverse is our knowledge about the Vedas as a result of Advaitvad.

Similarly, the Advaitin philosophy has not been able to afford clarity to, and state, the importance of the Bhargavi-Varuni-Vidya which Poornavad did. When we acquire a certain knowledge through erudition and penance and begin to doubt due to some adverse observations, the knowledge in such cases is not wrong but incomplete, and it cannot be completed only by erudition and penance. Poornavad afforded clarity to the above important doctrine which the Advaitin philosophy could not. Based on this doctrine, science made strides and adhyatma also progressed. When the best of adhibhautik (material) knowledge could not lead the world to success, it was not that there was something wrong with the knowledge but that it was inadequate for the task at hand. Man realized this fact quite early and that led to development in adhidaivat and adhyatma. Scholars should remember this. Furthermore, they should try to discern between the Vedic import of Vidya-Avidya and Brahmavidya and the distorted meaning owing to Kevaladvaitin conditioning and should co-worship Vidya and Avidya. This would ensure Poorna's experience and this is the basic objective of this chapter. As the *Mundaka Upanishad* (2.2.8) states:

भिद्यते हृदयग्रन्थिश्छिद्यन्ते सर्वसंशयाः।
क्षीयन्ते चास्य कर्माणि तस्मिन्दृष्टे परावरे।।

bhidyate hṛdayagranthiśchidyante sarvasaṃśayāḥ|
kṣīyante cāsya karmāṇi tasmindṛṣṭe parāvare ||

[He crosses the sea of sorrow and assemblage of sins. The knots of heart, i.e., improbability and adverse feeling of intellect when untied, he attains Brahman-experience and immortality.][18]

Here, it is distinctly mentioned as 'feelings of the heart' and 'doubts of intellect' respectively. Then is it the 'feeling' which is Avidya or is the 'doubt' Avidya? If both fall under Avidya then there is a possibility of speculating if Shruti says that at a given time, 'to doubt' is okay and at other times 'evil disposition is fine'. But the Vedas don't agree with this. Doubt or improbability can never be good; any one would say so, and so do the Vedas. If it is so and if feelings and doubts of the intellect are Avidya's activity, then how to worship (practice) Avidya as occurring in Ishavasya? Such doubt is quite natural.

The second doubt is: why is it said that with self-realization or comprehension of Poorna's form 'action is enfeebled' instead of 'action ceases'? The Atman is beyond fate and consequent fruits. Therefore, after the comprehension, if (*tasmin drushte paravare*) [it is] construed as Turiya Brahman then the import would be that 'He sees Himself' as 'I am This'. If this be so, the action ceases; but, instead, why does Shruti say that 'the action is enfeebled'?

If comprehension of form is Vidya, then 'feelings', 'intellect's doubts', 'determination', etc., turn out to be Avidya; action too is Avidya. Even if improbability and doubts are destroyed and they do so as a result of comprehension of Poorna through Vidya, good feelings and determination of heart and intellect do remain and those fall under Avidya. Therefore, worshipping (practicing) Avidya means destroying ill feelings and retaining good feelings; improbability and doubts are destroyed with comprehension of Poorna but good feelings and determination remain; shortcomings due to want of Vidya are destroyed, and not Avidya itself. So, the heart's and intellect's activity continues, karma or action continues, and is not destroyed. But those

---

18 Author's own translation.

actions or karma, being of pure form, are no longer binding and become feeble.

Description by sages like Vashishtha, and by seers of the past and present (and even of the future) is the outcome of a sharp intellect and not the sign of a non-functioning intellect. Therefore, the doctrine that, 'Avidya is not destroyed by Vidya' is correct and cannot be negated. Further, with respect to Vidya's worship, which aspect is to be worshipped? Is any one aspect to be worshipped and another, not? There is no command or restraint in this regard. Therefore, in day-to-day life there can't be an injunction or restraint, but it is imperative that improbability, doubt and heartless nature—which are due to lack of Vidya—should be necessarily destroyed with the aid of Vidya and the doctrine states that it does happen so.

The Vedas don't proclaim that all knots of the heart or knots of the intellect are necessarily Avidya; rather the shortcomings lying in Avidya due to want of Vidya are predominantly mentioned in this shloka as knots of the heart or knots of the intellect. Those are not Avidya but knots owing to want of Vidya and the Poorna's comprehension destroys them, such is the import of this shloka. These knots due to want of Vidya are not Avidya at all but are far from beneficial to Avidya and as those are destructible by Vidya also need Avidya. Therefore, worldly life needs spirituality and co-worship of Vidya and Avidya as this is in man's best interest.

It is important to know minutely the difference between Avidya, Vidya, knots of heart and knots of the intellect. All knowledge relating to (the material) adhibhautik is Avidya while that which is acquired by (spiritual) adhyatmik or (divine) adhidaivik penance is Vidya. We studied that by virtue of co-worship of Avidya and Vidya, direct perception, the experience of Poorna Purusha is possible. But there are stumbling blocks in the process and there are knots of the heart or knots of the intellect (improbability and doubt or suspicion). From this point of view, the subject of knots of the intellect lies in between Avidya and Vidya, much like the filling in a sandwich keeps the two [slices] apart, doesn't allow them to join. Even if we worship, rather co-worship Avidya and Vidya, owing to knots of the intellect they can't become one. And comprehension of Poorna's form does not become possible.

During the wakeful state, we experience the world through our sense organs. We experience God through feelings, that is possible. Direct experience of Atman realization, Brahman experience, i.e., 'Parabrahman experience', is through knowledge. However, Poorna's experience is by co-worship of Vidya and Avidya and collective Sadhana of action, knowledge and worship.

We ourselves seem to question the knowledge of Vidya and through penance, e.g., after the penance we got divine experience, we were happy, but later quite naturally, we wonder if it was an illusion. Suppose someone tenders us advice and convinces us from all angles, we are also logically convinced. But after reaching home we begin suspecting whether he had some self interest in it. Without anyone's intervention, we ourselves start brooding. In a way it can't be said that such doubts are due to want of Vidya! These are neither Avidya nor due to want of Avidya. Therefore, such knots of the intellect are to be untied by each of us by penance.

Just as it is important to apply action, knowledge and worship depending upon the situation, it is even more important that such knots of the heart and the intellect are eradicated by each personally. We must be able to do so. This is called strong resolve. So long as a person doesn't decide to become wise, no one else can make him/her wise. That person alone becomes wise who has the desire to become wise. By this rule, only one who has resolved to eradicate such knots of the heart and the intellect—by using knowledge, action and worship—can eradicate it. This task has to be performed by oneself only. Perhaps, the grace of God and Guru could afford such a person bit of courage and guidance but each has to personally undertake to eradicate these knots of the heart and intellect.

Here, the question is—having acquired knowledge and also with little bit of experience, why do such knots of the heart and the intellect occur? After gaining knowledge, why should there be doubts? The reply is: the knowledge acquired is not complete knowledge. Had it been complete there would have been no scope for any doubt. The fact that such knots of the heart and the intellect occur, indicates that acquired knowledge is not complete. Therefore, each one has to take it to completeness by one's own resolve. Once it is taken to that state of completeness, all doubts cease and this is the state of All Completeness, the Siddha state. It is this that Bhargavi and Varuni Vidya prove.

In the process of co-worship of Vidya and Avidya, once knots of the heart and the intellect cease to occur, Vidya and Avidya merge in each other, become one. It leads to Poorna's experience which settles a person into the Poorna state and that is why '*tasmin drushtey paravare*' as stated in *Mundaka Upanishad* means: he who is settled in Poorna state post his Poorna-experience, all that knots of the intellect and the heart are untied. Here, Vidya and Avidya become one form, e.g., one who stands on the banks of adhibhautik Avidya of the river of life, to such a person adhyatmik Vidya appears as though it is on the other bank that lies across the river. But he who can swim to either bank, crossing the river flowing between the two banks, for him there is no such thing like separation, no such thing like two banks and water in between; it is all just the same water. And hence, whether one is a householder or a spiritualist he swims effortlessly back and forth as needed. He attains success with natural joy.

One who is thus settled in Poorna has direct perception and comprehension of Poorna Purusha, for him it is the same whether it is adhibhautik or to dwell in the other world. Because, in whichever sphere he dwells, be it adhibhautik, adhidaivik or adhyatmik he is in the Poorna's world and joyous; and such division ceases to be of any relevance for him. From this state of his thoughts, he acquires the confidence of being able to attain whatever he decides, whether adhibhautik, adhidaivik or adhyatmik.

CHAPTER 11

Parabrahman: Lord of the Infinite Universe

PARABRAHMAN IS the reflection of the Shiva form of the 'Poorna', and is known as the spiritual aspect of Poorna Purusha. It is the maximum enlargement or the broader concept of self or jeeva. The individual soul is the minimum image of Parabrahman. From micro particles that are finite, to the larger extent of the infinite universe, they all are one and the same. The jeeva contains all those particles of the whole universe. To experience the Parabrahman it is essential to recognize the dual, i.e., the self ('I' that we experience ourselves as) that seeks to realize the Greater Self.

Experiencing duality is what gives us the 'material eye'. It is the 'material eye' that causes us to perceive the material world as 'real'; it is the material eye that transmutes into the Virat as shown by Lord Shri Krishna on the battlefield of Mahabharata (Kurukshetra). It is the Virat form of the jeeva's 'material eye' that reveals Ishwara's infinite form. This state is the highest degree of non-dual. It is a state of tranquility and is transcendental.

Journey Between Non-dual and Dual

Our life is a journey between the non-dual to dual. The journey of the jeeva starts from the womb of the mother, in a non-dual state. At birth the jeeva becomes dual, and upon attaining the Turiya state (the essential nature or Shiva, the Superior Brahman or Parabrahman) it becomes non-dual again. Thus, Parabrahman, Atman, Ishwara and jeeva are but one and the same; all are parts of the Poorna Purusha.

Poornatva is only absolute and pure Truth. This is the main hypothesis of Poornavad. When we define any such concept or contention we should know the proper meaning of each word so that we convey the exact, correct message. Knowing the meaning of 'absolute and pure Truth' comes first and then the concepts of Maya, Vidya and Avidya. In order to comprehend Poorna, rely on the fact that that the real/unreal, pure/impure, or Vidya/Avidya are not contradictory to each other but there is co-ordination between them. This is proved by the Vedas.

It is necessary to know which truth is the Absolute Truth. The Kevaladvaitins hold that Parabrahman and Ishwara are integral forms of the Poorna Purusha. Of these three forms (Parabrahma, Ishwara, and Poorna Purusha), the Advaitians speak more about the adhyatmik (spiritual) aspect and less about the adhibhautik (material) and adhidaivik (divine) aspects of the Poorna Purusha, which has been defined by the Vedas. Though the Advaitins have not talked about the adhibhautik and the adhidaivik aspects, to know the Parabrahman it is necessary to know about these two aspects of the Poorna Purusha. Immanuel Kant said that, 'Metaphysics is a dark ocean without shores or lighthouse upon which is strewn many a metaphysical wreck.' Poornavad accepts that metaphysics or spirituality (adhyatma) can lead to darkness, but only if unaccompanied by divinity (adhidaivat) and materiality (adhibhautik). Poornavad thus also stands with Aristotle's contention that knowledge of metaphysics or spirituality alone is not sufficient for the realization of ultimate truth and reality.

It is the main contention of Poornavad that without the material and divine dimensions of Poorna Purusha, any application of Indian philosophy becomes weak and irrelevant to modern concerns. The impact, in the sixth century, of Buddhism on Shankaracharya's Kevaladvait and Mayavad, reflects this. To prove the similarity between the Buddhism and the Sanatan Vedic tradition, Shankaracharya neglected the true Vedic concept of Poorna Purusha—which is really the relevant philosophy for the present age.

Poornavad made all efforts to reconstruct the neglected aspects and concepts of the Vedic tradition. Brahma, Parabrahman and the Poorna Purusha are one and the same according to the Vedas and Pooranvad. Human life is dominated by three dimensions—dnyan/knowledge (adhyatmik/spiritual) karma/action (material/adhibhautik) and bhakti-upasana/devotion-worship (adhidaivik/divine)—as per the Vedic and Vedanta traditions. Thus, all three aspects, the spiritual, material and divine, are equally important, no one aspect can be less or more important.

Chitta or Pure Knowledge

According to the Vedantic view, experiencing the Parabrahman is due to the pure knowledge provided by the Chitta '*dnyanat eva tu Kaivalyam*'. However, the Kashmiri Shaivas do not agree that knowledge is the means for the Parabrahman experience. They emphasize that knowledge is the cause of bondage, hence Shivaroopa is not attained by knowledge. Their contention is that where the process of knowledge stops, ends, settles, becomes still, at that point is Shivaroopa attained. The aphorism '*Dnyan Bandha*' in the *Shiva Sutra* substantiates this view.

In order to make it clearer, Shiva-Parvati's story is quite useful. Parvati was Daksha's daughter and the word 'dakshata' means being alert, this is the Chaitanya's quality—to be alert 24 x 7, to note whatever is observed, assimilate knowledge about it and experience it. This is called to be alert, and the Chaitanya ataVishisthmata [thought] or the jeeva (the prajnya [intellect] part of atman) does this job. The reference found in Shivsutra, the text of knowledge, for knowing the power and authority of Shiv and Parvati—Shiv is the power and Parvati is the knowledge—Shiv/Parvati i.e. Purush/Prakruti. They are opposite of each other. There is a struggle between the knowledge and power, therefore, it is explained mythologically and said that there was a tremendous quarrel between the couple. It can be linked up with the present system of universe which is dynamic and ever-changing—Purush and Pralriti's struggle affects the jeeva i.e. every being on earth. In other words, Vedas are environmental science, therefore, the Vedic system follows every universal law, right from Reality-Gravity, law of conservation of energy, antiparticle theory, etc.

Parvati is a form of potency (shakti), knowledge-power form, existence-form. Alertness is power, knowledge-power or satta is gained. Parvati was Daksha's daughter, Dakshakanya, i.e., born of Daksha. However, as long as she was Dakshakanya, Shiva didn't meet her because Daksha despised Shiva, treated him with indignity. But when Dakshakanya, abandoned her father Daksha's side, she became Dnyanshakti, unmovable, still like a mountain, settled, and then she became Parvati. She relinquished all hopes and desires and quietened the Prajnya-Atman's intellect. This state is the equipoise, Sthitapranjya state. When she reached this state, she attained Shiva's spiritual state.

Such is the philosophy of Kashmiri Shaivas. Therefore, they don't consider the Chitta/Pure Knowledge as transcending Chaitanya, rather Chaitanya according to them grace or development of Chitta (of the Satchidanand). From it is born the 'Chitvilasvad' of Saint Dnyaneshwar. Therefore, there is a Shiv Sutra *Chaitanyam Atma* because the Atman is Truth, hence the elaboration of Chitta in a way proves to be Truth. This is the view of Kashmiri Shaiva's and Saint Dnyaneshwar. But because Chittta-shakti according to them is a bondage for moksha or for attaining Shivaroopa, unless the Chitta-shakti settles in Truth, merges in Truth, becomes the Satyaroopa or Truth-form, the Shivaroopa is not attained. Although they consider Shivaroopa as Sacchidanandroopa, only Chittaroopa as firm and not the Dnyanroopa. This is the important point of difference between the Vedantins and Kashmiri Shaiva ideologies.

Because of the difference in the two ideologies as mentioned above, it is a mistaken belief that Saint Dnyaneshwar in his *Dnyaneshwari* advocates the Shankara philosophy. However, of the two, Acharya's view is closer to Poornavad. According to Poornavad, the difference is that the 'I' who has Parabrahman or Shiva experience is greater than truth, pervades it. Poornavad stresses that while contemplating on that Poorna

'I', just as the concept of Ishwara is found on this side of Parabrahman, it transcends Parabrahman and is seen as the Poorna Purusha or the Highest God, Parmeshwara.

Similarly, there is no causal relation between jeeva, Ishwara, Parabrahman and Poorna Purusha, rather it is the Form-Relation. And hence, these are not steps in a straight line but are different states of the 'Self' in a circular pattern. Therefore, even after the Poorna Purusha experience, man can complete the circle by taking birth in accordance with his wish or can serially experience the wakeful, dream, sleep and Turiya states and again retreat to jagruti (wakefulness). Or through the path of Bhu, Bhuva, Swaha, Maha, etc., the seven vyahritis (the seven worlds or planes of existence) go up to Satyam and again commence the journey back to Bhu.

The almighty desired to be many, assumed the world-form, created everyone. Therefore, it is natural to be inquisitive about our original form. Arising out of this is inquisitiveness about Parabrahman, inquisitiveness about Poorna, and by satisfying it, man enjoys well-being. The scholar should remember that except this difference, there is an identity of view between Shankaracharya's Kevaladvaita and Dr Parnerkar's Poornavad about other aspects. The ideologies of Acharya Rajnish, J. Krishnamurthy, etc., are also slanted towards Shaiva philosophy, but Ramakrishna Paramhansa's and Vivekananda's philosophy are in accordance with the Shankara view.

We have considered above, the difference of opinion between the Kashmiri Shiavas and the Advaitins. Such difference can be seen between Bimb-Pratibimbvad of the Vivarankars [Shankara or Shankaracharya] and Abhasvad of Vidyaranya Swami. Swami Vidyaranya considers jeeva and Ishwara as reflection of Chaitanya and therefore that is false (illusion). Vivrankars contend non-duality of bimb [image] with pratibimb [reflection] and that pratibimb is real (truth). Therefore, jeeva and Ishwara which are reflections of Chaitanya are also true.

Now let us see Vidyaranya Swami's Mimamsa ('to investigate'). In brief it is: Chitta is Brahmachaitanya and its reflection in the intellect's desire is Ishwara. Out of the three states—waking, dream and sleep—the intellect's condition is subtlest. Vidyaranya Swami states: intellect's desire and the reflection of Chitta (Brahmachaitanya) in intellect is Ishwara. But the subtle intellect acting during the waking and dream state, the reflection of Chaitanya (not the Ishwar Chaitanya Chitta) in that intellect, is jeeva. And that intellect active during these two states is called Vidnyan. Hence, jeeva is considered as having a Vidnyaynmaykosh. And because such intellect's desires are active during sleep are referred as with Anandkosh[1]. Therefore, Ishwara can be equated with Anandmaykosh.

From this discussion a question arises: during the sleep state there are innumerable intellect-desires and if the Brahmachaitanya reflected in intellect-desires is Ishwar, wouldn't there be many Ishwaras? To which Vidyaranya [Shankaracharya's Acharya] Swami's answer is: the Brahmachaitanya reflected in the intellect-desire-specific ignorance should be called Ishwara. The ignorance form of the sleep state of jeevas is same. That being the bliss form there is only one Ishwara. On the contrary, during the wakeful state each individual's intellect being different, jeevas are many.

Owing to this method being adopted by Vidyaranya Swami, the reflection of Ishwara (Brahmachaitanya) in the ignorance during sleep state and the reflection of this Ishwara during the wakeful and dream states (reflection of reflection) is jeeva. But due to this description, there is a hurdle in establishing non-duality of jeeva and Brahman. However, in the Bimb-Pratibimbvad, the reflection in ignorance of intellect's desire and that in the inner organ (antakaran; intellect of wakeful and dream state) being of the same Chitta and that being direct, there is no difficulty in establishing non-duality of jeeva and Brahman. Because there is no need to consider the Ishwara in between. It is like one Sun directly reflected in numerous mirrors.

Even if there appears to be a seeming difference with Shankaracharya, owing to the method adopted by Vidyaranya Swami, i.e., his (Shankara's)

---

1 Even in sleep, the state of transcendence, i.e., the bliss, remaining unaffected because Ishwara is always in the state of bliss.

advocated consciousness-specific-atman or jeeva and consciousness-transcending-Atman (pure Atman) concept appears to be mutually strange and even if there is difficulty in proving '*jeevo bramhaivana paraha*' [Jeeva is Brahaman and not another] there is no difference between the two. That which Shankara calls pure, intellect or 'nabal' Brahman and Vidyaranya Swami addresses as Brahman and from it coins the term Brahmachaitanya that eternal, pure, intellect, free, Turiya Parabrahman form; there is no difference whatsoever between these two forms.

Here, there is a consensus between Shankara, Bimb-Pratibimbvadis, Vivarankars and Abhasvadi Vidyaranya Swami. Whatever difference that we saw is not about Parabrahman but limited only to jeeva, hwara, kootastha, and jeeva—the Advaitins, do not consider Brahm kootastha [spirit of physical body] and Ishwara. While Vidyaranya Swami has divided Chaitanya into four parts: 1) Brahma, Isa and kootastha as one in their '*Drug Drushya Viv.ek*' treatise, which includes kootastha and jeeva. Therefore, they accept only three parts [Truth, Conscious, Bliss].

With reference to Chaitanya, jeeva also is of three kinds—real, empirical and illusory. That Chaitanya, which is undivided by gross and subtle, is the real Jeeva. It has predominant non-duality with Brahman and is filled with Parabrahma Chaitanya. The empirical jeeva is that imagined internal organ, antakaran, in the undivided consciousness enveloped by Maya, which has resemblance with mind that—endowed with ego in both gross as well as the subtle body—is the empirical jeeva. This jeeva is filled with Ishwar Chaitanya. The illusory jeeva is that whose basis is imagined as the empirical jeeva which is enveloped by the deep slumber form Maya. This illusory jeeva is filled with jeeva Chaitanya.

Brahma Chaitanya and Ishwara Chaitanya are mutually reciprocal illusions. The Vivarankars disagree with Vidyaranya's classification of jeeva into three kinds. Their contention is that the archetype is not separate from the (image) reflection, therefore there is identity between the archetype and the reflection. Therefore, reflection is real. Vidyaranya, however, calls reflection as illusion, therefore, it turns out to be false.

If we minutely examine the discussion, the reflection of Chitta in Abhasvad in fact cannot be called real nor can it be called completely unreal. Meaning it turns out to be inexpressible, not capable of being expressed in words; same way in Bimb-Pratibimbvad also it proves to be inexpressible. Because the reflection of the face in fact being close to face, it is seen deep distant in the mirror. The characteristic nature of the reflection proves to be inexpressible. Thus, the main cause (material cause), in both the schools, for inexpressibility is ignorance. From the spiritual standpoint, as the understanding of Brahman can be had through either school, the Kevaladvaitins don't seem to be insisting about any one in particular. One may accept that which he likes.

CHAPTER 12

Vedanta Philosophy

THE TRADITION of Vedanta philosophy starts from the end of the Mahabharata War. The Bhagavad Gita is the first work of Vedanta literature and it set the guidelines for further Vedanta literature. Buddhism also comes under Vedanta, because Buddhism considers concepts of Vedic philosophy such as Brahman as a 'Dhammakaya' (dharma body), Avidya, Maya, and Nirvana as Moksha. There is also a partial impact of Samkhya and the *Katha Upanishad* on Buddhism. Therefore, there is room to say that the Vedanta tradition starts from Buddhism. Shankaracharya has taken the concept of Maya and the Stoist tradition from Buddhism and there is maximum impact of Buddhism on Shankaracharya's philosophy. Fritjof Capra has mentioned this in his book *The Tao of Physics* (p. 95) in a chapter on Buddhism.[1]

Shankaracharya destroyed the importance of Buddhism and therefore he became the hero of Hinduism, but the real credit of re-establishing Sanatan Dharma goes to Vaishnavacharya. Unfortunately, the history of Indian philosophy did not take cognizance of this historical contribution of Vaishnavacharya says Dr V.R. Parnerkar. Poornavad, Dr Parnerkar's doctrine, posed some queries to scholars about the absolute non-duality of Parabrahman. According to Dr Parnerkar non-duality requires

---

1 Capra, Fritijof (1975). *The Tao of Physics*. Shambhala Publications, p. 95.

the presence of more than one component, whereas Shankaracharya accepted only Parabrahman—the unmanifest universe—the other part of the manifest universe, the material world, he denied as *'jagat mithya'* (the world is false). This does not match the Vedic concept of the three dimensions of Poorna Purusha.

The Purusha consists of three dimensions in the Vedas—Shiva (knowledge); Vishnu (the science of manifest and unmanifest universe, which is known as Brahman, and in the Vedas Brahman and Parabrahman mean 'Purusha'); and the third dimension of Purusha is Vishwa (the material world) that Shankaracharya denied the existence of, calling it Maya or ignorance.

It cannot be denied that there is an impact of Buddhism on Shankaracharya. Because Lord Buddha also denied the material world saying it was ignorance. In Vedanta philosophy every acharya has interpreted Avidya as ignorance. This is the main confusion in the understanding of the Vedanta acharyas. The Shiva-Vishnu-Vishwa trinity of Dr Parnerkar's Poornavad is his outstanding contribution. With this trinity he has introduced the non-duality between three dimensions. Shiva, Vishnu and Vishwa are inseparable, interrelated, and interact as parts of Poorna Purusha. Why did Dr Parnerkar say that Purusha was Poorna Purusha? He said this with reference to the *Rig Veda* and the *Ishavasya Upanishad*, both of which state that only the Poorna is Absolute Truth. The Poorna means the manifest and unmanifest universe, the animate and the inanimate, the form and formless, bright and dark, divine and devil, life and death—all are parts of Poorna Purusha, who is the only personification of the infinite universe.

Lord Buddha, as well as all the acharyas of the Vedanta philosophy have denied the importance of Avidya, deeming it as 'ignorance', which has led to much confusion between the Vedas and the Vedanta, says Dr Parnerkar. He refers to his study of the complete *Katha Upanishad* which says that following only Vidya or only Avidya throws you into the dark. Dr Parnerkar says that Vidya and Avidya are both important to make our life complete and flourish. Avidya is the knowledge of material life, a science which is the applied dimension of the Vedas.

The highlights of the Kevaladvaitin philosophy of Shri Shankaracharya and that of the Vaishnavas are as follows: the Kevaladvaitins consider only the truth-consciousness-bliss form to witness Parabrahman as the Absolute Truth, eternal, pure intellect, free. They view the world as 'mithya' or false and dub it the activity of Maya which they translate as ignorance. The Vaishnavas, etc., reckon the being, the world and Ishwara (God) as real. Both Kevaladvaitins and Vaishnavas rely on Shruti to substantiate their views. This confuses the lay student of Shruti and there is a strong possibility of his views about Shruti getting polluted.

However, we have seen earlier that Shruti considers that Atman possesses four states and the embodied atman with three states of wakefulness, dream and sleep is called jeeva (the being) by the Shruti and when the Atman is in the fourth state, i.e., Turiya, it is called the essential nature Shiva, witness Atman or Superior Brahman (Parbrahman).

As all these four states of Atman (wakefulness, dream, sleep and Turiya) are eternal, none of these is ever absent. In case one state is manifest, other three are latent. There is never non-existence of any of the states. If one state is manifest the other three are latent. The Jeeva is One and not many. And this immutable all-pervading sole Jeeva is called the 'essential nature' Vishnu or Ishwara (God). The Omnipresent all-powerful presiding over all actions, unborn, sole, immortal, doer, the regulator, Ishwara of which the jeeva form is a part, such Ishwara as enshrined in the Shruti, is the basis on which the whole edifice of Vaishnava philosophy rests. The whole emphasis of this sectoral philosophy is on the reality of jeeva, jagat (world) and Ishwara (God), rather than on establishing non-duality. In short, just as the whole emphasis of the Kevaladvaitins is on eternality (i.e., eternal with oneness, non-duality), the Vaishnavas' emphasis is on reality and service to God.

The five schools of thought under Vedanta are: Vishishtadvaita, Dvaita, Shuddhadvaita, Dvaitaadvaita, and Achintyabhedabhed. As for the Vedanta Acharyas, except for Ramanujacharya, the rest have become irrelevant now.

CHAPTER 13

Poornavad's and Vedic Science

In THE Vedas, knowledge includes science, there is non-duality between knowledge and science. There is a science of knowledge and a knowledge of science. Knowledge is the basic theory of universe and science is the practical form of knowledge; Dr Parnerkar's Poornavad is the interpreter of the Vedas and says that Vedic knowledge is relevant to modernity as it is the fusion of tradition and modernity.

Every concept of the Vedas is defined by Poornavad as scientific. For example, the Vedic concept of Poorna Purusha is based on the *Ishavasya Upanishad*, which states that everything in the universe is under Poorna. Nothing is outside of Poorna and nothing comes out of Poorna. This is parallel to the law of conservation of energy, which states that energy can neither be destroyed (i.e., decreased) nor created (i.e., increased) but remains constant. Further, the tenth model [Rigved 10th mandala, verse 10.1] of the Purusha Sukta hymn is the definition and explanation of the entire manifest and unmanifest universe, it is complete and it is personified as Purusha; Poornavad calls it Poorna Purusha.

Scientists have yet not been able to find a microparticle smaller than the Higgs Boson nanoparticle, but the Vedas have. The soul of every being is the smallest microparticle which is the 1/10,000th part of the tow of hair of head. Cut the tow of head hair into 100 parts, take one of these 100 parts and further cut it into 100 parts—such is the micro soul, which cannot be seen by any scientific apparatus. The micro soul of Being is the smallest particle of the universe and the Poorna Purusha is the macro particle. The Bhagavad Gita states (2.23):

नैनं छिन्दन्तिशस्त्राणि नैनं दहति पावकः।
न चैनं क्लेदयन्त्यापो न शोषयति मारुतः।।

[No weapon can cut the soul into pieces, nor can it be burned by fire, nor moistened by water, not withered by the wind.][1]

The Concept of Maya

This concept is also rational and scientific. Poornavad states that Maya is the system created by Poorna Purusha to envelop Him so that nobody can easily approach Him. Even scientists have not been able to uncover all the secrets of the universe, and this is because of the system of Maya, described in the Vedas. However, Maya is misunderstood by Vedanta philosophers. Another concept, Avidya, is also misinterpreted by Vedanta philosophers, as ignorance (while Poornavad reinterprets it as the material world). Vedanta philosophers have not only misinterpreted Avidya, but have also compared it to a woman, negating the power of women.

Let us see what Dr Parnerkar has to say about the vision of science described in the dialogue (in *Poornavad*, chapter 7, 'Dnyan Vidnyan') between Shaunak and the great sage Angirasa, who defined the science of universe in words such as: Dwaya Vidya, Veditaya Para and Apara (where Para is concerned with the unmanifest universe and Apara is concerned with the material world). Bertrand Russell in his *History of Western Philosophy* mentioned that 'Shunya' comes through the Arabs which is the Indian contribution to Western science;[2] but Dr Parnekar says that, 'Shunya is not an Indian concept, Shunya figure is the same

---

1 Author's own translation.
2 Bertrand Russell, *History of Western Philosophy* (London: George Allen and Unwin Ltd., 2010).

but vision is rational.' instead of 'Shunya' there is the concept of 'Poorna' which multiplies the figure, because Poorna can be multiplied in infinite 'N', which increases the figure. Shunya has no place in the Vedas. This is the contention of Poornavad.

Environment Science of the Vedas

Some of the Devatas belong to the environment, amongst the 33 Koti (cadre) of Gods: like this:

त्वं ज्ञानमयो विज्ञानमयोऽसि

त्वं भूमिरापोनलोनिलोनमः

त्वं ब्रह्मा त्वं विष्णुस्त्वं रुदस्तर्वमिंद्रस्त्वं अग्निस्त्वं वायुस्त्वं सूर्यस्त्वं चंद्रमास्त्वं

ब्रह्मभूर्भुवः स्वरोम्॥

In Rudra, the Poornavad theory of Form-Relation is confirmed. The Rudra Contains the Purva Paksha and Uttar Paksha of the Vedas.

अग्निश्चमे, इंद्रश्चमे, पूर्णश्चमे, अश्माश्चमे, मृतिकाश्चमे

Not just a couple of hymns but the entire Rudra Adhyaya sets forth Poornavad. If the non-duality of all entities with Rudra, as contemplated in the hymn of Namak, is considered as Purva Paksha, even then in the later part (Uttardha) chamak: '*agnishchame, Indrashchame, poornachame, poornataranchame, asmachame, mruttikachame*' Rudra himself has pronounced His non-duality with all three i.e. adhidaivik, adhyatmik and adhibhautik as the rejoinder (Uttar Paksha). In other words, whatever the devotee has praised, Lord Rudra Himself acknowledged it as true. Even if someone raises a doubt as to all activities being that of Maya, Rudra Himself states His form-non-duality with whatever is all that and with His Atman form. Here it states: 'That Atman form which we consider as the Absolute-Truth-Form also is God's activity', e.g., '*Manoyajnenkalpatam, vakyajnenkalpatam, atmayajnen kalpatam....*'

In the Vedas, 'vidnyan' refers to science and 'dnyan' refers to knowledge. So, every topic of science comes under dnyan-vidnyan.

In fact, epistemologically (by Western method) after defining dnyan and vidnyan and determining their values, had we studied the three philosophies (Adhyatmik—knowledge, Adhidaivik—divinity, Adhibhautic—materiality), it would have been clear to us as to what, out of the knowledge we acquired is dnyan and what is vidynan. However, this is not the Indian tradition. The sages and those learned ones studied first by penance and then by dhyana; acquiring empirical knowledge, translating (transforming) it by using philosophical method. Therefore, while studying Indian philosophy, it is important to understand this philosophy with a seeker's mindset, and having understood clearly, to deliberate as to which is dnyan and which is vidnyan. We are going to deliberate on dnyan and vidnyan from this point of view in this chapter with reference to our study so far.

There is a shloka in *Mundaka Upanishad* (1.1.3):

शौनको ह वै महाशालोऽङ्गिरसं विधिवदुपसन्नः पप्रच्छ।
कस्मिन्नु भगवो विज्ञाते सर्वमिदं विज्ञातं भवतीति।।

śaunako ha vai mahāśālo'ṅgirasaṃ vidhivadupasannaḥ papraccha
kasminnu bhagavo vijñāte sarvamidaṃ vijñātaṃ bhavatīti

[Shaunak, the dean of a large university with 88,000 alumni, such a great householder, having approached Angirasa very humbly, with samidhas (Wooden stick used for offering in the yadnya) in hand, duly asked: 'Oh adorable Sir, (which is that thing) which having been known, all these becomes known?'][3]

In the above question by Shaunak, the term '*Sarvamidam*' ('*sarvam*' all; '*idam*' this) is specially to be contemplated. The shloka mentions '*Poornam* (complete/all) *adah* (that), *poornam idam* (this)'. *Mundaka Upanishad* (1.1.3) above, includes *adah* and *idam* in '*Sarvamidam*'. Hence, Shaunak's question to Angirasa is what should be known, in order to know all that we see and experience. Unless and until the

---

3   Author's own translation.

scope of *Sarvamidam* is fully comprehended, the answer to the question cannot be unravelled.

The first Vaishnavacharya, Shri Ramanujacharya, attached special importance to this Shruti hymn '*Poornam adah, poornam idam*'. In his opinion, the doctrine '*Ishwar Sharirbhootam Jagat*' (this world is Ishwara's body), is based on this hymn. Shruti appears to be pointing out that 'knowing that' by which all is known should be construed as dnyan (knowledge). We realize that every school of Indian philosophy has defined dnyan and vidnyan in their own way. We take the philosophies of Poornavad, Ajatvad, Shankaracharya's Mayavad and the Vaishanva schools, into account to examine fundamental doctrines. Therefore, we are not concerned with what is stated as dnyan-vidnyan yoga in the Bhagavad Gita and with dnyan/vidnyan as a subject. Readers should please bear this in mind.

The Kevaladvaitins consider the direct perception of Parabrahman as dnyan; all Vaishanvacharyas generally consider dnyan as the jeeva's comprehension that he is the servant of God. The answer to Shaunak's question 'knowing that by which everything can be known' is provided by the Vaishnavas and followers of Ajatvad and Mayavad, as: '*Eke Brahma vidyate sarvamidam jagatmithya eva vidyatam bhavatiti*', i.e., by comprehending the (one) Brahman, one knows that all these (signified by *Sarvamidam*) the world etc., are all false, thus all these are Brahman form is realized. So, say the Advaitins. The sages who expounded the Vaishnava philosophy stated: 'We are all Hari's servants.' Once this is firmed up, then *Sarvamidam* conveys that animate and inanimate and all that is in this world is God's.

But those who have studied Poornavad would easily realize the incompleteness of both these answers, as well as the thought. The main objective of dnyan is the development and expansion of intellect. It widens the vista. In other words, the awareness of the fundamental principle is dnyan, and vidnyan is the application of dynan which, in turn, results in expansion of happiness. According to Ajatvad and Mayavad the knowledge of Brahman or comprehension of form is knowledge/dnyan. As for vidnyan, many Kevaladvaiti pundits assign different meanings to the term vidnyan such as conscience (antakaran), intellect, and vritti (tendency) and say that knowledge of the Brahman purifies these things (the conscience, intellect and tendencies) thus making life happier. Among the Vaishnava teachers, Vallabhacharya interprets vidnyan as animate consciousness. Just as dnyan is not proven, the same way vidnyan is also not proven independently.

In the *Mundaka Upanishad*, Angirasa has answered Shaunak's question quite differently from the Kevaladvaitins or the Vaishnavacharyas. This one fact is quite enough to prove the inadequacies of these two philosophies. To Shaunak's question 'which having been known, all this becomes known?' Angirasa answers: 'two Vidyas should be acquired one is para and other is apara. Knowers of Brahman say that there are two kinds of Vidya (knowledge) para and apara.' In short, that by which we comprehend our immortality is para or higher knowledge. Of course, our desire to be immortal is fulfilled by para. On the contrary, apara is dominant when one feels one has to live because one feels some duties are still left towards this world, one still has things one wants to acquire, one has tasks one feels the need to complete. But Angirasa calls both para and apara as Vidya; please note he doesn't call apara as Avidya.

Again, there are two parts of this apara, one is the jeeva (the being) and the other is the world in which are the objects of the jeeva's desires. He alone has to determine as to what he needs. This knowledge is called 'dharmadnyan' or knowledge of duty. How can it be acquired? Such knowledge which shows 'how' is nitidnyan or knowledge of ethics. This knowledge is AparaVidya.

Kevaladvaitins abandoned the traditional pairing of dnyan and vidnyan and created a new pairing—parokshadnyan (indirect knowledge) and aparokshadnyan (direct perception). Their definition of paroksha and aparoksha is that both are a reflection of the intellectual certitude of Brahman form. As a consequence, even if Buddhism was refuted and uprooted in India, resurrection of the Vedic path could not happen. This became possible due to the Vaishanava philosophy and the path of karma, at least to some extent survived.

The Poornavad doctrine holds that 'All Completeness is Absolute, Pure, Truth, Highest God'. This state is attained by following the path of knowledge, logic, yoga, upasana and karma (action) which includes all three Swakrut (one's own actions), sakrat (actions from the present) and sukrut (actions from past lives). This comprehension that the Poorna Purusha is the Ultimate Truth is dnyan, and vidnyan is to apply this dnyan to the six-faceted (shadang) practice in daily life. Vidnyan helps one to live artfully and to one's entire satisfaction (according to one's wishes) and with humanity. From the Poornavad point of view, to bring it into reality all that we need to do is to turn dnyan into vidnyan.

This is not possible without the three means (Adidaivik, adhyatmik, and adibhautik) and the grace of God. The decline of faith in God and in the Vedic path of karma, has been successfully arrested by Poornavad, as a result, the ignorance of adhidaivik/material knowledge is constantly ignited in the sacrificial fire of faith in God. He who has comprehended Poorna's form easily understands that the material, spiritual and divine are all forms of only the Poorna. With steadfast efforts and by surrendering to God in conformity with His designs, one can have all one's wishes fulfilled.

The desires of mind keep on changing with civilization, fulfillment of desires as aforesaid foster civilization and also harmonize civilization with culture. Therefore, while behaving as directed by the mind, one should look at the mind's form in the mirror of time, that is to say mind and time should go hand in hand. And because of this Poornavadi dictum, the dignity of Dharma is ever enhancing today. The reason for natural inclusion of both Paravidya and Aparavidya in Poornavad, is that in the hymn '*Poornamadah Poonamidam*', adah/that means the Parabrahman, while idam/this means 'all is this'; and in the Poornavad doctrine 'All Completeness is Absolute Truth Highest God' is inclusive of both adah/that and idam/this. Therefore, one who studies the Poornavad treatise in the sadhaka (seeker) state can easily attain Poornatva (All Completeness) or reach Poorna Purusha, as he acquires a clear understanding of Poornavad's dnyan and vidnyan.

One who abandons the pairing of dnyan-vidnyan, i.e., knowledge and its application and accepts the Kevaladvaitin pairing of paroksha-aparoksha (indirect and direct) dnyan tends to interpret the term vidnyan as intellect, conscience, tendency etc., however we shall now see with reference to *Katha Upanishad* (1.3.5), how very erroneous his interpretation is. Let us consider the below shloka:

यस्त्वविज्ञानवान्भवत्ययुक्तेन मनसा सदा ।
तस्येन्द्रियाण्यवश्यानि दुष्टाश्वा इव सारथे:

Yastvavijñānavān bhavatyayuktena manasā sadā
tasyendriyāṇyavaśyāni duṣṭāśvā iva sāratheḥ

The organs drive the chariot of body. But what path these horses should take is controlled by the intellect which holds the reins. But for him who doesn't understand the vidnyan of a philosophy, his mind intellect is always in an unsettled state, in two minds. Therefore, his senses are not in his control. He can't get the desired results from them, they are like stubborn horses (senses) that drag him anywhere. Even with whiplashes the charioteer (mind-intellect) finds it extremely difficult to keep the horses (senses) under control. In short, one who doesn't know dnyan cannot turn it into vidnyan, i.e., applied knowledge.

The two-fold nature of man's life is because of the anti-particles of the universe that affect the mind in a way that can take man from being constructive to being destructive or vice versa. The tangible result of thought is conduct, sounds like a good definition. But that is hardly the case in life. Normally, in man's life, it does not happen that a thought occurred and resulted immediately in action conduct. One can't think just because he wants to think. It has to be learnt; one has to take pains. Furthermore, because thought doesn't turn into deed immediately, one has to take pains and endeavour to act upon on the thought. It begins with 'obedience' inculcated in childhood which later helps control the sense and functional organs. Otherwise, as aforesaid, like stubborn horses become uncontrollable. Shruti calls such individuals as avidnyanwan, or those who do not know vidnyan.

But in the very next shloka of *Katha Upanishad* (1.3.6) the author states:

यस्तु विज्ञानवान्भवति युक्तेन मनसा सदा।
तस्येन्द्रियाणि वश्यानि सदश्वा इव सारथेः॥

yastu vijñānavānbhavati yuktena manasā sadā |
tasyendriyāṇi vaśyāni sadaśvā iva sāratheḥ ||

[He who is proficient in employing the organs to transform the thoughts into conduct, performs every task with full involvement, like good (trained) horses his organs obey his commands. Such an individual the hruti calls, a 'Vidnyanwan', 'one who knows Vidnyan'.][4]

Similarly, *Katha Upanishad* (1.3.8) states:

यस्तु विज्ञानवान्भवति समनस्कः सदा शुचिः।
स तु तत्पदमाप्नोति यस्माद्भूयो न जायते॥

yastu vijñānavānbhavati samanaskaḥ sadā śuciḥ
sa tu tatpadamāpnoti yasmādbhūyo na jāyate

[he Vidnyanwan, with alert mind and pure inner organ (in the respective philosophies) attains great heights and never descends from there.][5]

On the contrary, as stated in *Katha Upanishad* (1.3.7):

स्त्वविज्ञानवान्भवत्यमनस्कः सदाऽशुचिः।
न स तत्पदमाप्नोति सँ सारं चाधिगच्छति॥

yastvavijñānavānbhavatyamanaskaḥ sadā'śuciḥ
na sa tatpadamāpnoti saṃ sāraṃ cādhigacchati

---

4 Author's own translation.
5 Author's own translation.

[The Avidnyanwan (one who knows Avidya) is always with a gloomy mind and inauspicious. He never attains that highest goal and falls deep into abysmal depths (the rounds of worldliness).]

All the above shlokas from *Katha Upanishad* bring home the import of one who knows vidnyan. One who is able to immerse the self fully in any task (with full control on mind, body, intellect) is a person who has mastered the application of dnyan, i.e., has mastered vidnayan. The *Taittariya Upanishad* (2.5.1) states:

तस्मात्संसारमूलस्य भृशमुच्छित्तयेऽधुना।
यथाभूतार्थबोध्यात्मज्ञानं सम्यक्प्रवक्ष्यते।।

tasmātsaṃsāramūlasya bhṛśamucchittaye'dhunā |
yathābhūtārthabodhyātmajñānaṃ samyakpravakṣyate ||

[Vidnyan (is the action of) performing the yajna ritual (with offerings to the sacred fire accompanied by mantras). Accomplishment of the yajna lies in the knowledge [of it] leading to its execution.][6]

If one asks which is this yajna? The answer is as described by Shruti '*Yajnen yajnamayjant devaha*' [Rig Veda, 10th mandal, chapter 'Poorushsukta']. As a ceremony, a series of actions, Yajna is vidnyan (application of knowledge) and thus yajna is karma, but it is a karma that expands the fruits of righteous deeds. The thirty-three koti gods also cause such enhancement of karma by performing the worship of the Parabrahman. The Vedas call Vishnu, the regulator of this world, as Brahman Parabrahman. This proves that he who comprehends vidnyan (or knowledge applied) as Brahman commits no mistake in knowing Brahman. Such an embodied vidnyan-form jeeva destroys all sins. All the wishes of such a jeeva are fulfilled and he enjoys best of subjects.

This single *Kaushitaki Upanishad* shloka (3.2) gives three different meanings of vidnyan as: Vishnu, jeeva, and vidnyan:

---

6 Author's own translation

अथ खलु प्राण एवं प्रज्ञात्मेदं शरीरं परिगृह्योत्थापयति

[This prana truly becomes Pradnyanatma and embodied.]⁷

In the *Taittiriya Upanishad,* refers to vidnyan as Brahma in the *Kaushitaki Upanishad* prana is referred to as Pradnyanatma. This proves that the terms 'atma' and 'Brahma' are employed to convey 'Poorna Purusha'. However, as and when there is a need to indicate any particular aspect of Poorna, retaining the terms 'atma' and 'Brahma' (showing non-duality), the aspect-specific adjective is prefixed, e.g., when Sakshi (witness) is prefixed to Parabrahman, it implies the witness Poorna Purusha. In the same way the essential-nature-Shiva of Poorna Purusha is addressed as Anandmaya Atman (the Bliss-form Atman) and the essential-nature-Vishnu (with wakeful, dream and sleep states) and the jeeva (or being) atman pervaded by desires is called Vidnyanmay Atman. However, what is to be remembered is that even if the different aspects (forms) of atman or Poorna Purusha are indicated by different terms, there is no causal relation between them. The essential-nature-Atman, inclusive of all aspects (forms), is explicitly referred as Poorna or Poorna Purusha. The *Taittiriya Upanishad* (2.3.1) states:

तस्यैष एव शारीर आत्मा । यः पूर्वस्य ।
तस्माद्वा एतस्मात् प्राणमयात् । अन्योऽन्तर आत्मा मनोमयः ।
तेनैष पूर्णः । स वा एष पुरुषविध एव ।
तस्य पुरुषविधताम् । अन्वयं पुरुषविधः ।

tasyaiṣa eva śarīra ātmā . yaḥ pūrvasya
tasmādvā etasmāt prāṇamayāt . anyo'ntara ātmā manomayaḥ
tenaiṣa pūrṇaḥ . sa vā eṣa puruṣavidha eva
tasya puruṣavidhatām . anvayaṃ puruṣavidhaḥ

---

7 Author's own translation.

[This is that Vidnyanmay atman's embodiment of embodied manifestation. That Atman in the inner atman of this Vidnyanmay Atman is the blissful. Is pervaded by Poorna and is Purusha form.]

Indeed, this establishes His Poorna Purusha form. In the Kevaladvaitin commentary on the above shloka, there is a lot of deliberation on the suffix 'mayat' or Maya. Arising out of that, the Ananadmaya has been considered as Karmatma. But this thinking is not appropriate. Because, the very term Atman signifies the essential form, i.e., which negates the effect-cause relation. There is a mention in the shloka as '*Tenaishapoorna*' (He is Poorna). Therefore, the Anandmaya mentioned here is verily the essential form Shiva. The direct perception/comprehension of essential form of this witness—which is the 'truth-consciousness-bliss' essential form'—is knowledge. Here nothing seems possible post-knowledge. But it is not so in case of Vidnyanmay Atman. There, desire, action, object and satisfaction all three being present, the Yajna takes place—Vishnu is called as Yajna in Vedas. Therefore, that comprehension of Vidnyanmaya or the essential-form-Vishnu is vidnyan only comprising desire, karma and contentment or satisfaction.

In the eighth shloka in chapter six of Bhagavad Gita (6.1), Lord says:

ज्ञानविज्ञानतृप्तात्मा कूटस्थो विजितेन्द्रिय:
युक्त इत्युच्यते योगी समलोष्टाश्मकाञ्चन:

jñāna-vijñāna-tṛiptātmā kūṭa-stho vijitendriyaḥ
yukta ityuchyate yogī sama-loṣṭāśhma-kāñchanaḥ

[He who has acquired dnyan and Vidnyan both and has conquered his senses, is said to have attained the highest state. For Him a lump of earth, stone or gold all are same. Therefore, He is called a 'Siddhayogin'.]

Only 'dnyan' or only 'vidnyan' never occurs in Shruti, Smriti and the Puranas. Shri Shankaracharya also begins by first mentioning clearly,

'*Nishreyashetutaha*' [absolute], and then glorifies dnyan It is a serious mistake to expand the scope of Shankaracharya's 'dnyan' as 'dnyan-vidnyan' or construe it as 'all is this' i.e. *Sarvamidam*'. As Shankaracharya had clarified his stand, he cannot be held at fault. The main cause of this is, although knowledge (dnyan) and its application (vidnyan) on the face of it appear to be two, they are deeply interlinked. That is possibly why Angirasa tell is Shaunak: 'Those with Brahman-knowledge asked [for] the two Vidyas, para and apara to be studied.'

Despite representing *sarvamidam* (all is this), Vidya is only one; single. Over the centuries, for the purpose of study and understanding it has been called para-apara, dnyan-vidnyan, vidya-avidya. In the tenth chapter 'Avidya: Knowledge of the Material World' we studied that they are not opposed to each other and that Vidya does not eliminate Avidya. The Vedic injunction is to co-worship these two. This is the proof of co-worship.

All of us have experienced that 'knowing' doesn't encompass all that we are aware of, that we have studied and that some of it experienced. Similarly, what we are 'applying' isn't fully known to us. For instance, we switch on a fan, use a sewing machine, ride a bicycle, drive a car, fly an airplane. But that does not mean we know everything about their 'how'? While riding the bike, we maintain perfect balance, does it mean we have assimilated technically the principle of balance? No.

Poornavad states: 'the householder's duty with description in the interest of body (material) Jeeva (divine) and atman (spiritual) rather than being prapancha [our day today domestic life]; turns into (spirituality) Parmartha; whereas, even Parmartha with greed, jealousy and selfishness, be it devotion of That with form or Upasana of That formless turns to be prapancha (householder's life).' Therefore, dnyan-vidnyan, para-apara and vidya-avidya are one thing only, indicate one principle only, i.e., Poorna Purusha. This view of certitude is everywhere in the Vedas and that is why Poornavad says that 'mind and matter is one and same reality' and 'that is the essential form Ultimate Truth'. And that is why Poornavad considers Shankaracharya's Parabrahman and Vaishnavacharya's Shri Hari as truth. Readers, however, should bear in mind that Poornavad does not call that as complete truth, or truth of truths.

People who perform their duty steadfastly as a householder with humanity, some bit of charity and service to people doesn't mean that they have very little or no thought of Ishwara or atman. Because they have necessarily applied knowledge to some extent. But it cannot be said that what all they did was service to God. Therefore, without comprehending with Ishwara, to sing His praise or that of the divine (adhidaivik) plane, service to God or people does not amount to service to divine (adhidaivik). In a nutshell, dnyan-vidnyan, para-apara, vidya-avidya pairs are related to the same principle. Bearing this fact in mind, with further reading, the seeker (sadhaka) would have no difficulty in having the true experience of Poorna Purusha and his prapancha and parmarth would attain oneness, and reach all completeness (Poornatva).

Brihadaranyaka Upanishad (Bri 4.5) lays out in detail the vidnyan of Vidnyanmaya Brahma i.e., Vishnu-form Poorna Purusha thus:

स वा अयमात्मा ब्रह्म विज्ञानमयो ... यत्कर्म कुरुते तदभिसंपद्यते ॥

[He who possesses the three states of wakefulness, dream and deep slumber and who moves about in this and the other and many worlds, that vidnyanatma is reflected in the vital breath, eyes, ears, earth, water, fire etc. Five elements, same way devoid of fire i.e., beyond the five elements, in desires and beyond desires, in anger and beyond anger, in Dharma and beyond Dharma, in short in everything i.e., pervades all the manifest and unmanifest. In effect, it is Brahman.]

The Kevaladvaitin's stand that, 'consciousness reflected in ignorance is jeeva' is refuted by the above shloka. This Vidnyanmay Atman identifies with jeeva. It becomes one with the conduct of the jeeva. With the pious acts he becomes pious, and unpious with unpious acts.

Vishnu or the Jeeva as His part is obsessed with lust and desires, so say the sages. His resolves would be in accordance with his desires and the fruits would depend on the actions. What is conceived in the intellect is ultimately reborn. Therefore, the wise should resolve to seek the Poorna Purushas form etc. Generally, fruits are in accordance with man's action. Saint Tukaram says: 'Birth and desires emerge together', and the same is conveyed in the maxim: 'what is conceived in the intellect is reborn'. Therefore, to identify with the desire behind one's birth is one's duty. This is the first Purushartha (prowess).

In gist, the above discussion establishes the Jeeva's Brahmanhood by first stating all-pervasiveness of this desire-obsessed Purusha, the Vidnyan Atman or the Jeeva. And later, it is proved that sacrifice (yajna) is duty (kartavya), '*Yatha karama tatha kratuhu, yatha kratuhu tatha karma and yatha karma tatha bhog*' (to all our actions there is a reaction and every reaction has action, we receive result or fruit for all our actions.) From this, it is obvious that Shruti doesn't preach to belittle or ignore desires. Even Shri Krishna tells Arjuna in the Gita that 'Dharma viruddha kamosmi' (I am sexual activity in life which is not contrary to Dharma). Of course, Dharma or desires causative to birth and entire desires favorable to that desire are Vishnu-form. As such, it is everyone's duty to perform sacrifice (yajna); fulfill those desires. The fulfillment of the desires causative to our birth is the objective of this life (birth). Therefore, it is not that man sets the objective of his birth by consulting scriptures, studying the circumstances, consulting any wise and learned persons, but that it is predetermined. The objective for taking birth, however, is to be identified and one's conduct has to be in accordance with it but it is easier said than done.

Secondly, the essential element Shiva or Atman and the sacrifices-form (karmaroop) essential element Vishnu are eternal. Therefore, those are not separate because those are two forms of Poorna Purusha and that is why are eternal. And because of their eternal character, neither can ever be abandoned it is just not possible. The living beings harbor fear of death of course, to be immortal is the wish; similarly, all living beings seek to to live life their own way. The first desire (to be immortal) is the proof of essential nature Shiva; and the second desire (to live life one's own way) is the essential nature Vishnu—and both being fully awake (active), to live a successful life one must develop both. In fact, to put it philosophically, both aspects-material prosperity (essential nature Vishnu) and spiritual emancipation (essential nature Shiva) being eternal, i.e., not being optional, neither of these can be abandoned, it is not possible.

Shri Shankaracharya has in a predetermined manner expounded only one *'Nishreyas'* (absolute) of the two, but to accept only that as the Ultimate Truth is sheer insistency. A yogin means one who has non-duality with the Highest God, but that is precisely why the Gita describes him as *Dnyan-Vidnyanyukta* (who has acquired both dnyan and vidnyan.). Therefore, the Absolute Truth in the Vedas is Poorna Purusha alone. Vidya-Avidya and dnyan-vidya are one and the same, and are related to only one thing. One is in the form of experience and the other is as means. In Sanskrit, the Vedas are referred to as Purusha or Vedpurusha and the word Veda is masculine, while the word Vidya is feminine. The all-inclusive knowledge of the Poorna Purusha is found in the Vedas. Partial knowledge or knowledge of one particular form of His is referred to as Vidya, feminine. Vidya and Avidya both are kinds of Vidya only.

Arising out of this, the Shruti hymn: '*Ksharantva vidya yamrutantu vidya*' (going beyond the death is the fruit of Avidya while immortality is the fruit of Vidya) when viewed in the above perspective, feminine nomenclature vidya is assigned for the knowledge of essential form Shiva. That of course only shows that essential-form Shiva is one of the forms of Poorna Purusha. And that is why the Kevaladvaitin knowledge is not complete knowledge.

There is a specific kind of inquiry in *Chhandogya Upanishad* (7.17.1) about vidnyana:

यदा वै विजानात्यथ सत्यं वदति नाविजानन्सत्यं वदति विजानन्नेव सत्यं वदति विज्ञानं त्वेव विजिज्ञासितव्यमिति विज्ञानं भगवो विजिज्ञास इति ॥

yadā vai vijānātyatha satyaṃ vadati nāvijānansatyaṃ vadati vijānanneva satyaṃ vadati vijñānaṃ tveva vijijñāsitavyamiti vijñānaṃ bhagavo vijijñāsa iti

[Sage Narada requests of Santkumara that, when man comprehends Truth, The Poorna Purusha, completely then he speaks truth. He alone, who knows Him completely, can elucidate His true essential form (mere knowledge doesn't help) therefore one should desire to know vidnyan also. Oh, revered Sir! It is for this reason, that I specially desire to acquire knowledge of vidnyan.][8]

In the original shloka above the word 'completely' is not there. Nevertheless, because of the reference before and after, it has been employed for interpretation. The readers may not necessarily be aware of it. Therefore, in order to understand the core meaning of the shloka, this application is particularly appropriate.

'The knowledge of mere "Soham" makes one vociferous', so says sage Sanatkumara in part 16.[9] And that is why in order to be capable of true expression of truth, Narada expressed his particular inquisitiveness. When we examine that hymn closely, we are convinced about the appropriateness of employing the world 'completely'. In this regard, that shloka (*Chhandogya Upanishad*, 7.16.1) is given below:

एष तु वा अतिवदति यः सत्येनातिवदति सोऽहं भगवः सत्येनातिवदानीति सत्यं त्वेव विजिज्ञासितव्यमिति सत्यं भगवो विजिज्ञास इति ॥

eṣa tu vā ativadati yaḥ satyenātivadati so'ham bhagavaḥ satyenātivadānīti satyaṃ tveva vijijñāsitavyamiti satyaṃ bhagavo vijijñāsa iti

[Here Sanatkumar tells Narada that, 'He who talks only of the ativadati knowledge of 'Soham', is really stubborn and extremist'. Whereupon sage Narada confesses and admits, 'Oh adorable Sir! I am really an extremist.' And then Sanatkumara preaches to Narada that, 'Setting asides the one-sided knowledge, one should try to know the Truth completely.' Narada then prays with humility and denies being

---

8   *Poornavad; Reinterpretation of Indian Philosophy*, Dr V. R. Parnerkar.
9   Ibid.

adamant about any particular opinion and evinces his keen inquiry about The Truth.]

The above teaches is that it is imperative for complete knowledge of the Ultimate Truth i.e., complete knowledge of Poorna Purusha, to have knowledge of both dnyan as well as vidnyan. Knowledge alone cannot become the ultimate objective of man's life. Chanting of Soham means to contemplate on the subtle sound of 'Soham' with each breath and to concentrate on Soham meaning 'I am the Ultimate Truth'. But this Ultimate Truth according to the Vedas originally comprises both dnyan as well as vidnyan. As such, power, grandeur, the zeal of life, etc., are difficult to achieve if one disregards vidnyan and adheres only to dnyan. When Sanatkumara pointed out this mistake, Narada expressed his inquisitiveness about vidnyan and also learnt it.

It is indeed astonishing that despite such vital principles being so very lucidly laid down in the Vedas, Smritis and the scriptures, the 'one-sided attitude' has gained ground in society. The path of vidnyan as given in the original scripture is as follows: without intense desire for happiness, one doesn't perform action; one doesn't put in purposeful efforts, efforts with a resolve and an end in mind. Similarly, in the spiritual realm, faith doesn't seem possible without devotion; there is no reflection without devotion; nothing can be comprehended without reflection; and without contemplation and reflection Ultimate Complete Truth is impossible to know.

One who would understand this pathway to vidnyan should know that the beginning lies in an intense desire for happiness, which becomes the motivating force for resolute action. If there is no intense desire for a result or outcome that one believes will bring us happiness, the first action (karma) itself will be devoid of resolve and efforts may be devoid of results. Even if such irresolute efforts (karma) bear fruit, one is not able to believe in the relation between karma/action and its outcome nor is one inclined to reflect and undertake penance or seek acquisition of newer knowledge. On the spiritual path too when the karma/action is driven by the wish to manifest a desire and is backed by resolve, it firms up devotion, and personal belief is easy to come by. One must remember, action alone does not assure success, God's grace is essential.

There is no dispute that rather than being lazy, one has to perform karma. However, this is absent in the present generation. Helplessly living life, no matter what one does—good, bad or indifferent—is not living according to Dharma. Living in accordance with Dharma means to keep performing with resolve. Dnyan and vidnyan are two wheels of the same cart. Neither is inferior and neither is adequate alone. This is the message of the Vedas. The Ultimate Truth is dynamic, not static. The means to comprehend Poorna and for meditating upon it, as described in this chapter are dnyan and vidnyan. This alone can make one's life happy and lead him to continue towards the Ultimate Complete Truth. This is what is meant by Poornavad.

Truth is covered by untruth, that is reality. When speaking on bootstrap theory, my Master Dr Parnerkar explains the parallel between Western science and Vedic hymns regarding modern Physics and cites a short sutra from Vedic literature on Quantum and bootstrap theory.[10]

यथा पिण्डे तथा ब्रह्माण्डे

Yatha Pinde, Tatha Brahmande

[What is true of the microsm is true of the macrosm.]

Whatever in the universe is in every particle and every particle differs from the other while being interrelated. This network makes the universe a symmetrically inseparable and interrelated unity. The Vedas call it the Purusha. The form of the Supreme Lord, Dr Parnerkar further explained how Western science has yet not found the utility of different types of particles; specially the divine particles of universe.

My master says that the Samkhya school of Vedic philosophy is the ideal example of the antiparticle theory. He says that Buddhism, Jainism, Christianity and Islam are the antiparticles of Vedas, they are

---

10 *Poornavad; Reinterpretation of Indian Philosophy*, Dr V. R. Parnerkar

not parallel to Vedas, but stand opposed to the Vedas. The Vedas have been misunderstood by scholars with biases. Vedas never propounded to 'forget material and physical gains', but advised sublimation. The Poornavad way of divine life follows the Rishi tradition which follows the family system. But Buddhism and many religions have the stoniest traditions for their priests to follow, which is against the natural law and creates the possibility of malpractice. Dr Parnerkar never criticizes pluralism in religion as nature has created diversity in unity and unity in diversity.

The Vedas offer us the pure science of the Universal System. Poorrnavad, that worships the all-complete, includes the worship of universal energies in the form of the planets, the sun, fire, water, wind, sky—these are the gods of the Vedas—the Navgrahas, including Aditya; Agni, Varuna, Vayu, Anteriksha.

CHAPTER 14

Moksha: Liberation

MOKSHA OR liberation is not a state of transcendence to be enjoyed after death, it is the state of mind that gives one a spontaneous overflow of joy and bliss throughout life. It is the highest stage of spiritual and divine experience. There is tremendous misunderstanding about the concept of moksha among Eastern and Western scholars that Indian philosophy is liberation-centered; but this is just a misunderstanding. In the Vedic tradition moksha or liberation is one among four types of prowess (purushartha)—Dharma (duty), artha (money, finance), kama (sex, sexuality), and moksha (liberation). Vedanta teachers, such as Shankara and others who accepted the Vedic tradition only partially, did not dwell on acquiring all four types of prowess, but jumped from duty to liberation, neglecting money/finance and sex/sexuality. This happened because as celibate monks they had no interest in money/finance and sex/sexuality; they also declared that Avidya meant 'ignorance' and equated women with Avidya. It is a wonder how they negated women power, which the Vedas recognize and honour. Pointing out this lacuna, Dr Parnerkar states that Avidya (in the Vedas) does not construe ignorance, and that women power must be honoured just as is the power of men.

When I was presenting a paper on Poornavad's concept of Moksha before the World Congress of Philosophy 2018, in Beijing, the Chairperson asked me to talk on the other three types of prowess (duty; money/finance; sex/sexuality) as well. I asked the Chairperson, 'tell me who followed these Purusharthas? Did Shankara? Did Ramanuja? Did Madhava? They jumped from Dharma to moksha.' I gave the reference of the dialogue between Shankara and Mandana Mishra. When Mandana Mishra's better half, Saraswati, had asked a question on Kama, to Shankara, who, being a celibate monk, could not answer her and hence requested for some time to get back to her. He then conducted an experiment called 'Parkaya', wherein his soul left his body and transmigrated to another body where his soul gathered experience of conjugal life and of money and finance for fifteen days. Thereafter he returned to his own body and was able to respond to the questions posed to him by Mandana Mishra's wife. The tradition followed during the Vedic period was for all rishis to acquire all four types of prowess. Thus, these great sages had happy family lives too. Dr Parnerkar follows this Vedic tradition. He is married and lives very happily with his son, daughter, and daughter-in-law under one roof.

Let us see the concept of liberation in Dr Parnerkar's terms. Vidya-Avidya, para-apara, and dnyan-vidnyan are all related to a single thing, the Supreme Lord, but there are some important differences between them that we should try to understand one by one and experience as well. For example: (i) Vidya basically inspires one towards worldly activities, it is in the nature of motivation while dnyan or knowledge restrains one from worldly activities; it deters. (ii) There is diversity in Vidya. There are many kinds of Vidya and they reveal many truths. But knowledge is related to a single principle out of many. It is also related to that which is in our contemplation, the truth of truths. (iii) Vidya never turns into Avidya, but Avidya can transform into Vidya. Knowledge (dnyan) turns into application of knowledge (vidnyan). Knowledge attains completeness only after it is applied. A thought becomes complete after being complemented by action.

We saw in the preceding chapter that the complete, all-faceted knowledge of the Poorna Purusha is found in the Vedas. The Ved Purusha is masculine and is naturally inclined towards abstinence, restraint, emancipation, enjoying solitude, loneliness. Whereas Vidya is feminine, tends to expand naturally, desirous of impressing others, has a liking for networking. Man becomes learned and wise (a pandit) by acquisition of Vidya. (iv) Knowledge/dnyan culminates only when it is subjected to application, i.e., transforms into vidnyan; at its spiritual apex epistemological and empirical process both cease leading to bliss-form-satisfaction as witness and that is liberation. (v) Even when Avidya turns into Vidya, Vidya expands; it neither eliminates Avidya nor is it itself eliminated. Therefore, Vidya expands every principle even Brahman. As such Vidya doesn't tend to dissolve. (vi) Knowledge/dnyan is intellect-related, while Vidya is senses-related, it doesn't need a sharp intellect.

Those who would properly understand these six points would know that of the many truths revealed by Vidya, that which we egocentrically or in practical terms (according to our needs) determine to be the truth of truths, to know that is knowledge. Once that knowledge is transformed into application, with the completion of this process both processes (dnyan and vidnyan) end and what remains is bliss-form-satisfaction and contentment as witness—that is called moksha/liberation. In this state of liberation, man's mind and heart is relaxed. Here onwards, leaving behind the seeker state, man begins to take off towards the perfected master or siddha state.

He who would understand all these would understand the importance of the first sentence of this chapter. 'Moksha' (liberation), 'mukti' (freedom), 'amrutattva' (transcending immortality) all these terms are relative. Dr Parnerkar in his speech on Poornavad elaborates this sentence in the next paragraph. He says,

> Whatever man does either with mind, body or intellect that is all relative to life. Devoid of life, he who is conscious of neither the internal world nor the external world, nor internal consciousness

of mind, body and intellect, how does bondage, moksha or hell matter to such man? Of course, it is true that the Anandmaya means the essential form Shiva which is without any adjunct but all these adjuncts are there to the Vidnyanmaya or the essential form Vishnu. Besides, we saw earlier that this essential form Vishnu is eternal. Likewise, owing to co-existence of essential form, Shiva and Vishnu, according to the maxim 'Jeeva Bhootah Sanatanha' life is held as eternal and it becomes necessary to consider about bondage, moksha and hell.

Vidya puts forth many truths before man. It becomes man's duty to determine the truth of these, gain knowledge/dnyan from them and to apply this knowledge. At the point that the epistemological process ends, the result is bliss-form-void, the witness state, that according to Poornavad is liberation. Although Poornavad does not accept Shankaracharya's process, as long as the epistemological process is active the being is in a kind of bondage, and when this process culminates in acquiring the principle—be it about children's welfare or preparing for a long voyage or an examination or even spiritual progress and direct perception—liberation from bondage of that subject stands proved. Thus the bondage-form is a reality and Poornavad accepts this reality.

Once the seeker (sadhaka) state ends and the state of liberation begins, the mind is no longer stuck on the resolved issue or issues, a man attains the state of a perfected master. Of course, the state of liberation is relative to any subject—even knowledge with respect to Poornavad—is a buffer state between the seeker-state and the perfected-master state.

In short, liberation being the buffer between the seeker state and the perfected master state this small chapter has been penetratingly placed by Dr Parnerkar between dnyan-vidnyan and Poornadvait in his book.[1]

Of course, like Poornavad, the Kevaladvaitis and the Ajatvadins refute ignorance and its activity saying that the world never was (i.e.,

---

1   Parnerkar R. P. (2002), Poornavad, 1st edition, Vimal Prakashan, Pune.

never existed, hence does not exist) and negate the jeevadasha (the state of being). It proves that according to their doctrine they disagree with bondage and liberation process. However, the original Kevaladvaiti-Mayavad recognizes 'ignorance' as an entity and states that Maya and Avidya are its activities. These activities evolve the adjunct-form-effect Ishwara and the being/jeeva. Avidya is bondage for the being and relative to that, the direct perception of truth-consciousness-bliss-form is liberation. The Vedas describe the Vidnyanmay Atman Jeeva as eternal.

The Ajatvadins' negation of ignorance is true but their negation of the world and the jeeva (being), which is contrary to reality, is not acceptable to anyone. Once it is decided that the being (the jeeva) 'is' and there is no such thing as ignorance and Avidya. When Shruti indicates that the Vidnyanmay Atman is eternal, the being cannot be in a state of bondage. The Vedas concur.

No wonder that Poornavad does not accept the concepts of bondage and liberation, because except for Mayavad, no other school of philosophy accepts the concepts of bondage and liberation. Therefore, he who has acquired knowledge, and has applied it and attained liberation, his seeker-state ceases and he begins to tread the path of the siddha/perfected master. (It should be remembered that liberation being relative, Poornavad reckons the perfected master state as a state beyond even liberation. However, he needs to bear certain things in mind.)

Firstly, as the being/jeeva is eternal is static as well as dynamic. As such, just as this dynamism can be progressive, it can be regressive as well. The Vedas, Shankaracharya's Mayavad and other philosophers agree that there are two movements to the being: progression and regression, and that is a reality. The being having completed or reached the end of the seeker state has to therefore be cautious that his movement is in the direction of progress and not regression. There is no point in having a false belief that owing to acquisition of knowledge, downfall is impossible. The being shouldn't forget the reality that one with knowledge, a dnyani, is not above temptation. In real life too, we observe prosperity as well as downfall and the extremes of this in spiritual parlance are called heaven and hell. And this has come down to us since the time of Vedas.

Secondly, the being as a dnyani, having reached the end of the seeker state, should remember that when by virtue of knowledge he experiences the state of non-duality, the witness of monistic state realizes 'oneness' by 'isness' and he experiences oneness that exists in all beings. He views everyone in one form. However, in practical life, he observes plurality, diversity, duality; their mutual conflicts, etc. For example, as the head of the house when we say 'this is my home', it signifies all the members in the house, the rooms, the paraphernalia in each room etc., i.e., oneness. Our feeling is 'we have authority over the members, rooms, the arrangement, a certain discipline'. But in reality, each member has a different room, different furniture, his/her unbridled authority over it. This diversity is contradictory to the 'my home' feeling. But this doesn't help. As the original owner, we try to visualize a certain harmony and it is due to our reliance on this feeling that this many-ness or plurality does not bother us, we are not fed up of it.

Just like the above, there are two experiences: (i) the oneness of many felt owing to knowledge; and (ii) their diversity in real life. A seeker who is at the far end of the seeker state should be able to strike a balance between these two. If he can't do so, the diversity could cause him disgust, trouble and boredom and as a result he would seek escape. Consequently, in a way he loses his authority in the house. At this juncture, i.e., at the fag-end of the seeker state, he should balance both; he must never allow an imbalance to occur. He should understand that just as there is oneness in reality, there is manyness (diversity) too.

Just as his experience of plurality of beings on the material plane, one with knowledge has an identical experience on the divine plane too. There are thirty-three main deities in the Vedas and each deity has a separate world. It is said that the devotee, with the grace of his deity (personal god), enjoys temporal life till death and attains his deity's world later. It is also said that the unpious and atheists go to hell, there too there are destinations. However, one who has acquired knowledge should not be affected by all this experience of plurality but rather should harmonize it with affinity much like the arrangement of flowers in a vase. Rather than being troubled by plurality, the knowledgeable being (the dnyani) should master the art of experiencing unity.

No being, not even one who has acquired knowledge, wants death or sorrow and therefore it is essential to proceed on the path of progress. A knowledgeable being should remember that the state of a perfected master lies beyond even attaining liberation by knowledge. Hence a knowledgeable being should employ a three-faceted approach that includes action (karma), upasana, and spiritual practices and disciplines (sadhana), prior to acquiring knowledge. This three-faceted path, which is an ideal blend of the spiritual (adhyatmik), material (adhibhoutik) and the divine (adhidaivik), can help a being to attain the state of a perfected master, a siddha. Thus a knowledgeable being should never shirk action. By realizing unity in diversity, he should try to put in the best of efforts.

The being should not think that he is knowledgeable, that he has realized unity, that he has nothing to do with the diversity of other beings and can leave them to their fate. Espousing asceticism and dwelling in the liberated moksha state, is not proper. Remember, the liberated or moksha state is relative. There is always the possibility of falling into the abyss instead of rising to siddha state, the state of a perfect master. The knowledgeable being should never shirk karma. He should never lose sight of the Vedic concept that life is upasana, or is an ongoing yajna (a sacred fire ceremony with ritual offerings).

Each being, with or without knowledge, should constantly remember that as long as s/he has to live and survive in this world, action and upasana are essential. Upasana enlightens both material and spiritual planes and yields success. Therefore, even ascetics like Shankaracharya and Ramakrishna Paramhansa after direct perception of the Divine, didn't abandon worshiping the goddess with form and attributes. Goddess Shardamba is worshipped in Acharya's monastery even today.

The Kevaladvaitin philosophy was imbibed by people under the mistaken belief that the human birth was to attain liberation; their saints didn't lag behind either when they advocated devotion as life's ultimate goal. In fact, the life's main objective is to understand and execute one's Dharma. This is done by identifying the innate desire that lay behind one's birth and to endeavour by all ethical means to fulfil it. But in order to make it happen i.e., to make life successful, the Vedas point out the need for knowledge and devotion, without which the purpose of life won't be fulfilled.

Life needs many things. Only those qualities that one possesses is not adequate. Just developing one's inherent qualities will not suffice. It is essential to acquire qualities that one doesn't possess. What all qualities of Poorna are in us which are latent, to know this and to worship the respective deities for their grace. But one must have knowledge of Poorna for this, without that such upasana doesn't yield fruit. Therefore, in order for our personal upasana to be fruitful, knowledge of Poorna, of Poornavada and of the Poornavad treatise is extremely important.

The Vedic injunction is that before beginning anything, one should remember the great god Ganapati, the Poorna. The word 'gana' means 'attendants' and 'pati' means 'chief of' or 'head of'. Hence, Ganapati is the lord and master of all attendants. The gods have their own attendants and are the chiefs or heads of their own attendants. Ganapati, however, is head of all attendants (including those of the gods) and is their master. Of course, He is the Poorna Purusha. To comprehend Him first, and to then worship the deities yields fruits rapidly. The Master of Vidnyan Brahman and Anand Brahman (direct perception is the experience of Anand Brahman i.e., truth-consciousness-bliss form) is Lord Ganesha, who is also known as Bramhanaspati.. This is what remains in ten directions despite pervading the world-the Parbrahman. In the zero of this ten, even if everything is embraced, in zero-form, unintelligence-form, the one of self-sensitivity still remains (outside) but post Poorna's experience, the one of Poorna overlapping One of self-sensitivity, all three i.e., Adhiboutik, Adhyatmik and Adhidaivik are experienced. Just as direct perception of ten (10) is included in eleven (11), it is that of Vishwa and Ishwara also. Therefore, the master of Vidnyanmay Brahman and Anandmay Brahman is the One Poorna PurushBrahmanaspati. While proceeding from the seeker to the perfect master state, we have to go to absolute non-duality (Poornadvaita) i.e., to the Poorna Purusha. Liberation is the intermediate state between the seeker state and the perfected master state. Therefore, in order to proceed from liberation to the perfected master state, the knowledgeable being, the dnyani, should perform action and that action is 'swaDharma-karma', i.e., action in accordance with one's predetermined duty. Poornavad, just like the Bhagavad Gita advocates the same. If we consider the relationship of chapters in Poornavada, there are nine chapters, whereas there are eighteen chapters in the Gita, i.e., exactly twice. Chapter 7 of Poornavad is 'Dnyan-Vidnyan' and Gita's seventh chapter also is 'Dnyan-Vidnyan Yoga'. Gita's message is that the knoeldgeable being, dnyani, shouldn't shirk action, karma, the same message in Poornavad. Therefore, Poornavad is no less important than the Gita or the Varkari sect's *Dnyaneshwari*, from Poorna's point of view. It would not be an exaggeration to say that Poornavad is a step ahead of the Poorna-Siddha state.

To sum up, just as the upasana of our personal deity is life's essential form of upasana, in the same way the concept of a complete life, i.e., the concept of swaDharma (duty innate to oneself) is essential. One's innate duty is linked to the innate desire causative to birth. Hence the innate duty must be fulfilled first and then the other three types of prowess—money/finance, sex/sexuality, and liberation—must be acquired. Achieveing the object of one's life, adhering to Dharma, even if inferior, assures fulfillment and brings success.

The objective (Dharma or duty) for which man is born, that very Dharma has godly potency to fulfil it. But the man of today looks for the purpose of his life in scriptures, circumstances, craves for success and becomes disappointed in the end. So long as the desires to fulfil which one is born and also other incidental desires are not fulfilled, no matter what one does, satisfaction is far away. Death, whether due to an accident, old age or any other natural cause, will occur in in a state of dissatisfaction due to unfulfilled desires, and that is not an auspicious death. Rebirth is imperative for fulfillment of such desires. One is born again and again. The sense of dissatisfaction and indifference in old age signifies non-fulfillment of desires, and in the absence of knowing one's innate duty (swadharma) the fulfillment of this Dharma is just impossible.

Readers may be wondering as how to identify this swadharma, one's innate duty. And even if identified, how one would be motivated to act upon it? It is difficult to know, what one's innate duty is, and once known to act accordingly is also difficult. It feels difficult because it has been stated through the highest self-spiritual point of view, that one must first determine the essential form Poorna by knowledge. Then one has to apply that knowledge and the point where the epistemological and empirical processes culminate, the seeker state attains completeness. Once man settles in that liberated, moksha state, he can comprehend in an unbiased manner, the desire behind his birth and his innate duty, his swadharma.

Consequently, his only remaining objective is to act upon that swadharma, disregarding all pros and cons; acting upon it steadfastly, ritually and with humanity. Just as 'knowing' and 'applying' is important; with regard to swadharma, 'identifying' and 'performing' is important. Even after direct perception, an ascetic continues to live in this world, it only means that there is still a possibility of fulfilling the desire that caused his rebirth. As such, after comprehending Poorna, fulfilling the desire (that led one to take rebirth) with proper conduct, when man merges in Poorna with name and form, then alone he will be able to take birth when and where he wants.

This becomes possible only when man, in this life itself, lives according to his wishes and these are fulfilled. In practical parlance, whatever he desires happens, and this happens repeatedly and constantly. This would mean that he has attained the state of being of a perfected master. Man may attain liberation following the processes outlined by other philosophies, he may be liberated from the birth-death-cycle, but he still can't be born where and when he desires. Ishwara grants everything to man, but to be born when and where he desires or to die naturally is granted only after man comprehend's Poorna. Therefore, the Poorna-state is the step after liberation.

For a lay man it is difficult to identify swadharma by following the spiritual path alone. Dr Parnerkar mentions the following in 'An introduction to Poornavad': (i) vision of syllables while descending from Samadhi; (ii) chanting the Gayatri mantra 24-lakh times as penance; (iii) God's or Guru's grace. There are many who have had God's vision but only the very few, like Arjuna have asked God: 'what is my swadharma?' In view of this, Dr Parnerkar has made this still easier by advocating 'synchronizing mind with time is the conduct according to swadharma'. He also advises one to keep in mind poet Waman Pandit's composition *Susangati sadha ghado* (May I have good company always).

When you say study of time, its scope is quite wide and includes: Civilization, scientific discoveries, progress in education, political upheavals, fruits of civilization viz. TV, mobiles, computers, etc.; a variety of jobs, progress of economies etc. etc. Whereas the mind includes recurring desires, things causing sorrow, mental habits, nature, vices, etc.

One important fact to be remembered here is time has no affinity for mind. Disregarding mind, time keeps moving ahead. The mind has to keep pace with it. By doing so, gradually, the mind is able to exercise some authority over time. Same way action or karma has no affinity for knowledge. Action, with or without knowledge, brings its fruit all the same. Therefore, knowledge has to co-exist, get adjusted with action, karma. In order to bring about synchronization of mind, time and action, control over one's senses, freedom from addiction, obedience are essential. One must decide whom to listen to, and having decided whether we agree or not to obey him or her, we must keep our senses under control and act according to his or her wishes. In real life too, we first ascertain who is a good doctor or a good teacher and having gone to him, regardless of the fact whether we agree or not, we have to listen to him. This is not intellectual servility.

An individual who has such control over his senses can bring about the co-existence of time, mind and action, and with faith in the task and a pleasant mind behaves in accordance with his own innate duty, his swadharma. This is the path of the material (adhibhautik) world. Just as having knowledge and applying it is important; in swadharma 'identifying' and 'performing' the dusty with the right conduct is important. If one is not motivated, that does not mean refraining, similarly restraints or abstinence doesn't mean there can't be motivation again. 'Today's enemy can be a friend tomorrow', said Dr Parnerkar to the author once.

Comprehending swadharma is important but what is more important is to act accordingly. To do what is expected, when expected and how expected and to carry out our tasks happily and enthusiastically is the conduct according to one's innate duty swadharma and its result is peace and mental satisfaction. Even Brahman can't render a better definition than this.

In short, study and exercise during childhood, harmonious relations during youth, for fulfillment of wishes, proper upsana for spiritual upliftment acquiring conditioned knowledge, assimilating in the atman deliberation of Poornavad, living satisfactorily at the far end is 'swadharma acharan', conduct in accordance with one's innate duty. Even a Godlike individual should adhere to this. Only then he will attain siddha state and reach absolute non-duality. The Shruti hymn (Poornavad, Moksha, Chapter 8):[2]

वायुरनिलममृतमथेदम् ... कृतंस्मर।

vayuranilamamrtamathedam ... krtamsmar

[Now the breath: Pradnyanatma in the dying body of my Purusha and the nectar-filled-joy-witness and anil vidnyanatma Jeeva may reach the Universal soul (sarvatmaka). And may my body consigned to fire turn to ashes, the *Dharmapurusha Kratu*, dwelling in Om–form-heart and eager to merge with Poorna Purusha and remember also your

---

2 Parnerkar V. R. (2016), Poornavad: Reinterpretation of Indian Philosophy, BBC Publications, New Delhi.

actions. Oh being, remember your Dharma and conduct, such is the repetition here.]³

In this hymn '*Om krutosmar krutam smar*' clearly shows that if your conduct has been in conformity with Dharma, then emancipation lies ahead. Therefore, in order to know what is next? You recollect your past life from which you yourself would know. This single hymn is enough to bring home the point as to what is a successful life. And how is emancipation or heaven attained. Not to leave any doubts about the concept of Dharma, quoted below is the hymn:

अग्ने नय सुपथा राये अस्मान्विश्वनि देव वयुनानि विद्वान
युयोध्यस्मज्जुहुराणमेनो भूयिष्ठां ते नमउक्तिं विधेम

[God Agni, lead us on the auspicious path. Oh Lord! You are omniscient. You know who has worshipped which deity and how are their actions. You know if conduct has been in conformity with swadharma or otherwise. Take away ugly sins from us. We do worship you now by offering prayers.]⁴

Here actions other than those that align with one's innate duty are referred to as sin. Therefore, Poornavad has newly defined sin, fatigue and worry in 'Tondolakh'.⁵ As per Shruti, liberation resultant from direct perception does not breed new desires; and the desire causative to birth once fulfilled by action post knowledge, makes a man truly eligible for complete liberation and as aforesaid his death occurs in a contented state.

---

3   Author's own translation.
4   Author's own translation.
5   Parnerkar R. P. Tondolakh (Marathi), Vimal Prakashan, Pune. 'Tondolak is a Marathi introductory text, *Poornavad in Practical Life* by Dr R.P. Parnerkar' (edited).

CHAPTER 15

Fear of Death

THE BIGGEST fear in life is the fear of death. This fear can be removed by studying the Poornavad philosophy which is the rational interpretation of the Vedas. Once you comprehend Vedic science, you will not have any fear.

Western scientists and philosophers had hitherto rejected the existence of the soul, which is immortal, and is a micro particle of the universe. Macro is the Supreme Lord. And if we understand the reality of oneness of the universal God, it will be easy to digest Eastern mysticism, i.e., the Vedas. By rejecting the existence of soul, Western science and philosophy had become partial and one-sided. The Vedas have the scientific justification of the existence of the soul, which has now been accepted by scientists.

In the cycle of life after life, death is the gap between two lives. The Vedas call it the chain of prebirth and rebirth. Once a Principal of a Science College asked me how I could justify rebirth. I explained to him that darkness befalls only at the end of the day. And the night then converts into a bright day. There is constant rotation of day and night. On the same grounds, there is rotation of life and death. In fact, because of this Lord Buddha says life is impermanent; but the Vedas say life is immortal. Therefore, man is also immortal. Death is not the dead-end of life. Lord Buddha has also explained his previous births, saying that He is the twenty-fourth prophet. The same with Jainism. The Vedas have had an impact on Buddhism and Jainism.

Now we will turn to the Poornavad view. Once I asked my Master, Dr V.R. Parnerkar, why does Poornavad talk less about death? He instead asked me, 'why do we take birth? To die or to live? Poornavad talks more on life than about Brahma, God,' he said and explained that Vedas were optimistic, positive and practical therefore, he said, 'Poornavad states that we don't worship God for the sake of God but we worship God for our sake, he said. 'Therefore, focus...' 'focus on the present, don't think of death. If your present is harmonious your future birth will also become harmonious. Your next birth is based on the balance of karma from your present birth. This is known as Karma Siddhant; it means your rebirth is the reaction of present birth.'

What we think on the fear of death, reality asks us not to fear death and has given references from Upanishads.

Knowledge of Death

Katha Upanishad is the source of the knowledge of death for the departing soul. In this Upanishad, Rudra (another name for Shiva) imparts the knowledge of Tarak Brahman. The jeeva (the being), as a result of the knowledge of Parabrahman, attains the immortal state and is freed from the sorrow of death. Therefore, the entangled being should always worship Lord Rudra during one's lifetime, he should not forsake it. 'Is it so important?' Brihaspati asked Sage Yajnawalkya, who replied: 'Yes, it is very much so'.

Shankaracharya in his commentary has interpreted it differently. Instead of 'lifetime', he says, 'till comprehension of Brahman'. But when it is categorically stated that, 'Rudra imparts the knowledge when man breathes his last', its meaning and purpose ought to be that 'during lifetime till death', the being should worship Rudra. Here, there is an emphasis on the adhidaivik (devotion to the divine) aspect. The plain and clear meaning is that by virtue of worship the Form-Relation being firmed up, by the grace of Poorna man gets the knowledge of Tarak

Brahman at the time of death. The *Jabala Upanishad* has a special commentary on the sanyasa (ascetic) phase of life. When an Upanishad dealing with sanyasa asserts the devotional form of worship then what should be the Absolute Truth? Of course, it must be Poorna Purusha only and not the Parabrahman. Otherwise, that which cannot rid itself of the adjunct Maya, how could it at an appropriate time, impart knowledge to the dead to relieve him of the sorrow of death and also give him knowledge of the essential form of Parabrahman, the subsequent state? At the most Ishwara should have taken the dead to His own world in Kailasa and there elevate him to the liberated state.

Thus anvay-dnyan (perception associated with senses of cognition) is not the only means to attain self-realization; self-realization can be attained through devotional worship also. Atman realization is the knowledge of one of the forms, the adhyatmik or spiritual form, of Poorna Purusha. With the grace of Poorna, which the being obtains by devotional worship, it can have such a realization at the time of death. Devotional worship of Rudra, i.e., Poorna Purusha, frees the being from the fear of death at the appropriate time and gives him Brahman-realization with the comprehension that he is immortal.

Earlier, we saw that man naturally attains the Turiya state at the time of death. In this phase, if a man recollects his devotional worship, his personal deity can impart knowledge of atman transcending even the Turiya state (i.e., Parabrahman) in a very short span of time. Atman realization or Brahman realization are in fact relevant for realizing one's deathlessness or immortality at the time of death. As this knowledge is not essential in our day-to-day life, Shruti calls it impracticable. With this background, the meaning of Omkara's three syllables A-U-M (respectively waking, dream and sleep states in the *Mandukya Upanishad*) and the fourth is turiya state for which there is no quarter or rather signified by the unuttered crescent. There is only a reference to it in the Upanishad. The witness hood experience is in this state. Let us see what is stated about this in the *Mandukya Upanishad* (12):

अमात्रश्चतुर्थोऽव्यवहार्यः प्रपंचोपशमः शिवोऽद्वैतएवमोंकारःआत्मैव,
संविशत्यात्मनाऽऽत्मानं य एवं वेद य एवं वेद।।

amātraścaturtho'vyavahāryaḥ prapañcopaśamaḥ śivo›dvaita evamoṅkāra ātmaiva saṃviśatyātmanā"tmānaṃ ya evaṃ veda ||

[The fourth, Turiya, witness-Atman without sound (or parts) is beyond 'relativity'. 'Beyond relativity' does not signify agnostic. Because the very next word is 'prapanchopshama'. Of course, this atman is the ultimate stage of the desired filled worldly activities and that is the state of dying".][1]

Therefore, in the shloka from the *Jabala Upanishad*, referred to earlier, it is stated that the Rudra communicates knowledge of Tarak Brahma, to the man in his dying state. Crest jewel among the saints, Saint Tukaram, having had the experience speaks thus: 'I verily saw my death with my own eyes, that event of bliss is simply unparalleled.' Therefore, this being the experience in the dying state, it has no usefulness during one's lifetime. Hence the Shruti calls it as 'non-essential in empirical relations'. Furthermore, the cognition of duality ceases in this state; therefore, it is called non-dual, auspicious and good.

Of course, the dying state is not inauspicious and when Shruti suggests that although this 'Turiya witness' is wholly in Omkara, it is Omkara. Thus, he who comprehends this has the experience of this during the lifetime itself. As such, when one experiences this state during one's lifetime and comprehends that 'this is the state of dying', all fears of death leave him. Incomprehensibility is always terrifying for man and that is why he fears death. But as stated earlier, with the comprehension (experience) of death there remains no cause for his fear. This knowledge can be acquired through direct experience or as explained in *Jabala Upanishad*, by devotional worship of Rudra. Thus

---

1 Author's own translation.

even for ascetics (sanyasis), the Upanishad advocates Shiva's worship and it is seen to be very much in vogue.

Of the threefold form of Poorna Purusha, the adhyatmik or spiritual form is called Shiva, Shankara, Rudra etc.; the adhidaivik or divine form is called Vishnu, Indra, Vaishvanara etc.; and the adhibhautik or material form is known as Jad, Vishwa, Brahmadev, Prajapati. Shankaracharya's Vedanta falls under the adhyatmik or spiritual form and deals with the witness Brahman. It is called Shankara Vedanta and he being the teacher of this philosophy is honest with the Shruti.

Now we shall consider various shlokas from *Svetasvatara Upanishad* which deal with Parabrahman's form, here the shloka (6.19):

निष्कलं निष्क्रियं शान्तं निरवद्यं निरंजनम्।
अमृतस्य परं सेतुं दग्धेन्धनमिवानलम्।।

*niṣkalaṃ niṣkriyaṃ śāntaṃ niravadyaṃ nirañjanam
amṛtasya paraṃ setuṃ dagdhendhanam ivānalam*

[That which is partless, actionless, tranquil, free from all modifications, faultless, taintless, causeless, self-existent, Supreme bridge to immortality, because of Whom the experience of dying state is gained.][2]

Even if the Vedas call the inanimate or adhibhoutik as eternal, owing to the transformation from one state to another, experiencing immortality is very difficult. End of one state and the advent of another is virtually the death of the former. Here owing to suspicion, certitude is difficult. However, due to Its 'Absolute' characteristic there is no reason to doubt or suspect that the 'states' or transformation are non-existent. Therefore, this Atman, Parabrahman, has been called the ultimate limit or test of immortality. Even if a man is not convinced about his immortality by anything else after self-realization there is a certitude about his

---

2 *Principal Upanishads*, S. Radhakrishnan.

immortality. Once we are convinced about our immortality, it is quite enough to convince us about our non-difference with Ishwara.

After funeral rites (consigning body to fire), the inert body turns into air and from there again there is a possibility of that turning into inert body. There is a principle in physics that 'matter can neither be created nor can it be destroyed'. At the most, its form or state may change. And now of course, we are told that it can be transformed into energy. And that matter cannot be destroyed. Similarly, once man is convinced by experience that he is immortal, such knowledge is quite adequate to convince him of his non-difference with Ishwara.

CHAPTER 16

Aum: Powerful Mantra of Immortality

THE BIGGEST fear in life is the fear of death. Dr Parnerkar's Poornavad gives us assurance and relieves us from this fear. In the very beginning of the Poornavad doctrine in the Heart to Heart; he explained that Poornavad should be read and studied because it gives the perfect interpretation of the Vedas and the practical benefits therein, and removes the fear from death. At the beginning of every Vedic ritual is a starting mantra of 'Sankalpa', i.e., the 'determination' mantra. The primary objective of the Vedas is to use physical ability and the will to live life in a way that bestows confidence to gain material prosperity.

Dr Parnerkar introduced the divine aspect of the Vedas, which is beneficial for everyone who trusts and studies the Vedas. He notes that in the name of religion, people only talk about spirituality and ask others to sacrifice something from their dogmas, whereas the Vedas never ask that one sacrifice anything. Veda advises on various ways to acquire prosperity and the stability of life by way of some divine mantras, because mantras are more powerful. In day-to-day life, we require wisdom rather than intellectual knowledge. Dr Parnerkar's Poornavad explains that the Vedas hold practical benefits that can make our life easier and more comfortable. Poornavad also says that God is not mere intellectual curiosity; rather, His grace is like another material need, an utmost important need. If we want to realize the complete form of the Supreme Lord—the Poorna—then we should know the complete form of God and AUM is a means to understand the complete form of God.

16.1 The Knowledge of › AUM

A hymn[1] in the *Mandukya Upanishad*, which, when contemplated, brings into light:

ओमित्येतदक्षरमिदं सर्वं तस्योपाख्यानं भूतं भवद्विष्यदिति सर्वमोंकार एव।
यच्चान्यत् त्रिकालातीतं तदप्योंकार एव।।

[Syllable Om is everything and that is being elucidated. All that which is taking place in this world is, for certain, Omkara. Anything beyond Time, the One in many is only Omkara. Omkara is the name of the Lord. Therefore, when Lord is eternal so is Omkara eternal. In short, Omkara means the Lord. This (Om) is all this (world) and the indescribable Bramhan. Here, 'Bramhan' is not stated as the form of the Lord and the world as its activity. If it were so, at least here it should have been clearly mentioned, because the purpose is to show Om and the Bramhan. Therefore, here, too, the reference to non-duality pertains to non-duality of form.][2]

When we say 'Atman is consciousness, knowledge and bliss', it means that consciousness, knowledge and bliss are one with the Atman. In other words, they have a non-dual relationship of form with Atman. Likewise, is the relation of the world and Bramhan with the Lord (where Brahman means the Lord). They are one. The Taittiriya Upanishad (*Principal Upanishads*, S. Radhakrishnan) Having stated in one hymn: 'all [is] pervaded by Omkara', stating in the very of next hymn, 'all [is]

---

1   Man. 1, Principal Upanishads, S. Radhakrishnan, pp.695.
2   Author's own translation.

pervaded by Bramha' lays down the same hypothesis and therefore, both words are used to convey the same meaning.

सर्व हि एतत् ब्रह्म सर्व जगत ब्रह्म अयं आत्मा ब्रह्म

All this (existence) is verily Bramhan this Atman is Bramhan; this same Atman has four quarters (places of manifestation, namely, jagrit or awakened, svapna or dream state, susupti [susupti is the state of deep sleep] and turiya). The point is if the 'manyness' (diversity) of the world makes us reluctant to call it 'form', then Atman also is divided into four quarters: visvam (world), taijasam (awakened), prajna (dream) and turiya (transcendental consciousness) which Shruti describes as '*santamsivamadvaita/n Chaturtham*' and that has been dealt with especially at length by Sri Shankaracharya.

We have just dealt with the identity of Bramhanand Omkara. Let us consider the hymn (Mandukya, Upanishad chapter 8, verse 1) which asserts the very same point and the non-duality of Bramhanand Omkara. This Om is verily The Complete, i.e., the world, Bramhan and the Atman. Hence, predominance from the standpoint of syllable Om. The syllable that signifies the Lord is Om. Those which constitute the four quarters of the Atman (visvam, taijasam, prajna and turiya) are the matra on Om and the letters a, u, m.[3]

State	Sound	Quarter
Jagruti	a	Visva
Swapna	u	Taijas
Susupti	m	Pranja
Turiya	soundless	Turiya

A bindu or dot in the crescent over the syllable Om as written in Sanskrit is called by some as ardhamatra.

---

3   Man.9,10,11. *Principal Upanishads*, S.Radhakrishnan.

Know Thy Roots

The following hymn in the *Chhandoga Upanishad* (Ma.1 16,21), likewise, elaborates on the meditation of Om by discriminating between the form of Om and its effulgence.

ओमित्यदक्षमुद्गाथमुपासीत। ओमिति हृद्गायति तस्योपव्याख्यानम्।

'Esabhootanamprithvirasah' (anything beyond time) in this way, the beginning which is from the 'material', describes the variants of worship relating to the mental and spiritual planes.

As such, owing to the diversity of forms in the world, the *Bramhan Upanishad* goes on to explain the different types of meditation and the fruits thereof. This Upanishad consists of fourteen parts and eight chapters. It is a Bramhan Upanisad of Chhandogya branch of Samveda. It emphasizes the concept of Poornavad, which integrates knowledge, duty, and meditation. For actions to be meaningful, there must be a sense of unity between the world and the divine. Meditation, when performed by Ishwara (the supreme being), is considered devotion. Ignorance can only be overcome by knowledge.

But the Samhita Upanishad and the Bramhana place knowledge, action and meditation on the same platform and elucidate that any one of the three, singly, would not serve the purpose and there is no recourse without the practice of the triad in entirety. From the means standpoint the proposition pointed at is 'Poornavad' only. The Upanishad highlights that seeing the temple's cupola is as significant as seeing the deity inside, emphasizing the importance of holistic practice.

Meditation by Means of Om: The Way to Realization

The actual means of meditation which a spiritual teacher imparts to his disciple is described unanimously in the Upanishads as being the symbol Om. It is also to be noticed that Om is described as not merely the supreme means of meditation, but the goal to be reached by the meditation itself. The Om occupies in Indian philosophy the same position which the Logos occupies in Christology. The Upanishads repeat from time to time the efficacy of meditation by means of the supreme symbol.

'The word which the Vedas declare and which is the subject of all austerities, desiring which men lead the life of religious studentship, that word, I tell thee, is briefly Om; that word is the Supreme Brahman; that word is the Supreme Symbol; that word is the Supreme Support'. In these terms, the Katha Upanishad identifies the means of meditation. The symbol in short - stands for both the means and the end of spiritual life. The *Chhandyoga Upanishad* declares that all speech is interwoven on this symbol Om, in the same manner as the leaves of a tree are woven together on a stalk.

The *Mundaka Upanishad* tells us by the help of a very happy simile that: we should take into hand the bow of the Upanishads, and put upon it the arrow of the Soul, sharpened by devotion. We should next stretch it with concentrated attention, and penetrate the mark which is the Supreme Brahman. The mystic symbol Om is the bow; the arrow is the Soul; and Brahman is the mark to be pierced. We should penetrate it with undistracted attention, so that the arrow may become one with the mark.

We are told here how devotion is necessary for the wetting of the point of the arrow, how concentrated attention and undistracted effort are necessary for making the arrow of the Soul pierce the target of Brahman, how, finally, the arrow is to become so absorbed in the target that it ceases to exist as a separate entity. If unitive life is to be expressed by any metaphor—and all verbal expressions, it must be remembered, fall short of the experience of reality—the metaphor of the arrow and the target invented by the *Mundaka Upanishad* must be considered a very happy one, as most fittingly characterizing the communion of the lower and the higher selves so as to involve the utter destruction of the separate individuality of the lower self.

Further, the Om has not merely an individual, but a cosmic efficacy as well. It not merely serves to help the meditation of the individual person, but the Sun himself, we are told, travels the universe, singing the symbol Om.

Finally, the moral efficacy of meditation by means of Om is brought out in the *Prashna Upanishad* where Satyakama inquires of his teacher as to what happens to a man by his continuing to meditate by means of that symbol till the hour of his death, and the answer is given that 'just as a snake is relieved of its slough, similarly is the man who meditates on Om relieved of his sins, and, by the power of his chants, is lifted to the highest world where he beholds the Person who informs the body, and who stands supreme above any living complex whatsoever.'

16.3 The Mandukyan Exaltation of Aura

The *Mandukya Upanishad* supplies us with a unique exaltation of Om and its spiritual significance. We are told there that Om consists not merely of the three more A U M, but that it contains also a fourth morale's part. The reason for this fourfold division of Om lies manifestly in the author's intention of bringing into correspondence with the parts of Om the states of consciousness on the one hand, and the kinds of soul on the other. The Om is supposed to represent in miniature the various states of consciousness (wakefulness, dreaming, deep sleep and the Supreme Self-conscious state which is called turiya) as well as the various kinds of soul. (namely the vaisvanara the enjoyer of gross things, the taijasa the enjoyer of the subtle, the prajna 'the Lord of all, the all-knowing, the inner controller of all, the origin and end of all beings', and the Atman which is the Mandukyan equivalent of what philosophy calls the Absolute). The morale's part of Om has correspondence with the fourth dimension of psychology, namely the turiya, as well as with the fourth dimension of metaphysics, namely the Atman. The Atman, is described as:

> '... neither inwardly nor outwardly cognitive, nor yet on both sides together. It is not a cognition-mass, and is neither knower nor not-knower. It is invisible, impracticable, incomprehensible, indescribable, unthinkable and un-pointable. Its essence is the knowledge of its own self. It negates the whole expanse of the universe, and is tranquil and blissful and without a second.'

The spiritual significance of the psycho-metaphysical correspondence of the parts of Om lies in the great help that is supposed to be given by meditation on it in intuiting the Atman in the Turya state of consciousness after a negation of the other kinds of Soul in the other states of consciousness. Nowhere else as in the *Mandukya Upanishad* do we find such an exaltation of Om,.

Contemplation of Aum

Aum iti brahma, aum itidarhsarvam, aum ityetadanukrtir ha smavdapyosrdvayetydsrdvayanti, aum itisdmdnigdyanti, aum somitiiastrdnisamsanti, aum ityadhvaryuh, pratigarampratigrndti, aum iti brahma prasauti, aum- ityagrtihotramanujdndti, aum itibrdhmanahpravaksyann aha, brahmopdpnavdniti, brahmaivopdpnoti.

Aum is Brahman. Aum is everything. Aum is the sound of assent, of harmony, of cosmic agreement. When someone is instructed, "Recite," they begin with Aum. When a Brahmana begins a sacred recitation, he starts with Aum. Though Aum is just a sound and, by itself, lacks awareness, its spiritual significance is immense, just like an image used in worship. The divine presence (Ishvara, the Supreme Being) accepts the intention behind it and grants the fruits of devotion. Aum is the symbol of both Brahman and Isvara and represents the path to divine.

CHAPTER 17

The Dream of a Universal Religion

WE ARE living in a supersonic and technological age, but still face rivalry and violence between different religious groups. Despite material progress on the global level, the common man is not enjoying absolute happiness in life. How can such crisis occur in such a supersonic and technological age—this is the challenge before global thinkers. It is time to define and explain the concept of a global citizenship that ensures the welfare of the common man, who only wants to live peacefully without any wars that create crises for humanity.

As citizens of earth we don't want any boundaries, whether national or religious that go against the law of natural justice. Unfortunately, the present global leadership is becoming more ambitious and selfish, desiring to dominate other nations and their religions. The rulers of many countries are becoming aggressive, offensive and crueller than animals, because even animals are bound by natural laws. Countries are encouraging terrorism for their own gains. Barking and shouting every day for war, such rulers are becoming enemies of humanity.

To end wars that are fought on the basis of religion global thinkers, secular and intellectual thinkers, are dreaming of a Universal Religion. This will require some redefining, reconstructing and reinterpreting of all the traditional philosophical systems, Oriental and Western.

The Vedic tradition provides for just such a utopian society. Some Western thinkers have pointed this out, amongst them the German indologist Hermann Oldenberg, German philosopher Arthur Schopenhauer, American historian and philosopher Will Durant, German author Kersten Holger, and Austrian-American physicist Fritjof Capra.

Holger, the author of *Jesus Lived in India*, wonders how Christianity has constantly denied its connection with India.[1] Durant has recognized India as the motherland of European race, Sanskrit as the mother of European languages, and even of philosophy, mathematics, and self-government.[2] Oldenberg is said to have stated that the roots of Christianity lay in Buddhism and the roots of Buddhism lay in Vedic philosophy, which was the most ancient philosophy known to man. If so, we can say that Vedic philosophy is the root of all philosophies of the major religions of the world and that we can find some solutions to the present crisis before the world today. The major point is that we have failed to understand the concept and the difference between 'religion' and 'dharma'.

In his *Constructive Survey of Upanishads*, Indian scholar-philosopher-saint Ramachandra Dattatreya Ranade lauds Christian missions in India for instituting research in various departments of Indian thought, and the close attention they paid to the Upanishads—even though their views were bound to be in the interest of Christianity.[3] Thomas E. Slater's book, *Studies in the Upanishads*, published by The Christian Literature Society for India: London and Madras, in 1897, is a very good and clever production. Only Slater does not hold that the Upanishads are capable of supplying the ideas of a universal religion.

---

1 Holger ([1930], 2001), *Jesus Lived in India*.
2 Will Durant (2015), *The Case for India*.
3 Ranade, D.R. (1926), *A Constructive Survey of Upanishadic Philosophy*.

If the dream of a universal religion be true (and we have but one science of the universe); if the fatherhood of God and brotherhood of man be true, there can be but one bond of spiritual union for such a family—and such a religion cannot possibly be based on the Upanishads. If you make them your religion, then you must be content to see it confined to a small corner of the globe, and to a select coterie even in that corner. For if as it has often been urged, this ancient system can be properly understood only in the original Sanskrit, then true religion at its highest, depends not only on superior intellect, but also on special linguistic talent.

It is the Vedas and not the Upanishads that define and describe the science of the entire universe and the unmanifest and manifest world. This is the stand of Poornavad philosophy. Therefore, the interpretations of Poornavad philosophy on Vedic concepts can be compared to a universal religion for better hermeneutical understanding between the religions of the world.

Religion is belief in worship of and/or obedience to a supernatural power or powers considered to have control of human destiny, as among the Christians. As a system of worship and faith, it is thus a formalized expression of belief or a group of certain beliefs. Religions may or may not be limited to a certain group or nation. Dharma is of protean significance in the Sanatan Vedic context. It is derived from the root 'dhr' (to uphold, to sustain, to nourish). Dharma is the norm which sustains the universe, the principle, the virtue of a thing. It is also used to denote religious rites.

Dharma is referred to in the *Chhandogya Upanishad*, which speaks of the three branches of Dharma relating to the duties of householder, the hermit and the student; and in the *Taittiriya Upanishad*, which asks us to practice Dharma—it refers to the duties of the stage of life to which we belong. In this sense it is also employed by the Bhagavad Gita and in the *Manusmriti*.

Dharma, for the Buddhists, is one of three jewels (*Triratna*) along with the Buddha and the Sangha (the community). According to the *Poorva Mimansa* it is desirable object defined by a direction, the

Vaisheshika Sutra defines Dharma as that from which happiness and beatitude arise.

For our purpose we define Dharma as the duty of man in relation to the fourfold purposes of life (dharma, artha, kama, and moksha) and the four stages of life: brahmacharya (student life)), grihasta (life as a householder), vanaprastha (retired life), and sanyas (a life of seclusion). The supreme aim of this social order is to train a human being to attain a stage of spiritual perfection and sanctity. Its essential aim is directed, towards developing social conditions that leads the mass of people to a level of moral, material and intellectual life in accord with the good and peace of all.

Religion is not so much a revelation to be attained by us in faith, as much as it is an effort to unveil the deepest layers of man's being and get into enduring contact with them.

Dharma is both that which we hold to and that which holds together our inner and outer activities in its primary sense. It means a fundamental law of our nature which secretly conditions all our activities. Each being, type, species, individual group has its own Dharma. Secondly, there is the divine nature within us that must evolve and reveal itself. In this sense, dharma is the inner law or guiding principle that governs this growth and unfolding in our being. Thirdly, there is the law by which we govern our outgoing thoughts and actions and our relations with each other so as to best help both our own growth and that of human race towards the divine ideal.[4]

While the concept of religion concerns itself with a certain group of beliefs, the concept of Dharma is wider and is no way concerned with the concept of modern religion. Many thinkers believe that the present crisis before humanity is concerned with religious pluralism. But if we look into the roots of world philosophy, more than five-thousand years ago there was only one belief or religion in the world, i.e., the Vedas.

---

4   'Sri Aurobindo and the Sanatan Dharma: A 11-part series by Alok Pandey'. https://auromaa.org/3-dharma/#:~:text=Dharma%20is%20both%20that%20which,group%20has%20its%20own%20dharma.

The solution to the crisis we are facing, can come from Poornavad that is derived from the Vedas and provides a solution to this crisis.

Our life is dominated by thoughts, both positive (aka divine) and negative (aka devilish). We are more concerned with divine or divinity. In this frame we will focus on the Poornavad Vedic philosophy, which is the modern interpretation of the interpretation of Vedic philosophy made by Vedanta teachers.

The Background of Poornavad Philosophy

Every man, dissatisfied with his present state of affairs, must work hard to attain a higher status in life both socially and economically. At the same time, in order to protect his own culture both internally and externally—i.e., to maintain an internal tranquility and to satisfy the demands of higher planes of his own existence—he must refrain from all sorts of undesirable deeds to achieve this goal.

Vast progress in science and technology, civilization and culture, has failed miserably in achieving the goal—that every person should be free to live in a way they like and in whatever way they choose, and thus enjoy a happy and contented life. To live as per one's own choice seems to be the basic instinct of man and any amount of religious literature has not been able to modify or belittle it. The Poornavad philosophy states that, 'to live and to live one's own choice are two basic instincts of man and they cannot be modified under any circumstances.'

By civilization we refer to the vast technological progress that has taken place, the innumerable commodities of human comfort brought into market (creating materialism), the different forms of democratic and socialistic governments which shape the finance, law, education and defence and general law and order situations established throughout the world. By culture, we not only mean the history, the languages, the historical places, places of pilgrimage, temples, ancient arts such as music, dancing, painting, and religious faiths, but also the adjustment of this normal natural life to modern techniques of civilization. It is the way of life adopted to bring our old natural life in line with the new modern developments. It is a change in our lower-self, in our very nature, performed consciously, to use the modern amenities to our fullest advantage and prosperity.

It is true that God has not given a particular piece of land to a particular man, or the rights of using a well or river to a particular group of people; but for administrative convenience, every type of government is forced to take such decisions. The talk of a free society is alright in theory, but with advanced civilization, more and more restrictions become inevitable. People are unhappy because they cannot live the way that they want to, while others who have nothing to live by, struggle to survive and have to live according to the whims of others. Thus man is entangled in a mesh created by himself, whilst desiring to adopt a culture that will satisfy his higher soul.

Today, brilliant hard-working students are not sure of their success in examinations, those who are successful, are not sure of getting admission to colleges, those who have completed college education with merit even, are not sure of being selected for suitable posts. 'Luck' and 'chance' seem to rule everywhere and hard work and honest conscious efforts to raise oneself to higher planes of existence seem to have no meaning whatsoever. This breeds sorrow, misery and suffering. Sufferers often have no place to complain or express their sorrows, because support systems such as God, faith, guru and even parents have been cast away. This brings extra stress leading to nervous breakdowns, mental disorders, whimsical attitudes and erratic behaviours. Hence the only way left out is for man to analyse nature in which perfect regularity is observed.

Such an analysis was also attempted in the past and it brought forth two basic principles namely 'jad' (matter devoid of consciousness) and 'chetan' (mind and higher planes of mind that gives us consciousness of matter). Now all Eastern and Western philosophies accept any one principle of the two as real, eternal, everlasting and look upon the other as derived from, or temporarily existing on the one they have selected as eternal.

Shankaracharya held that 'chetan' was real and ever-existing and the world full of matter was only a hallucination, a false impression, on the original sea of 'Satchidanand' (truth, consciousness, bliss). The materialists take the reverse view and say that matter is the eternal substance and 'chetan' or 'mind' is temporary. Thus 'Brahma satyam, jagat mithya' (Brahman is real, the world is false) is the slogan of Eastern philosophers, while 'Dust thou art and to dust thou returnest' is the outcry of Western philosophers.

Poornavad does not uphold or criticize either view. It simply states that whatever is seen to exist is Poorna or Complete. If it is matter, it is that kind of matter from which a consciousness/an awareness, a 'chetan' or 'mind' can evolve; and if it is 'chetan', it is that type of 'chetan' from which inert matter results, so that the 'chetan' can distinguish itself as 'chetan' (i.e. a a mind that can perceive the inertness of matter).

Thus, Poornavad states that 'Chetan (mind) must be in existence to recognize, and to have a feeling of the matter (jad) as inert matter devoid of any consciousness.' It further states that 'Ordinarily chetan (mind) cannot be experienced without the aid of some type of matter, may be the invisible particles of cosmic material.' It is man who has a body and can say that earth is full of matter and can also proclaim that I have become Brahma or Brahmaswaroopa. If we say that matter can also exist without 'mind' or 'chetan', again it is only the mind which can make such a statement. So Poornavad states that 'Whatever exists or we feel as existing, is Poorna or complete entity.'

Thus Poornavad says, 'Whatever exists is complete and being complete, it has power to create both mind and matter and anything else which is seen or experienced.' Hence basically mind and matter are one and a complete entity. So Poornavad proclaims that for 'jad' we must lead a material life and keep pace with others, and for 'chetan' we must be able to detach ourselves completely from material world (mentally) and raise our consciousness to the highest plane of joy and bliss. With the help of Vedic hymns and mantras 'chetan' deity's consciousness is invoked and invited to enter the 'jad', i.e., the idol. This is then prayed to, which is referred to as 'murti pooja' or idol worship.

'Life is an art' is what Poornavad states. It is the art of transforming human life by—which is nothing but the feeling or experience of 'jad'—

increasingly merging into 'chetan'; and this 'chetan' exists with the help of 'jad' (i.e., the mind exists in the 'jad' human body).

Since whatever exists is a complete thing, the object of Poornavad is not merely the development of the inner being but also the development of one's outer nature and life. To attain this object, man must become conscious of himself and of the different parts of his being and their respective functions and faculties. Since man in his essential being is nothing but consciousness only, its analysis reveals that self-consciousness or 'I', has three parts, each distinct from the other—the consciousness of material body (the material I), the consciousness of mind (the mental I), and the vague consciousness of something beyond mind (the divine I).

All these three aspects of human personality get a particular joy by their mutual actions and reactions and this joy is named as 'jivanananda' or 'the natural joy of life' states Dr Parnerkar. He claims that this joy is no less than what one gets when he becomes one with Atman or Brahma. Because in this latter case his consciousness dwells permanently in the 'divine I' rejecting all other experience as 'Maya'. The ordinary man on the other hand has no experience of the 'divine' or even 'pure mental' consciousness and therefore his consciousness dwells only in the 'material'. Such a man thus enjoys only 33 per cent of his 'natural joy of life.'

The object of Poornavad is to develop all these three aspects of human beings simultaneously, thus leading to a complete developed being, the 'Uttam Purusha' or 'Poorna Purusha' as described in the fifteenth chapter of the Gita.

Thus, Poornavad does not aim at 'liberation' or 'moksha' but believes only in leading a complete divine life on this earth. Since the 'divine I' is also developed side by side, at the time of death those who are interested can liberate themselves by keeping their consciousness permanently fixed in the 'divine I'. But it is difficult to conceive that the object of this whole universe is just 'liberation' and merging into the static immutable Divine Truth, i.e., Brahma.

Integral Approach to the Divine Way of Life

Poornavad not only believes in God but states that we all are here just to experience His grace and lead a complete divine life. Divine is all light, bliss, knowledge and power, nothing is impossible for Him. The whole world along with its natural laws form His outer material body or Vishwaroopa; the personal gods of popular religion or the great seers of truth, living on the plane of spiritual universal mind, form his mental aspect.

The Nirguna or static immutable Brahma is the inner core of the Vishwaroopa. This supreme God was originally alone in a state of divine existence, divine knowledge and divine joy. To experience His own light, joy, and knowledge more explicitly, He manifested as many.

Therefore, Dr Parnerkar holds that God's grace must result in a favourable change in the material life of an individual, coupled with a corresponding level of inner mental satisfaction. A sudden favorable change in a person's material circumstances is undeniable proof that divine grace is at work. But before the grace intervenes, good unobserved preparation is necessary and once divine grace has intervened, one has still to put in a good deal of work to keep and develop what one has got. Thus, we see that for our complete development, personal efforts, in addition to divine grace, are also important.

Hence the common man should make a humble beginning in this direction by acquainting himself with this Poornavad philosophy. In personal life he should pay proper attention to the words he uses and the language he speaks. This will help him to develop his intellect. Then keeping the principle of human unity in view, he should exercise proper care in keeping good relations with people around him. The knowledge that they are all parts of Vishwaroopa (material form of God) will help him to keep his internal balance and tranquility. At times, he should completely detach himself mentally from his surroundings and study the whole thing in a scientific manner just to understand his own problems specifically. He should think, experience, or undertake things in the spirit that whatever he will give to the world will be received by God in his Vishwaroopa form.

He should also have a place when he can freely complain about his suffering and seek guidance in moments of difficulties. Remembering the Poornavad thesis that 'Whatever exists is complete', he should try to assess carefully the things he has got and learn to derive maximum pleasure and satisfaction from them. Without sacrificing the demands of his higher planes of existence, he should always try to acquire higher status in life both socially and economically. Thus having made a good preparation he should pray for divine grace for the fulfilment of his wishes.

Here, spiritual practices and disciplines, and worship as well as his approach to the divine are very important. Feeling joy and satisfaction for the good things we already possess, and an internal conviction that whatever we are demanding will make us happy, generally does the job. Thus, once we get a proper material change in our surroundings, we should try to consolidate the internal satisfaction and peace achieved, and be always striving to ascend to higher planes beyond mind. This is an integral approach to a 'divine life' as detailed by Dr Parnerkar.

He was unique in that he never spoke publicly about his thesis until he had tested it through practical applications - first with a scientific, experimental mindset, and later as a confirmed theory, presented in five or six Marathi books for the general public. So Dr Parnerkar's Poornavad leads to the Poorna or complete entities described in the following Sanskrit verse:

ॐ पूर्णमदः पूर्णमिदं पूर्णात्पूर्णमुदच्यते।
पूर्णस्य पूर्णमादाय पूर्णमेवावशिष्यते।।

Om Puurnnam-Adah Puurnnam-Idam Puurnnaat-Puurnnam-Udacyate|
Puurnnasya Puurnnam-Aadaaya Puurnnam-Eva-Avashissyate ||
Om Shaantih Shaantih Shaantih

[What is visible is the infinite. What is invisible is also the infinite. Out of the Infinite Being the finite has come, yet being infinite, only infinite remains.]

Noted scholar Prof. S Pannerselvam opines that the Poornavad philosophy can change the life of both, the individual and society. In the Poornavad philosophy, nothing exists outside of it. Everything is included in it. It does not believe in mere theoretical understanding of life, but gives a practical orientation to life. Man is said to be the combination of both matter and spirit and most of the time, man is immersed in material side of life and spirituality is often neglected. Spirituality gives identity to human beings. Poornavad philosophy takes the human being to the higher planes of life, namely spirituality with divine power. This is the first experience to give more pleasure in all respects. This makes Poornavad philosophy more relevant to the twenty-first century and as a philosophical method, it offers a guiding principle to life.

S. Pannerselvam on Hermeneutics

In his work, 'Cultural Paradigm and Social Critique: A Tamil Perspective', S. Pannerselvam explained the meaning and reference of hermeneutics with reference to the *Tirukkural*.

> Hermeneutics is a method of philosophizing used in the eighteenth century for the interpretation of the texts. Though initially it was used for interpreting the religious texts, later it was extended to the philosophical texts. For example, Schleiermacher who used hermeneutical method in theology defined it as the art of avoiding misunderstanding. Savigny, Boeckh, Steinthal, and Dilthey developed the method of Schleiermacher. Dilthey, who was a historian and the biographer of Schleiermacher, stressed that there is no presuppositionless understanding. The foundation of human science, according to him lies in understanding. Later, Heidegger explained the need for all interpretation to rise from a previous understanding. He openly refuted the idea that understanding can be presuppositionless. 'All interpretation is grounded in a fore-sight, and a fore-conception,' says Heidegger. Hermeneutics is concerned at its

core with the eternal foundations of all meaning and values. It insists on the relation between the parts and the whole, for correct understanding is possible only by studying the relation between the parts and the whole. We can understand the parts of the text only if we understand the whole; similarly, the understanding of the whole becomes complete by understanding the individual parts. Gadamer, in the Truth and Method, attempts to refound the notions of tradition and heritage, and also to discover its real nature and foundation. For him, hermeneutics is centered on a theory of interpretation, of the transmission of the stored-up riches of the tradition. Interpretation is always open-ended, which means that no interpretation is ever final, thus allowing always a new interpretation. Our understanding grows out of a particular context.

Prof. S. Pannerselvan on Poornavad and, Tradition and Modernity

One of the great contributions made by Dr Parnerkar is his attempt to reinterpret the Vedas and Upanishads. This is the need of the hour and many contemporary thinkers like Swami Vivekananda, Sri Aurobindo, Tilak and many others have worked for the upliftment of man using the reinterpretation as a mode of understanding the texts. No doubt, as a contemporary Indian philosopher, Dr Parnerkar has worked out a methodology in this direction thus paving the way for liberation of the entire humanity. He is a synthesis of tradition and modernity. No doubt, he is a great follower of Indian tradition.

Tradition is the finite unfolding of an infinite content, a history of finite actualization of an essentially inexhaustible, or infinite, truth. To put the same in Gadamerian terms, it is "inescapable facticity". Every re-telling of it is a renewal of the tradition. Our belongingness to tradition is our primordial ontological condition. Tradition is the locus of understanding. We are shaped by our past in various ways and this has a tremendous influence on our understanding. The past and the present are related and become a continuous process through the tradition. In tradition, we think in our own concepts. Tradition is the tool which he applies for his understanding of the texts. Dr Parnerkar, though follows the tradition since he comes in the great tradition of Sankara, Ramanuja and Madhva, he deviates from Gaudapada or Sankara with regard to concepts like Maya or *Ishwara*. In this way one can say that Dr Parnerkar embraces modernity. Wherever necessary he deviates from the orthodoxy to make the text more relevant to humanity. His modern understanding of the Upanishads proves this. His methodology takes us to two further questions. They are (1) What does the word "modernity" mean? (2) Are tradition and modernity not irreconcilably opposed to each other? There is answer available in Dr Parnerkar's Poornavad. The modern philosopher J. N. Mohanty says that if modernity means outright rejection of tradition, then of course, there is no promise of fruitful dialogue and mediation. There are two ways of understanding modernity. First, modernity consists in addressing oneself to what is contemporaneous. It is a contemporary ongoing dialogue. The second aspect is the idea of criticism. Tradition demands respect and continuity. Dr Parnerkar tries to understand modernity in this way. He addresses what is contemporaneous and also criticizes when the given interpretation by the predecessors are found unacceptable, thus making the tradition a living one.

Indian Tradition has no Dogma
The Indian philosophical tradition is a commentarial tradition. Indian philosophical discourse has developed through the commentaries. The commentaries are interpretational in nature. Following this one can say that Dr Parnerkar, in his interpretation of the Vedas and Upanishads adopts hermeneutic-analytical method. The *prasthanatraya* is the source for Vedanta which rests on *shruti, smriti*, and *tarka*. The *Upanishads* represent *shruti-prasthana*, the *Brahmasutra* represents *tarka-prasthana*

and the *Bhagavad-Gita* represents *smrti-prasthana*. The texts are connected with the commentaries or interpretation. The texts are expository and they are to be commented. The role of interpreter starts here. The commentaries are as important as the texts. In fact, the commentaries do much work than the texts, because sometimes the texts are not only brief, but also elliptical in nature. The interpreter, as a way of his commentary, explicitly analyses what the text says and interprets according to the need and the historical conditions. Thus, it is not a mere interpretation but an interpretation mingled with historicity. It is inevitable for the interpreter or commentator to take into account of his historical conditions and other factors. Thus, the text when it is written may have one goal or intention, but the commentator has to interpret the text taking into consideration various factors. In fact, these influential factors are already implicit in the act of interpretation itself. The interpreter need not wait or search for the historicity to operate on him, while interpreting a text. It is automatic. It is because historicity simply operates on and the interpreter simply exists in it. The interpreter not only understands the texts, but also presents in a different way so that more people can have easy access to it. The text written by the author is not always elaborate and hence cannot pass the message to the reader; whereas the interpreter, who has a better understanding of the text, interprets and presents in a better way than that of the author. Thus, the interpreter has a more important role to play than the author does. Here, the author is transcended but not the text. In other words, the text becomes more meaningful in the hands of the interpreter. As a great interpreter of Indian tradition, Dr Parnerkar explains the need for reinterpretation of the texts which is explained through the Poornavad philosophy.

CHAPTER 18

Waves of Bliss

As HAS been mentioned earlier, it is for the first time after the ancient Mahabharata War that the optimistic and scientific vision of Vedas has been presented to the world by Dr Ramachandra Parnerkar, in the Form-Relation doctrine of Poornavad. As also discussed at various points earlier in this book, Buddhism has had an impact on the philosophy of the majority of religions present in the world today; specifically, the Buddhist concept that believes, 'life is misery, suffering, sorrowful and impermanent'. This is negative and pessimistic; a partial truth but not the absolute truth. Through the doctrine of Poornavad, Dr Parnerkar proves that only the Poorna Purusha is the absolute truth, the ultimate reality.

Citing the *Tattiriya Upanishad's* statement '*Anand vai Brahma*', Dr Parnerkar shows that the Vedas maintain that bliss is God and God is bliss. Though world is made for pleasure and bliss, Poornavad, concurring with the astrophysics theory, states that every atomic and subatomic particle has its own anti-particle and that anti-particle is the cause of adversity in the material world Poornavad explains that divine bliss is truth and its antiparticle is experienced as misery, uncertainty and sorrow.

Dr Parnerkar was a scholar of Sanskrit and studied the Vedas as well as astrophysics, cosmology, along with other modern sciences and thereafter established his Form-Relation doctrine of Poornavad, which is the science of the inseparable oneness of Poorna; the entire universe including the unmanifest and the manifest material worlds. It proves that the Poorna Purusha is the sole cause of the world which has a form relation with the Poorna Purusha.

18.1 Bhrugu Undertakes Investigation of Brahman[1]

> *bhrgurvaivdrunih, varunampitaramupasasdra,*
> *adhlhibhagavobrahmeti, tasmdetatprovdca,*
> *annamprdnamcaksussrotram mano vacant iti.*
> *tarn hovdca, yatovdimdnibhutdni jay ante, yenajdtdnijlvanti,*
> *yatprayantyabhisamvisanti, tad vijijndsasva, tad brahmeti*
> *satapo' tapyata, sa tapas taptvd.*

Bhrugu, the son of Varuna, approached his father Varuna and said, 'Venerable Sir, teach me *Brahman*.' He explained to him thus: matter, life, sight, hearing, mind, speech. To him, he said further: 'That, verily, from which these beings are born, that, by which, when born they live, that into which, when departing, they enter. That, seek to know. That is *Brahman*.' He performed austerity (of thought). Having performed austerity, the father Varuna teaches his son Bhrugu, the sacred wisdom. This fundamental definition of *Brahman* as that from which the origin, continuance and dissolution of the world comes is of *Ishvara* who is the world-creating, world-sustaining, and world-dissolving God.

Cp. T 'am the first and the last and the living one.' Revelation XIII. 8.

Brahman is the cause of the world as the substratum *(adhisthdna)* (S), as the material cause *(upaddna)* of the world, as gold is the material cause of gold ornaments, as the instrumental cause *(nimitta)* of the world. Madhva.

---

[1] Subsections 18.1 to 18.6 have referred to S. Radhakrishnan, *Principal Upanishads*, Harper Collins, 2006.

Austerity is the means to the perception of Brahman, *tapas* is spiritual travail, *brahma-vijndra-sddhana*. S. Cp. Aeschylus, 'Knowledge comes through sacrifice/ *Agamemnon*, 250.

18.2 Matter is Brahman

annambrahmetivyajdndt, annddhyevakhalvimdnibhutdnjdyante,
annenajdtdr.jivanti, annamprayantyabhisamvisanh
tad vijndya, punarevavarunampitaramupasasdra,
adhihbhagavobrahmeti.
tarn hovdca, tapasd brahma vijijndsasva, tapobrahmeti,
satapo' tapyata, sa tapas taptvd.

He knew that matter is *Brahman*. For truly, beings are born from matter, when born, they live by matter, and into matter, when departing they enter.

Having known that, he again approached his father Varunj and said, 'Venerable Sir, teach me *Brahman*.'

To him he said, 'Through austerity, seek to know *Brahman Brahman* is austerity. He performed austerity; having performed austerity,

The first suggested explanation of the universe is that everything can be explained from matter and motion. On second thoughts, we realize that there are phenomena of life and reproduction which require another principle than matter and mechanism. The investigator proceeds from the obvious and outer to the deeper. The pupil approaches the teacher because he feels that the first finding of matter as the ultimate reality is not satisfactory.

18.3 Life is Brahman

prdnobrahmetivyajdndt, prdndddhyevakhalvimdnibhutdnijdyante,
prdnenajdtdnijlvanti, prdnamprayantyabhisam.visanti.
tad vijndya, punarevavarunampitcramupasasdra,
adhihibhagavobrahmeti
tarn hovdca, tapasd brahma vijijndsasva, tapobrahmeti, satapo'
tapyata, sa tapas taptvd.

He knew that life is *Brahman*. For truly, beings here are born from life, when born they live by life, and into life, when departing they enter.

Having known that, he again approached his father Varuna, and said: 'Venerable Sir, teach me *Brahman*.'

To him he said, 'Through austerity, seek to know *Brahman Brahman* is austerity.'

He performed austerity; having performed austerity.

[See C.U. I. ii. 5; VII. 15. i; K.U. III. 2-9; B.U. IV. I. 3.]

While the material objects of the world are explicable in terms of matter, plants take us to a higher level and demand a different principle. From materialism we pass to vitalism. But the principle of life cannot account for conscious objects. So the pupil, dissatisfied with the solution of life, approaches the father, who advises the son to reflect more deeply.

Matter is the context of the principle of life.

18.4 Mind is Brahman

Mano brahmetivyajdndt, manasohyevakhalv imam bhuiani jay ante, manasdjdtdnijivanti, manahprayantyabhisam-visanti.
tad vijndya, punarevavarunampitaramupasasdra,
adhihibhagavobrahmeti,
tam hovdca, tapasd brahma vijijndsasva, tapobrahmeti,
satapo' tapyata, sa tapas taptvd.

He knew that mind is *Brahman*. For truly, beings here are born from mind, when born, they live by mind and into mind, when departing, they enter.

Having known that, he again approached his father Varuna and said: 'Venerable Sir teach me *Brahman*.'

To him, he said, 'Through austerity seek to know *Brahman*. *Brahman* is austerity.'

He performed austerity; having performed austerity. When we look at animals, with their perceptual and instinctive consciousness we notice the inadequacy of the principle of life. As life outreaches matter, so does mind outreach life. There are forms of life without consciousness but there can be no consciousness without life. Mind in the animals is of a rudimentary character.

See *'Aitareya Aranyaka* II. 3. 2. 1-5. Cp. *Milindapanha* where *manasikdra*, rudimentary mind is distinguished from *panna* or *reason*. Animals possess the former and not the latter. Even mind cannot account for all aspects of the universe. In the world of man, we have the play of intelligence. Intelligence frames concepts and ideals, plans mean for their realization. So the pupil finds the inadequacy of the principle of mind and again approaches his father, who advises him to reflect further.

18.5 Intelligence of Brahman

Vijndnambrahmetivyajdndt,
vijndndddhyevakhalvimdnibhutdnijdyante, vijndnenajdtdnijivanti,
vijndnamprayanty a bhisamvisanti.
tad vijndya, punarevavarunampitaramupasasdra,
adhihibhagavobrahmeti;
tarn hovdca, tapasd brahma vijijndsasva, tapobrahmeti;
satapo' tapyata, sa tapas taptvd.

He knew that intelligence is *Brahman*. For truly, beings here are born from intelligence, when born, they live by intelligence and into intelligence, when departing, they enter.

Having known that, he again approached his father Varuna, and said, 'Venerable Sir, teach me *Brahman*.'

To him, he said, 'Through austerity, seek to know *Brahman*. *Brahman* is austerity.' [He performed austerity; having performed austerity].

Intelligence again is not the ultimate principle. The categories of matter, life, mind and intelligence take us higher and higher and each is more comprehensive than the preceding. Men with their conflicting desires, divided minds, oppressed by dualities are not the final products of evolution. They have to be transcended. In the intellectual life there is only a seeking. Until we transcend it, there can be no ultimate finding. Intellectual man, who uses mind, life and body is greater than mind, life and body but he is not the end of the cosmic evolution as he has still a secret aspiration. Even as matter contained life as its secret destiny and had to be delivered of it, life contained mind and mind contained intelligence and intelligence contains spirit as its secret destiny and presses to be delivered of it. Intelligence does not exhaust the possibilities of consciousness and cannot be its highest expression. Man's awareness is to be enlarged into a super consciousness with illumination, joy and power. The crown of evolution is this deified consciousness.

18.6 Bliss is Brahman

Dnandobrakmetivyajdndt, dnandhyevakhalvimdnibhutdnijdyante, dnandenajdtdnijivanti, dnandamprayantyabhisamvisanti, saisdbhdrgavivdrunlvidyd, paramevyomanpratisthitd, yaevamvedapratititsthati, annavdnannddobhavati, mahdnbhavati, prajaydpasubhir brahma-varcasenamahdnkirtyd.

He knew that *Brahman* is bliss. For truly, beings here are born from bliss, when born, they live by bliss and into bliss, when departing, they enter.

This wisdom of Bhrugu and Varuna, established in the highest heaven, he who knows this, becomes established. He becomes possessor of food and eater of food. He becomes great in offspring and cattle and in the splendor of sacred wisdom; great in fame.

The higher includes the lower and goes beyond it. *Brahman* is the deep delight of freedom.

The Upanishad suggests an analogy between the macrocosm, nature and the microcosm, man, an equation between intelligibility and being. The ascent of reality from matter to God as one of increasing likeness to God is brought out. While man has all these five elements in his being, he may stress one or the other, the material or the vital or the mental or the intellectual or the spiritual. He who harmonizes all these is the complete, everything.

My Master Dr V.R. Parnerkar explains how bliss is God: the entire universe is made up of thoughts that are positive and negative, optimistic and pessimistic, constructive and destructive as a result of the divine particles and the anti-particles. But if our vision is divine and sublime we can convert any pessimistic thought into an optimistic and encouraging one. The entire universe has three dimensional energies: constructive, destructive, and divine. We never think about or recognize the divine particles of the universe that have tremendous power to convert our destructive energies into divine energies, causing us to think and act in a positive and constructive manner.

He agrees with the Astro-Physics theory that every particle has its own anti-particle. Anti-particles are seen in daily life in the form of the devilish, destructive mind. This destructive angle is the reality of our life and even if we don't think of bad things, we fear them. But Dr Parnerkar doesn't support escapism. He says hope for the best and prepare for the worst. Our mindset should become pro-conflict, i.e., prepared to tackle adversity. Bliss is God, while sorrows, miseries and adversity are the devil. Conquering the devil restores real pleasure and joy to life. Therefore, life is a challenge as well as an opportunity. Think about the opportunity; convert every penalty corner into a goal and win the match of life, says my Master.

Patience and concentration of the mind make us stable and confident. There is bliss in confidence and sublimity. See the sublime in the eyes of mother feeding her child; the confidence in the eyes of a Captain who wins the match. See the sun rise in the morning. Look at the birds singing in the air and the cosmic rays dancing on the waves of sea and striking the rocks. Listen to their music and enjoy their dance. Nature is the major source of divine bliss. Sages who follow the Vedic tradition sit in contemplation in the pre-dawn hours under the open sky. Sky above and mud below. The rays of the rising sun reflect divine and joyous bliss and these sages transmit their divine bliss to us. Nature creates bliss, but we have moved away from nature. When divine particles become part of any personality they transform that person into someone who contributes greatly to humanity, such as Lord Rama, Krishna, Jesus Christ, the Buddha.

Bliss is real. The Vedas are bliss-centric literature and we should develop/create a bliss-centric vision. Poornavad has investigated this optimistic vision of the Vedas. Dr Parnerkar says the Poorna contains both, divine bliss and earthly sorrow. These are two sides of the same coin. We should think of the reasons behind sorrowful events. We see with our material eyes and see a material world, whereas the world is three-dimensional: intellectual, divine and material.

Dr Parnerkar explains that the materil world is governed by divine energies and the Vedas, too, speak of prayer to the divine energies—the sun, the fire, etc. These are divine forms of the universe. By denying this reality, we face severe miseries. On the other hand, if we are able to perceive through our third eye (i.e., see the divine) we feel and realize the world of bliss, experience waves of bliss.

In 1913, Dr Rabindranath Tagore was awarded the Noble Prize in Literature, because of his sublime expression of divine nature in his work *Geetanjali*. He expressed the beauty of bliss that lay in the inner mind. Irish poet, dramatist and author William Butler Yeats, who was awarded the Noble Prize in Literature in 1923, wrote about his habit of contemplation for a couple of hours before sunrise every day. He had studied the Upanishads and this was the impact of the Vedic tradition on him. Tagore, too, could experience divine energy and bliss that he expressed through his great work *Geetanjali*. Dr Parnerkar too, always asks us to create a vision of sublime divine beauty and bliss.

Reading Rabindranath Tagore's *Geetanjali*, gives us the strength to strike the root of the heart. Our heart is full of divine bliss, it's just that we have to remove the cover of ignorance and fear. Dr Parnerkar says that bliss is real; it is sorrows that are unreal. Don't say that our world is unreal, an illusion. It feels unreal because we ignore the true nature of the material world. We fail to understand Avidya and label it as the cause of sorrow. Avidya is the knowledge of material world which has been denied by Buddhism and later by Shankaracharya and that denial still has an impact on world philosophy. Therefore, Dr Parnerkar asks us to refer to the *Katha Upanishad*, which tells us that after passing through the six vyahrities (Bhu, Bhuva, Swaha, Maha, Janah, and Tapah) one ascends to the seventh layer of space which is Satya, the world of Brahma; the root of the bliss of universe.

Bliss is universal. Anyone can reach this root of universal bliss by performing yogic practices like meditation, contemplation and penance, all of which make the heart pure and sublime. The Vedic sages reached that seventh stage, which is also known as heaven, the world of God. Now it has been discussed by modern physics also. The stage of realization of Ultimate Truth is the state of transcendence. It means only bliss, waves of bliss. Bliss is immortal and sorrows are mortal. See the beauty of the Lake Geneva in Switzerland, the beauty of the Mansarovar of Mount Kailasa. My friends, I pray that the waves of bliss may strike your heart so that you realize the bliss not needed. Bliss is the pure form of consciousness. Because of my master, Dr V. R. Parnerkar, I have become the beneficiary of the infinite waves of Bliss from the Supreme Lord.

CHAPTER 19

Divine Experiences in Worship

THE HIMALAYAS are a popular destination for those in search of peace of mind and silent solitude. Therefore, we see that people from the East and West seek the shelter of such a divine land. But Dr Parnerkar's Poornavad states that it is not necessary to go to the Himalayas in search of peace. Peace lies within you. You only have to realize it through the different paths—devotion, yoga and worship—and by the grace of God through the Guru.

We have very little understanding of the unmanifest all living beings on earth being influenced by unmanifest energy. We usually think only of the superficial manifest causes and so see the effects also superficially. When Dr Parnerkar states that human problems can be solved by intelligence, effort and help from others, he includes the unmanifest as well through the medium of the divine. He has given deep thought to the question of what should we do to gain control over life so that we can live a successful, happy life. Today our understanding of philosophy is centered on spiritual intelligence. The roots of our thoughts and the solutions to our problems can be found in the universe, because the entire universe is made up of thoughts.

Dr Parnerkar shares with us the secrets of the composition of the universe, which, he says, has 50 per cent constructive energy, 30 per cent deconstructive energy and 20 per cent divine energy. When there is an imbalance between constructive and destructive energies, the 20 per cent divine energy gets activated. This 20 per cent divine energy turns to our side only if we take some action with regard to the divine, such as worshipping or invoking the grace of God through a Guru such as Dr Parnerkar, who himself realized the unmanifest Nirguna Brahma and Saguna Shri Ganesha and was divinely directed to help needy disciples in their religious, moral and material life.

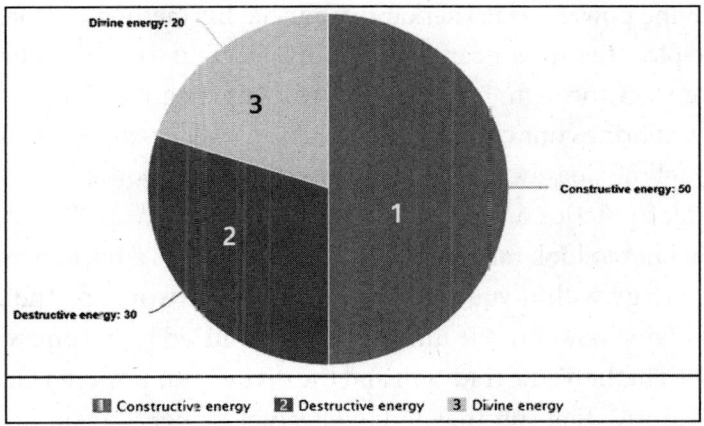

Universal Energy

Dr Parnerkar says when our efforts are insufficient, the divine energy in the universe helps us through our worship. All the religious leaders give only spiritual talks, but Dr Parnerkar says we do not need spiritual talks and spiritual thoughts as much as we need a divine solution which will help us to be successful in life. Material power is double-edged: both constructive and destructive; while divine energies are always constructive. However, we do not know how to harness the divine energies fully, and the same goes with spirituality. With the help of the Guru, we can access divine power and use its 100 per cent positive and active energy. This energy exists in the unmanifest universe. The unmanifest is more powerful than manifest and the Guru helps disciples through worship because he knows how to divert and utilize this divine power.

Worship is the regular chant of a specific deity given by the Guru; a sort of meditation. The power of your daily chanting of the mantra given to you by the Guru, combined with the divine grace of the Guru, can create success even in an emergency. People normally call such happenings miracles, but Dr Parnerkar calls this utilizing the divine power of the Guru. He notes that most intellectuals and scientists do not acknowledge the existence of such a divine power in the universe. Having acquired this divine energy by doing some yogic practices for a long time and after some practical experience of the application of such divine power, Dr Parnerkar introduced his method of worship to his disciples. The author can vouch for the fact that we can acquire such divine energy through the method of worship taught by Dr Parnerkar, and that it brings our constructive efforts to a successful conclusion.

Though he does occasionally expose his divine power, but it is not his regular practice and Dr Parnerkar strongly advises disciples and followers not to look for or depend on miracles. His advice is: build up divine energy within yourself by way of regular worship. The 20 per cent of divine power of the universe can be utilized by anyone who has deep faith in the Vedic tradition and the divinely empowered Guru. Dr Parnerkar says that spiritual and intellectual thoughts are of no use to the common man, who wants some assurance and moral support from the divine; someone to say 'Don't fear, I am with you.'

Dr Parnerkar also says worship alone won't work in regular practice, five other characteristics—Naipunya (expertise), Yojakta (planning), Loksangrah (public contact), Lokmat (public opinion), Kaal Dnyan (sense and knowledge of time)—must be added. And as for God and religion, Dr Parnerkar advises not spending more than fifteen to thirty minutes a day. He asks his disciples to be technocrats and be proud of their country, and for those who live abroad, he says they should be honest to their adopted homeland and prove their ability and utility in that country.

This chapter shares some experiences of disciples with the divine powers vested in the guru. Some have been narrated to the author who has shared them below and some have been shared by the disciples themselves. The author shares his own experiences too. The first two examples belong to the period of the Founder of Poornavad Dr R.P. Parnerkar and then of his successor and son Dr Vishnu Maharaj Parnerkar, 1980 onwards. Dr R.P. Parnerkar was called as 'Bhau', and Dr Vishnu Maharaj as 'Dada' by followers.

Mrs Yesu Godbole's Death Avoided (as told to the author)

Mrs Yesu Godbole, a disciple of Dr Parnerkar's, was visiting her brother in Kanhur when she went down with fever. Her health started deteriorating as both her lungs were weak and the fever would not abate. The fact that she was pregnant, complicated matters more. As her condition worsened, a physician Dr Kale had to be called in. By the time he reached, she was gasping for breath and he gave her an injection that helped her to breathe. The situation had been brought under control, but she felt that her time was running out. She, therefore, called her husband and told him to call Guru Parnerkar. 'I want to touch his feet at my last moment,' she pleaded. 'I do not have much time. My last moment is coming closer. Please call my Guru.'

Her husband immediately requested her brother, Mr Gokhale, to go Srirampur where Dr Ramachandra Parnerkar had gone on a visit. Upon reaching Srirampur her brother told Dr Parnerkar everything. Realizing his disciple was in trouble and possibly on her deathbed, Dr Parnerkar immediately packed his bags and left with Mr Gokhale. En route, at Nagar, he asked civil surgeon Dr Pawar to join them. Once they reached Kanhur, Guru Parnerkar asked the Dr Kale to be called so that he and Dr Pawar could both examine Yesu and give their opinion.

The doctors did so and told him that both her lungs were not working, she was anaemic and could pass away at any moment. Thereafter, Dr Pawar took his leave to return to Nagar. Next, Guru Parnerkar called Bhaukaka (senior member from Poornavad family). He asked him to go and see Yesu, but himself remained seated. Bhaukaka went near her and began to smile. Guru Parnerkar asked him why he was smiling. Bhaukaka replied, 'Yesu can't die even if she falls on a rock!' He said he saw Yamdev standing there and Guru Parnerkar doing pradakshina (circumambulating, i.e., going around, the deity a certain number of times in worship). Soon after Dr Parnerkar also left Kanhur, but before leaving told Bhaukaka, Gokhale and Yesu's husband to start chanting the *Vishnu Sahasranama* (the thousand names of Vishnu) thrice a day ten times each for thirteen days, and then give Yesu holy water (tirth) to drink.

While all this was being carried out, Dr Kale came to examine Yesu every day. On the twelfth day, the patient's health improved without medicines. Thereafter, she recovered completely and had a normal delivery. Doctor Kale was so impressed by this incident that he started worshipping Guru Parnerkar too.

Dr Kale's Diabetes is Cured (as told to the author): Dr Parnerkar's Siddhis and Practice

Having been introduced to Dr Parnerkar in such unusual circumstances, Dr Kale went to Srirampur for a proper Guru darshan and told him about his own health problems. 'Maharaj,' he said, 'I have problems with my blood pressure and I have diabetes. Please suggest something.' Guru Parnerkar replied kindly, 'Don't worry. Have some tea with me before you leave. Nothing will happen. Have this sweet tea with me for fifteen days.' On the fifteenth day Dr Kale did a urine test for sugar and checked his blood pressure. Both were completely normal without him having taken any medicines. Thereafter, he never faced any problem regarding his health.

Dr Parnerkar had acquired eight siddhis by the practice of Vedic yogic methods. He had first tried these out on himself. After getting positive results, he used these for the benefit of the disciples. Realizing that supernatural divine powers had been awakened, he started helping others. He cured many of disease, by giving them holy water to drink. Some were saved even from death. But instead of making this a habit, he taught them how to worship, so that their divine powers awakened. He gave mantras of specific deities to his disciples and advised them not to look always for miracles. Miracles were the exception and not the rule.

People tend to use Gurus for these divine miracles, but by using these powers again and again they lose their divinity. The power to handle mundane problems depends on each one's worship. Keep your problems in front of God while you worship. Communicate with God and He will definitely help you. This experiment by Dr Parnerkar is his outstanding contribution to Vedic philosophy in the modern perspective. The divine experiences that the disciples get, are the positive results.

Author's Introduction to Poornavad and His Own Divine Experiences

In 1969 December, at the Datta Janma (birth anniversary of god Dattatreya) celebrations, my professor at Poona University, Dr N.C. Joglekar, introduced me to the founder of the Poornavad philosophy, Dr Ramachandra Maharaj Parnerkar. I was highly impressed and influenced by the bright and divine appearance of the Master and touched my forehead to his holy feet. Since then, I became the undual part of this divine philosophical family and have followed the instructions of my Master.

The first thing that impressed me was his text on 'Sangharsh: The Conflict', which he calls 'the First Mantra of the struggle for excellence'. He says if you want peace and prosperity then prepare yourself to face conflict in life. He says that Lord Rama, Lord Krishna and even the Goddess Durga, used their weapons to fight evil and protect their children (mankind) from harm. The second instruction my Master gave me was to perform daily meditation and worship.

From 1980 onward, I came into contact with my Guru's son, Maharaj Dr Vishnu Parnerkar who became the head of the School of Poornavad Thought, following the demise of founder and Guru Dr Ramachandra Parnerkar.

Dr Vishnu Parnerkar, too, urges his disciples to meditate for half an hour, alongside ten to fifteen minutes of worship, as this strengthens our divine aspect. One who wants to be successful and satisfied in life should follow this path. Early morning is the best time to get positive and perfect results. One should learn the mode of worship and the mantras from a Guru. The fruits of this practice can be seen at three different levels—intellectual, divine and material—because the manifest Ishwara, Vishnu, represents the science of divine and material life, which provides us divine peace, prosperity and satisfaction. It is this author's experience that one can gain the transcendental experience while doing worship and meditation as per regular schedule.

We can get satisfaction of all the material pleasures by using our intelligence, but we cannot get peace and satisfaction. Many rich and famous personalities in the world are unhappy. Such famous personalities find it difficult to go to a psychiatrist or even to divine gurus and teachers. Hence Dr Parnerkar says the Vedas have suggested many ways to be self-reliant and complete. Dr Parnerkar himself learnt all these ways, got eight siddhis and then helped his disciples to succeed in life. He suggested a path to the divine that he had proven by experiment and experience.

Dr Parnerkar had attained to ability to not just see but to help advanced practitioners to see God and at least 5 per cent of his disciples experienced direct perception of God. At the end of his life, before departing, he transmigrated his eight siddhis to his son and successor, Dr Vishnu Maharaj Parnerkar in the guru-shishya tradition mentioned in the Vedas. His son was at that time practicing at Indore High Court as a Counsellor and Advocate. Upon becoming his father's successor, he took charge of the Poornavad family and became the Master Guru and the Chancellor of the Poornavad School of Thought. As a scholar of Sanskrit and the Vedas he helped his disciples with the advantages of these by adding a modern touch to them. And still he is obliging many of his disciples while working twenty out of twenty-four hours at the age of eighty. His followers are spread all over the world and giving their contribution to corporate sectors for the betterment of human excellence.

While discussing about these eight siddhis with the present Guru, I mentioned to him when Ramkrishna Paramhansa was on his deathbed, his favourite disciple Swami Vivekananda asked him whether he had used these eight siddhis. Swami Ramkrishna

Paramhansa said no. Swami Vivekananda then asked what good if would do if he took them, as both Guru and disciple were sanyasis and stoics. Dr Parnerkar says that Swami Vivekanand should have utilized these siddhis for the nation fight for Independence and for the prosperity of the nation.

Dr Parnerkar says that the Vedic tradition was the rishi (i.e., sages) tradition. All the rishis were married and the gurukul (or guru's family/lineage) was the rishi's household that accepted disciples as members of the family. These disciples studied, learnt and participated in all household activities. The importance of domestic life as shown in the Vedas also shows: (i) the importance given to women in that period; and (ii) that the way to happiness and prosperity is through the coordination of men and women. In the Vedas the women are found as daughters, sisters, wives, mothers, and as highly educated sages in their own right.

In his critique of Vedanata, Dr Parnerkar has asked if Lord Shiva and Goddess Parvati, Lord Narayana and Goddess Laxmi are married, then why did the Vedanta acharyas (teachers) not emulate them? Why remain unmarried and accept the sanyasa tradition? He says men and women living alone is against the laws of nature and the tradition of sanyasi rishis goes against the Vedic tradition, against the Vedas. It goes against production and creation. After marriage one has to often face more struggles (such as supporting a family etc.), he notes; the Vedanta acharyas taking sanyas can be misunderstood as running away from struggle.

Where there is life, there is struggle and conflict he has pointed out. He suggested a mindset that is prepared to overcome, to struggle as and when needed. Dr Parnerkar, having studied Particle Physics and accepted the theory of anti-particles in the universe, concluded that everybody had their own anti-mind too from which conflicts arose. Men-women, husband-wife, father-son, brothers, sisters and friends all struggle with each other from time to time. The *Shiva Purana* mentions a struggle between the divine couple Shiva and Parvati, who fought but did not go to the extreme of divorce. Other couples reflecting the Vedic tradition are Pandurang-Rukmini, Balaji-Padmini, Sita-Ram. All the gods and goddesses are married. Dr Parnerkar was a strong advocate of family life and advised people to find a way through the difficulties faced in family life by following Vedic traditions.

To be happy and successful one needs a guide, and Dr Vishnu Parnerkar suggests worship as a key to success. Today the way of yoga or of devotion are outdated. Today yoga means only physical exercises. The level of yoga that pierces six chakras and awakens the Kundalini is difficult to practice today, so Dr Parnerkar suggests worshipping the divine for just ten to fifteen minutes daily as this will help in solving our problems in daily life. Not just this, but such daily prayer helps us achieve bigger purposes and gives success in bigger tasks. More than God, Dr Parnerkar suggests, man needs God's grace. Those who pursue the path diligently and become worthy can realize the divine as Saguna and Nirguna (form and formless). I learned the major part of the Poornavad philosophy in the Vedic guru-shishya tradition with full devotion and deep faith in Dr Vishnu Maharaj.

First divine experience: I had different types of divine experiences when my Guru taught me meditation. I practiced daily in the evening. I enjoyed pleasant travel in space (astral travel) during meditation, by the grace and guidance of the Master. There is an invisible cord linked up with our spinal cord and the Guru protects this cord while his disciple is astral travelling. In the beginning Guru backs you and observes your ability and progress during meditation, and gradually he goes ahead and the disciple has to follow the Guru. The Guru increases his speed and looks at disciple to see how he follows him. There is an intuitional communication between the two—whenever the disciple finds any obstacle the Guru is automatically alerted and he helps the disciple. Such is the journey of meditation. This is the primary step of penance. Nevertheless, these are advanced techniques in themselves and one should not attempt such experiments.

In meditation, I saw beautiful colours and clouds around the stars and planets. I saw a group of white cows on an evergreen lawn on a hill and a bright sun, but the overall effect was cool and gave unimaginable pleasure. And only the Guru can ensure your soul's safe return to the body after astral travelling. The ability and divine power of the Guru is beyond our imaginations and capacity. The Guru is the Almighty God Poorna Purusha, who, because of his disciples, steps down and gives us parental affection. I am always obliged to His divine grace.

Second divine experience: After practicing the daily meditation for couple of years, one fine evening I was blessed with the vision of 'Smiling Ganesh' seated before me. There was no dialogue between us. But since then, I became ever joyous. My heart is filled with waves of bliss. I am never depressed by any adversity, what more does a happy and lucky man require in his life? I could write this book, *Know Thy Roots*, because of His teachings and His Divine grace for me.

Third Divine Experience: It was near about 2007 and we had gathered for Poornavad Parayana, a seven-day function. During this time we would hear the Philosophy Lecture Series presented by Guru Dr Vishnu Maharaj at Jagannath Puri—where Jesus Christ had learnt Sanskrit and the Vedas. During one of these lectures my Master said we should perform Vedic rituals with a sankalp (a special determination made for any purpose) and repeat A+U+M Mantra eleven times. He taught all of us about what a sankalp is and how to make it, and then told us about the most powerful mantra of Aum and how it should be pronounced. He also taught us the philology and phonology of Mantra. It was thus:

अथातो ब्रह्म जिज्ञासा, अथातो जीव जिज्ञासा, अथातोपूर्ण पुरुषअपरोक्षानुभूती,
भोगुरू अभिवादये

[I have curiosity to know thee Brahma. The Universe I have curiosity to know thy Dharma (this means Swadharma, which has nothing to do with the present concept of religion. It can be realized by the grace of God and Guru). The third curiosity to know the Jeeva, every being. Thus, the Trinity of Brahma (Science of Divinity), God of the

Universe (Dharma, spiritual knowledge), and the Jeeva (material life) plus its art of living (Avidya).][1]

I was following the instructions of my Master and performing the A+U+M mantra. During this period I, along with my better half Mrs Shobha, went to the Mahakaleshwar Temple in Ujjain in 2010 to worship and perform Abhishek of Shiva's Pindi. After performing worship, we came out from that main part of the temple and stood before the Nandi. Through him I was able to see the Shiva Pindi again and surprisingly I saw bright golden rays occupied the whole Garbhagriha (sanctum sanctorum) and from head to toe I saw Lord Vishnu in the form of Poorna Purusha with the Trinity of Vishnu, Vishwa and Shiva.

When I realized this divine perception of the Supreme Lord of Universe, Poorna Purusha, my Master complimented me and supported the divine perception. Such is my Master Dr Vishnu Maharaj who has given me everything which I desired. He can do anything beyond our imagination. Therefore, I experienced that reality is more beautiful than our imagination.

Incident at Niagara Falls, where Dr P. Kant and the author were present: We had gone to see Niagara Falls when this strange incident happened. A seagull sat observing Dr Kant (whom I address as Dada), where both of us were sitting. He observed him for an hour and Dada observed him too. Then he said, 'he won't leave without taking Prasad. Get whatever is there in the car.' After eating some puffed rice (murmure) and chanas (futani) from his hands, the seagull did three revolutions (pradakshinas) around Dada, touched his beak to Dada's feet as if to bow and then flew off. Dada was very happy. He said we had found a new person to carry on our work in America. In future Poornavad would expand here. **Saved from a storm in the sea:** In 2000, we paid a twenty-day visit to Australia from 1 to 20 May. It was raining there and it was also foggy at some places but we never had any issue.

---

1   Author's own translation.

'What is thy color, oh water? Just as that in which it is mixed.' I had a similar experience regarding Dada on this visit. The programmes had fewer disciples but more visitors. These visitors did not know even how to sit. I used to get irritable but Dada never reacted. He used to tell me, 'Slowly they will learn.' Such a great personality, but never shied away from adjustments. Dada gave a lecture on the topic 'Mother' on Mother's Day which is celebrated in that country on 14 May.

During this visit we planned to visit Ledim's grave (Ledim was a famous graveyard) on a boat with the Pingale family from Brisbane. My Swiss friend Catherine had warned me in advance to stay away from water. Yet we did not change our programme. It was Shri Bhau's (Dr R. P. Parnerkar) death anniversary. It was also supposed to be Jupiter's set and rise. We easily reached there and did Shraddh. It was already quite dark while returning, when a storm started suddenly and the sea became very rough. Very high waves took us up and then slammed us down forcefully. All the glass on the boat broke. There was water all over. No electricity and no way to contact anyone. There were almost 180 people on the boat. Except for me and Dada, everyone was vomiting. Mr Pingale's youngest daughter vomited on Dada's clothes.

We were as though seeing our deaths. Everyone was restless, including the captain. Dada said, 'The sea will rest only after meeting me.' I had a different doubt, so I told Dada, 'If required I will jump into the sea.' He just asked me not to worry. The captain suggested all should wear life jackets as the boat could break into pieces at any time. Dada told him to wait and said let us all chant the Ram Raksha stotram. Others were tired because of vomiting. Dada was peaceful. He touched the water after completely chanting Ram Raksha stotram. Having raged for almost two-and-a-half hours, the storm stopped. This reminded me of the Ganges, eager to touch Lord Shri Ram's feet, or the Yamuna, eager to touch Lord Shri Krishna's feet.

This was a very big spiritual experience for me. After the storm quietened, Dada asked the captain of the boat, 'Do you believe in God?' He said, 'Yes, I believe now.' That was the Jupiter set first and then rose.

This incidence showed me the father figure in my Guru, in a new light. Finally, after four hours the boat reached the shore and Dada said, 'Today God saved us all.'

Prof. V.P. Apte, Retd. Principal, Engineering College, Dombivli (in his own words)

I have heard of many disciples getting God realization but have not heard of anyone getting the divine experience. After peacefully listening to me, Maharaj told me to start doing the 'Shri Krishna Mantra' jap 108 times daily. This was Tuesday, 2 December 2003. I started the worship as directed by Maharaj and on 28 February 2005 I had the most unforgettable day of my life, because on this day I saw Lord Shri Krishna Himself in Vishnuroopa.

This is what happened: I was a little unwell. It was a very cold night and all my brother disciples were shivering with cold. In the darkness of the night, suddenly I saw a light and Lord Shri Vishnu appeared in front of me. The Lord hugged me and told me not to worry. Immediately, in a moment, there was darkness all over. But I can still feel that experience, that touch to date. I can prove this scientifically as well. After this 'Sagun Darshan' (a vision of the form of the Lord), I collapsed due to weakness and was admitted to the intensive care unit (ICU) in Shrikrishna Hospital.

The next day, Maharaj's youngest son came to meet me in the hospital with sweets. He conveyed Maharaj's message that I would be discharged from the hospital in the next two to three days and that my experience was indeed the divine experience. The doctor who had advised me to remain in hospital for five to six days, allowed me to go home in the next two to three days. Maharaj himself was waiting for me along with my family at home, even before I could reach home. My feelings after seeing the Guru who had helped me to see the Vishnuroopa, were beyond words.

After that, Maharaj called me to his house in Pune on 15 October 2006 and instructed me to worship Lord Shiva for the Formless Divine Experience (*Nirguna Sakshatkar*). Based on my experience I can safely say, nothing is impossible for Guru, who has the power to give everything. However, we should be worthy of receiving it. This is why, one should never challenge the divine Guru.

Mr Sunil Panditrao Jamkar, Hingoli (in his own words)

I would like to narrate an incident that happened with me. Guru helped me come out of a very big problem. This happened on 25 January 2000. I had shifted to Hingoli in 1999 for my children's education, from my village Hatala. We are a family of four; my wife Manisha, my children Mandvi and Rangnath, and myself. We had rented a two-room house and I used to go to Hatala sometimes to look after the farms. My parents also used to visit us at Hingoli time to time. Since my elder sister Vandana also lived in Hingoli, my mother used to visit her for a day when in Hingoli. On 25 January 2000, I picked my mother up from my sister's house and dropped her at home and since the next day was Republic Day (26 January), I went to Hingoli market and bought some stuff. At around eight in the evening, I parked my bike in the compound and entered my house. Upon seeing my mother there, I asked her, 'who got you here from sister's house?' Everyone thought I might have misunderstood something.

Later I started feeling heaviness in my head and went to sleep without breaking my Friday fast. The next morning I had to get up early and drop the children to school for the Republic Day function. I dropped Rangnath to school and on the way back I realized I was not able to see anything, but somehow managed to reach home. I told the whole thing to my wife. We called up the owner of our house and together went to meet Dr Bhale. Upon checking, the doctor said this was due to haemoglobin deficiency and recommended medicines. Despite taking medicine for two to three days, I still continued having the same condition. Then I told my father in Hatale, who got worried.

After thinking it over a thought we decided to speak to Maharaj. Next day he was to visit the village Selu. So, we all went to my aunt's house. Maharaj was staying close by. As we reached Maharaj's meeting and entered, he said, 'Come Sunil babu.' I went in and was helped to sit in front of Maharaj. My father narrated the whole thing to Maharaj, who asked for a Panchang (an ephemeris). He looked through it and told me to start repairs on the house on 11 February. I was not able to understand as I couldn't see anything. But Maharaj insisted on the repairs and went inside his room.

After a while he called for me to massage his feet. As I was going in, I stumbled on the threshold of the room and fell at his feet. He asked me if I really could not see and I said yes. He asked me to massage his feet. As I started doing that, he described to me the place where this happened. He told me to go visit Dr Deshpande in Aurangabad. All this was happening due to the bad energies around. He said the stone that he had asked me to wear on my finger had saved me, otherwise this problem could have been bigger. He further asked me to do Bhoomipoojan on 11 February and do some construction work till I exhausted all my money. Then I was to do a pooja (prayer ceremony) in that house and then go and live in that house. He assured me that after this, till the time I was alive, nothing could go wrong with me. He said, 'I will always be at your back.'

I did as per Maharaj's instructions on 11 February and surprisingly, that day onwards I could see clearly.

Mrs Chaya Hinge, Nagar (in her own words)

Before going out of station, we would always seek permission from Maharaj. When we wanted to go to Badrikedar on 14 June 1999, Maharaj was at Shrirampur. I went there to seek his permission. He gave me a five-rupee coin, a red flower and his blessings, saying, 'have a safe journey'. Whichever temple we used to visit, he used to give us money to give at that temple. That day he gave money but didn't tell me which temple that money was to be given. After reaching home, I realized that in my hurry to leave I had forgotten to ask him this. However, I placed the money and the red flower in a plastic bag and kept it in my purse.

We actually do not understand what is God's will. Sometimes what happens is way different than what we decide should happen. God being very kind, keeps giving us signals. But we should understand that and behave accordingly. We experienced this when we went to Badrikedar.

This is what happened: we departed on 14 June 1999 from Nagar for Haridwar. At seven in the morning on 16 June 1999, we left Haridwar by cab to go to Kedarnath, and reached Gaurikund at 4.30 p.m. after a difficult journey of 225 kilometres (km). Gaurikund to Kedarnath is a distance of 14 km. The next morning after taking a bath in the hot springs at Gaurikund and after the pooja, we decided to leave for Kedarnath darshan. Since no vehicle is allowed to go up to Kedarnath temple, one has to cover this distance in a palanquin or sedan chair, or on horseback or simply by walking. The route at that time was very narrow and unmetalled. My husband and I were to go on horseback while the kids decided to walk. The previous night there was non-stop heavy rain and thunderstorms. When we left in the morning, it was still raining. Our children Abhijeet and Smita had left earlier as they planned to walk.

We then went to the 'rent a horse' stand to go to Kedarnath, and mounted the horses. The horses must have walked hardly a few steps when suddenly my mind got a signal. I told the horse owner, 'we want to get down from the horse.' He kept saying, 'Don't worry madam! Nothing will happen.' But on my insistence, he helped me get down. Though my husband's horse was fine too, I asked him to get down as well. He was confused as to what exactly was the matter. But as soon as he got off the horse's back, just about five to seven feet away we saw a landslide had begun. Suddenly there was a lot of noise. All the horses started getting wild and running all over. That moment I thought had we not got down from the horses, we would have been under these huge rocks. A chill went down my spine with this thought.

By God's and Sadguru's grace, we were saved from a life-threatening situation. We simply touched the step there leading to Kedarnath temple, apologized to God for not being able to go for darshan and simply folded our hands. We somehow managed to escape from the crowds and went and sat in a small roadside hotel. The rain had started pouring down again. Just then some people came in saying there had been landslides on the mountains and so the roads were closed. The people who had reached there had to come back leaving their journeys halfway. Our children had left early in the morning and had not yet returned.

Throughout the landslide in front of our eyes, I was constantly chanting Sadguru's name and my heart was filled with gratitude. We were not able to understand what to do. Injured people were being brought down. I was still chanting Sadguru's name but as a mother I was scared. I was certain my children would be fine yet many thoughts were crossing my mind. And even as I was praying, Abhijeet and Smita returned, but they were unhappy because we were not able to go to Kedarnath. We were feeling sad because we came this far for a darshan and had to return without due to a natural calamity. But thinking that He and Sadguru saved us, we bowed down to them.

Mr Ajay Jagirdar, Hyderabad (in his own words)

'In 1997, I started worshipping Maharaj. Before that, an astrologer had told me that at the age of thirty-one, I could face a threat to my life. This had always stayed at the back of my mind. Once I had a nightmare and I felt it was a bad omen. In December 1997, I went to Parner and told Maharaj about my dream. He simply said, "Don't worry. I am with you." I was relieved and returned home.

'In the first week of January 1998, I had an asthma attack. My wife, Anushree, informed my younger brother Ashwin. At 3 a.m., he came with our family doctor who prescribed some medicines for me, gave me an injection and left. Within a few moments, I collapsed. I was shifted to a hospital with the help of our neighbours. With Maharaj's grace, I received the timely treatment and was saved. For three days I was in the ICU. Maharaj spoke to my sister and brother-in-law in Aurangabad and conveyed his blessings. I am completely aware that I owe my second lease of life to Sadguru's blessings. He has gifted me this life and so I dedicate everything to his feet. I only wish my conduct will be as per his guidance.'

Mr Prashant Aade (paraphrased in author's words)

I have been following the work of Dr Parnerkar since 1981. As the years passed, my bond with Dr Vishnu Maharaj deepened through numerous blessings and shared experiences. He recognized my spiritual progress, once gifting me a beautiful idol of Lord Ganesha, subtly indicating our evolving relationship. His words and actions always held layered meanings, offering guidance through unspoken understanding. Whether it was during my daughter's serious accident, where she saw the divine form of Maharaj offering her comfort, or his spontaneous offers of help during financial difficulty, his presence was constant, compassionate, and transformative. Every moment shared with him, from poetic gatherings to miraculous escapes from danger, felt charged with grace. Even when I lost a precious bracelet during an interview journey, it was his teachings that kept me steady and joyful, reminding me that divine work and discipline always prevail over worldly setbacks.

Over the years, Dr Vishnu Maharaj's divine interventions continued to shape my life: from arranging my daughter's marriage on a spiritually significant date to reviving me after a paralyzing stroke. In moments of despair, he infused me with new life and purpose, guiding me not just through spiritual paths but even practical life decisions like purchasing a new home. His blessings were not limited to rituals; they were acts of real, grounded support, like arranging the publication of my book or visiting my home to personally bless my space. His divine energy was always near, often making its presence felt through subtle signs or powerful dreams.

My journey with my Guru has been one of miracles and transformation, anchored in humility, devotion and trust. Words can hardly encapsulate the scope of his omnipresence in my life, but my soul continues to bow at the feet of this extraordinary master.

Mrs Geeta Hemant Dashrath, Pune (in her own words)

One question that the entire human race is facing since the evolution is 'what is right and what is wrong' and I am no exception to this. Our happiness or sadness, our success or failure, our satisfaction or regrets depend mostly on taking the right decision at the right time, but again we are faced with yet another question, what is right and which is the right time? To answer these questions and to guide us, to lead us on the right path we need Guru, guide or a mentor. I feel so fortunate that I have been blessed with a Guru, Dr Parnerkar Maharaj, who is also my guide, my mentor, my constant source of inspiration. All those questions have been answered by his philosophy called Poornavad.

As a child I was a very ordinary person, very average in studies, didn't have any great talent, didn't have any great ambitions. On finishing schooling, that too with average marks, my parents decided to send me to Fergusson College in Pune for further studies. When I came here all the more I realized that I was good for nothing. In the first year I didn't make any good friends, because no one would really notice me. I felt very insignificant and spent most of my time alone. I even wanted to give up studies and go back to my hometown Nanded.

As a child I had always heard that whenever you have any problem, if you are unwell or feeling sad remember to chant Guru Maharaj's name and ask for his help with great belief and be sure that he will help you; so I would do the same. Every time I was feeling weak and helpless I would pray to Dr Parnerkar Maharaj and ask him to give me strength and guide me. In eleventh standard I barely passed with very less marks. My parents were disappointed and worried about my future, for the first time I felt very small and could not face the disappointment of my parents. That year when I went to Parner for the Utsav, I heard stories from people, how their lives had changed by wearing a particular jewel given by Dr Vishnu Maharaj. So I thought I should also get one.

Luckily that year he had come to Pune, so I went for his Darshan and asked for a jewel. He asked me why I wanted it, and I said I want a good and happy life for myself and also to be good at studies so that my parents are not disappointed with me. He gave me jewel to wear in a ring and said, 'Do everything with focus and the result will be good. Don't worry about marks just study well you will get good marks.'

Those words were really life changing for me, my life took a right turn after that. I started to do well in studies, my parents were very happy. I also took the path of worship that year, because of which I started doing everything with mindfulness. For the first time I was comfortable with my own self. Like everyone else, my life has been a roller-coaster ride, there have been many ups and downs. But Dada Dr V.R. Parnerkar has always guided us and has assured us that if you do worship regularly with great belief, you will sail through any difficult situations. Those words are really magical and have given me strength to keep looking forward.

By God's grace and blessings of Dr V.R. Parnerkar I am living a good purposeful and meaningful life, supported by my husband Hemant Dashrath. Both my children, Rajat and Riya, have taken worship, and are walking on the right path which would lead to an incredible life of success, happiness and peace.

Mrs Shampa Tushar Joshi, Jacksonville in Florida (in her own words)

It is my great pleasure to share my divine experience of being a Poornavad disciple with you all. In the nine years spent in USA we always experienced the Gurukripa (Guru's mercy) every day. My husband used to get a new project in a new city every year, but the transition from one state to another state used to be so smooth. Challenges used to get solved and people used to wonder how come you guys are so lucky and happy even though you have to keep moving so frequently? And how come you have so many family friends in each state? But the thing is, I really love to visit new places and meet new people, and that has been possible because of moving from place to place.

I would say it is Gurukripa that we could stay in and see so many places in USA like California, Texas, Georgia, New York, New Jersey, Maryland, and Florida. We met Poornavad family members at each place. My parents came here and we could take them everywhere we had such a wonderful time together. My most memorable moment I would say is the New York trip with my parents. That could very much possibly be because of the blessings of My Most Revered Guru Maharaj.

People experience loneliness but we never ever experience it, in fact we meet so many families, that it is like home away from home.

Each and every desire, whether small or big, has been fulfilled because of blessings of my Guru Dr Vishnu Maharaj Parnerkar. We never felt strange anywhere, in fact all our efforts were successful and we had such a wonderful experience everywhere. I would definitely say with my own experience that I learned how to live life happily with maximum satisfaction because of my Guru Vishnu Maharaj Parnerkar.

CHAPTER 20

Mother

My MOTHER was a pivotal force in my life. She was my strength, my guide and an amazing woman. I lost her on December 1969—a very sad day in my life. It was the final year of my graduation and within couple of months I had to face my examinations. I was thrown into an ocean of tears, with most of my time spent in recollecting her memories. My examinations started and the first paper was English Literature, and the first question was an essay. There were five to six options, and I chose to write on the option, 'The Personality I shall Never Forget'. I thought about writing it on Mahatma Gandhi, the father of the Nation. But just as I started writing, I remembered another personality that had shaped my life, who was intelligent, gentle, caring, and upon whose teachings I strive to lead my life and wrote instead about 'Mother'.

The personality of a mother is unforgettable, unparalleled and I wrote 'Mother is the first heroine of the world.' It was truly a divine experience that helped me to write further on Mother. I suddenly recalled a mythological story about Lord Ganesha's childhood. He and his brother Lord Kartikeya were told by their parents that whoever of the two circumambulated the three worlds first would win. Lord Kartikeya at once set off on his vehicle, the peacock, confident that his brother Ganesha would not be able to complete this challenge on his vehicle, the tiny mouse. How he would manage to win the race on a small mouse?

Meanwhile, Ganesha sat calmly and quietly sitting behind his mother, Parvati who began telling him to hurry up. But Ganesha was still calm and quiet. The mother was worried, and thought what is this child all about!? By this time, having gone around the three worlds Kartikeya had almost reached home, when Ganesha finally got up, he circumambulated his parents thrice and then sat down again. His mother asked him the logic behind his taking three rounds of his parents and Ganesha explained that parents were the universe. Mother Parvati was deeply moved and from that day on Ganesha is worshipped first among the gods. Before starting any Vedic rituals, Lord Ganesha is worshipped. And he is known as 'Maha Ganapati', Brahmanaspathi, Lord Ganesha. He has become the trademark of knowledge and wisdom.

The roots of Lord Ganesha's wisdom lie in his mother Parvati - the mother's womb is the root of our thought of wisdom. Dr Parnerkar mentions that the Vedas have given priority to the mother as '*Matru devo bhava*' (revere your Mother as God). The mother is the first to whom we should bow deeply. Dr Parnerkar says that everything in Poornavad is three-dimensional, including the mother energy. Every form of Devi (goddess) is worshipped, as a daughter she is Kanyakumari, as a wife she is Laxmi of Narayana, the Lord Vishnu. And in the mother form she is the mother of Lord Ganesha.

An ideal example of mother is Mother Anusaya, the mother of Lord Dattatraya who is the symbol of Trinity of the Poorna Purusha—Brahma, Vishnu and Mahesh—the integral forms. Mother is the hallmark of trust and faith in India. Because of its strong mothers, their unconditional love and sacrifices, India has had many talented generations. Therefore, because of their extraordinary characteristics, Dr Parnerkar says that power of women should not be neglected. It is the subject matter of Avidya, he says.

The elephant-head of Ganesha is also the symbol of a cool head with mystic wisdom—one who knows all the secrets of this universe and its applied benefits. The instrument in his hand is the symbol of self-control and self-management. He is the master of all the Vidyas and Avidya, and you will always find his wives Riddhi (wealth, prosperity) and Siddhi (success, accomplishments) beside him at all times. Those who worship Lord Ganesha and his mother can get all the means to attain prosperity and peace with the bliss of transcendence.

CHAPTER 21

Some Thoughts in Closing: On Literature, Life, Philosophy and Poornavad

DR PARNERKAR explains the importance of literature in human life; and philosophy being part of life, it is interesting to think about it in a comparative manner, with literature. Literature plays an important role in making human life well-cultured. Literature impacts social interactions whereas social interactions give birth to literature. But the ideal character, as explained in literature, living an ideal life, is never seen in reality. For example, there has been no Rama except in the Ramayana and there is no second Dnyaneshwar outside the *Dnyaneshwari*. Literature is considered to be the mirror of society as it depicts society as it is, during any particular time-frame.

When social changes bring new needs into human life, it is philosophy that tries to answer questions that question civilization. Life can be created out of philosophy. There is a lot of scope for experiment in philosophy. Philosophy holds high values whereas literature narrates virtues. So one can understand and learn virtues. Philosophy explains biographies of people living now. Since this is based on reality there is no scope for imagination, as in literature. Literature narrates biographies of people who are no more. Of course, there can be some exceptions.

Literature awakens one's emotions. One should just enjoy and appreciate literature. Because the intention of literature is to create interest, as per the reader's intellect. Though literature discusses life issues, it is not same as life itself. There is a huge difference between literature and life. Yet, the reader experiences literature assuming it is life. However, these things cannot be experienced in real life. The author awakens the reader's emotions first. Ideally, the one who works hard should get the pleasure, but in case of literature the author works hard and the reader gets the pleasure. God has created the life in such a way that everyone has to work hard.

It is a myth that literature gives meaning to life. It is an art to paint life, so one should not get intoxicated by literature. The techniques to live life and to create literature are totally different. An incidence in literature can turn out to be immortal, but in reality, after living an entire life nothing can be immortal. Hence, we should learn to come out of the intoxication of literature and look at life. Otherwise one drifts away from real life. Normally people differentiate between philosophy and real life. They mistake philosophy as something meant for intelligent people and to be studied when one is old.

Philosophy is a part of thoughts, and thoughts are born out of human need—so philosophy is also a part of human life. Even if philosophy is born out of daily human need, it is as per the requirement of that particular time.

Science is created to tell us about the 'how' and 'why' of things. Answering the question 'how' is an art. Many sciences attempt to describe the 'how'. But answer to the question 'why' is called philosophy. All the questions in human life may not be solved by thinking, hence combining experience with logic, i.e., adopting a scientific attitude, works well. Logic gives meaning to experience. The importance of logic is proven by experience. Nobody is satisfied with a principle which cannot be adapted. Human life and philosophy progress hand in hand. And it should be so.

Role of Philosophy in Life

Modern rationalist Kant tried to combine human life with ethics but he realized this could not be done by common rationalism so he supported theory of pure rationalism. But he could not successfully explain this. At the beginning of the mechanical age, philosophers like Kant and Karl Marx promoted thinking that matched the modern mechanical age. They tried creating a culture as per the times. So 'Survival of the Fittest' was their belief. Whereas Herbert Spencer, through the theorem of 'Struggle for Existence' represented the struggles one had to face to survive. Absolutism or Spinoza's Neutralism appeared to be showing non-dualism between inert and consciousness. But there was no clear distinction between the individual and the complex.

In religious China, Confucius warned the rulers not to trust the divine powers or miracles, or it would lead to disaster. In short, he meant, a person can be made individually or socially well cultured or well behaved by teaching him. He also can be made ethically perfect by making him virtuous. One should not worry for one's life whilst making humankind virtuous to take care of ethical values. Original thoughts of this philosopher are: human being are teachable, improvable and perfectible through personal and communal endeavour, especially including self-cultivation and self-creation. A main idea of Confucianism is the cultivation of virtue and the development of moral perfection. Confucianism holds that one should give up one's life, if necessary, either passively or actively, for the sake of upholding the cardinal moral values of Ren (humanity) and Yi (righteousness).

This interpretation shows that by thinking only in an objective one-sided way, one can progress and success metaphysically, but one is deprived of the satisfaction arising out of spirituality. Any one-sided thinking leads to deterioration and to remove that, a holistic thinking philosophy is required. Indian philosophy has progressed uniformly from Upanishadic times to the thirteenth century. After that the literature of the saints spread all over India in Prakrit, the language of the common man. This literature describes the importance of ancient thinking; the saints did not add to the philosophy but they successfully managed to keep society alive by taking care of the ancient knowledge.

Every individual experiences his or her own independent existence. This experience is possible because it is given to them by society and the person's own behaviour and his or her expertise in a chosen specialty is what brings them respect. Through the relations of such individuals and society, is the respect of individual life and progress of society made possible. The ancient Indian term for this is Dharma and modern term is culture.

The result of political captivity of India was that the life expectancy of Indians was greatly reduced and, in many cases, lost. To bring it back to normalcy, Dr Parnerkar studied many Eastern and Western books scientifically, experimented practically and then presented this thesis of the vitalist philosophy of Poornavad in Sanskrit, at the Spiritual University which is the oldest university in Varanasi, and was awarded a doctorate in 1948. One important aspect of Poornavad is that it artistically brings together the reality of literature and truth in philosophy. Poornavad is inspired by the literature of the saints as Dr Parnerkar studied the Vedas in detail.

The responsibility of any new philosophy is that it has to clear any misunderstandings that are already present.

Indian Philosophy at the Dawn of Poornavad

Indian philosophy has two main streams of thought: the Poorva Mimamsa and the Uttar Mimamsa. Poorva Mimamsa is Maharshi Jaimini's just representation of Indian thought and is the first philosophy which is action-oriented. Gautam Buddha's philosophy, which predated Jamini's by a few hundred years, had given relief and peace to humans, but had also brought with it turbulence—what was there to live for? What was one to look forward to? Buddhism emphasized that everything was impermanent, transient and that all desires brought only sorrow and suffering. For the not-so-spiritual, it even brought depression in its wake.

About seven to nine-hundred-years after Budhha, came Shri Shankaracharya, who applied his logic that 'nothing can come out of nothing' to prove the fact that 'I am today because I was before', i.e., 'because I was, so I am, and so I will be'. Just as existence cannot come out of non-existence, non-existence cannot arise out of existence. Shankarachrya proved the immortal existence of soul. He showed his belief in God through his conduct, but in thoughts accepted that the existence of God was not known. This disparity of thought and conduct angered the Vaishnavacharyas (Vaishnava teachers). Shri Shankaracharya could successfully refute non-Vedic beliefs and conduct, but could not promote Vedic beliefs. Later the Vaishnavacharyas did this work. Conditions make one think, so any thoughts are as per as the requirement of the time.

The Poornavad philosophy falls under Uttar Mimamsa. Poorva and Uttar Mimamsa together form the complete thinking of Indian philosophy. This thinking is nourishing for individuals as well as society. It should be considered God's wish that Poornavad was approved by thinkers in 1948, just a year after India got Independence.

Poornavad doesn't follow the method of refutation and promotion. It follows the method of subjectivity and objectivity. Vedas are non-humans i.e. universal thought, i.e., not created by any human intellect and have been passed down as Shruti (directly heard) and Smriti (passed down by memory or tradition). And the doctrine of Poornavad is based on them.

The focus of Indian or Eastern philosophy is primarily on the unmanifest, whereas the focus of science and Western philosophy is on the manifest, which teaches us to live in the objective manner. But the reality of human life is not single-dimensional, subjectivity and expression also go hand-in-hand along with objectivity. Because of objectivity we get pleasures of life. But the satisfaction we derive from them depends on the subjectivity; and a happy life is an expression of this satisfaction.

Poornavad gives six steps known as the Shadang Sadhanas. They are: (i) skillfulness, (ii) connectivity, (iii) gathering people, (iv) opinions of people, (v) time and (6) worship. Vyahriti means changing the impractical to practical. It is changing the unmanifest to manifest and unknown to known. This means it is changing feelings to reality.

The doctrine of 'Poorna Purusha' as expressed by Dr Ramchandra Maharaj Parnerkar in his book on Poornavad, is in the Vedas as: (i) spiritual, (ii) material and (iii) supernatural. Although the Poorvacharyas thought of spirituality and supernatural is jada [jada is material aspect]. The Vedantian philosophers and the rest of the contemporary world philosophers consider spiritual and divine aspect and ignored material aspect, which is the reality and necessity]. Although Poornavad is an Indian philosophy, its speciality is to assert the Truth of the Root.

Dr Parnerkar has suggested pious behaviour to keep the condition responsible for success or failure, stable. To turn your destiny favourable, he suggests regular worship. Also, instead of worrying about how people behave or how they should behave, one has to do whatever is in one's hands to do. Running our family life decently is like serving society. This genuine behaviour could save three generations of the family. Honest behaviour gives shine to the earlier generation, which in turn keeps the present generation content and strengthens the next generation.

Poornavad or the Completeness Theory is one which brings the Western philosophy of just enjoyment in life, and the restraining philosophy of the East together and then propagates the completeness. This book introduces this theory. The perusal of this book will dissipate the fear in mind and once the fear is gone, one can experience the completeness of life.

Science of the Supernatural

Life should aim at bringing a culture and civilization together. Why does the common man become vulnerable and turn to God and religious teachings? The answer of this is available in an ancient literature on supernatural science. As people pursued prosperity through the rationalism of science, they encountered heightened vulnerability, leading them to turn to God and religion. The foremost duty of a believer is to cultivate theism in the world. A theist's failure in life reflects poorly on God. One who is satisfied with whatever God has given becomes eligible to receive God's grace.

State of Being Fearless

His Holiness Dr Parnerkar asks devotees to worship God faithfully. He says God is with you because He is highly gracious. He also says that having a firm belief that 'I pray to God every day, hence he will never turn me away,' is a state of being fearless. Acquiring this state of fearlessness would be the first fruit of worship. This state of one's being is a pure essence of spirituality. One should pray to God for oneself. One who has the full grace of God will never feel vulnerable in life.

Manifestation of Reality

The book titled *Sangharsh: The Conflict is* all about the manifestation of reality. Failure comes when there is no knowledge of reality.[1] This scripture is like Lord Krishna and the role of the scholar should be like that of Partha or Arjun. The book not only narrates the condition of a failed man but also explains the ways to overcome the failure.

From birth onwards a man is dependent on others for a long time. His unquenchable desire to live life spontaneously keeps going on. One can't live unintentionally, but it seems to be the reality. One wish comes true and another comes to mind. Man thinks only from his own perspective, but in reality there is much more than what he thinks. To live life, if there is no aim in life, means one is living just because death also far away and this leads to vulnerability. Such a man, whether he is involved in political, social, religious or other activities in life, he gets bored because of an urge for easy fulfilment of desires. This leads one to think that all his desires remained unfulfilled and this makes him upset. Ignoring such a person, thinking that he only thinks of his life gives scope for his sense of failure. This was discussed by Indian philosophers but it was on a superficial level.

---

1 Sangharsh (The Conflict) by Dr R. P. Parnerkar.

It is not advisable to nurture a wish to lead a spontaneous life when one should struggle to know their real purpose of life. To keep such desire indicates a weak state of mind. This entire subject is related to the study of mind. It's like; one feels hungry inside, while the food to fulfil this hunger is available outside i.e. in the nature. Hence, efforts are required where one cannot live spontaneously. Every creature that comes in this world is saved by others. But when one becomes able, one has to obtain the necessities of life for oneself Civilization and culture were born out of the effort to make this journey easier. But with this human discovery, life became easier but then he had to compromise on his spontaneity.

This book is not about the struggle mentioned by Herbert Spencer's 'Struggle to Existence' philosophy. It is about man's own struggle with a manmade civilization that has become a hindrance in his desire to live life freely. In the course of time, human beings have become dominant but their independence is gone. An obligation is laid down to follow the rules of society. In some societies this has led to the feeling of helplessness in the minds of the people as they have been weakened by the power their society wields over them. As a result, such social systems have deprived man of his personal happiness.

Struggle as Part of Life

Many distortions are born in society by not considering considering the happiness and sorrow of individuals. This is extremely dangerous for the overall well-being of the society. The desire to get freedom is the mother of all struggles. If one realizes this, one will easily embrace struggle as a part of living. Conflict is not a belligerent attitude; when, what a person thinks does not happen, conflict begins. Where conflict begins, that is where the struggle begins. It is not possible to turn our backs to the world and no matter how much we try to avoid it, the conflict will not go away. Conflict is an eternal part of our existence because it is self-created. But man considers it impermanent. Conflict is seen as part of temporal reality, so time is called its mirror. Look at some thoughts presented by His Holiness Dr Parnerkar in his book *Sangharsh: The Conflict*:

1. Considering the reality, life is an endeavour, but the unquenchable desire to live life spontaneously resides in man.
2. Acceptance of struggle itself, is the freedom from struggle.
3. Man keeps asking for peace to get rid of struggle; in reality, peace is the shadow of conflict.
4. There are two forms of struggle, one expressed and the other unexpressed. The first evidently realizable, while the second is inexplicably present in everyone's life. Although the expressed struggle is fierce, it is conciliatory, but even if the unexpressed struggle might appear soft, its nature is fierce. Lust for intense survival is the tendency to struggle.

Realization of Reality

His Holiness Dr Parnerkar has written the benefits of studying this book. The one who reads *Sangharsh* with a studious attitude, will have a realization of reality, and the one who reads it with faith and zeal and tries his best to reap the rewards, will get the fruits of his worship. Dr Parnekar expresses the feeling of success that I have achieved by writing this book. There are twenty-one innovative verses in all, that begin with poetic illustration of success, using struggle of life as their subject. The verses include twenty-eight 'Aryas', poetic prayers, those Sanskrit shlokas that you can sing. Through these Aryas, life has been studied in the form of questions and answers. These verses, designed to teach perfectionism to the common man, also teach how to deal with conflict in life. The welfare of the disciple is the soul of these verses by the Guru. One should study these verses with pure devotion. Unlike verses written by saints that express their experiences, these verses by the Guru, reflects a longing for the well-being of the disciples. These verses are timeless.

The focal point of these verses is human life. Dr Parnerkar, himself a philosopher, thinks about life just like a common man with pure devotion. Absolute philosophy is expressed in these verses. By reading these verses one feels purity of thought that leads one to think in a broader way, thereby, leading towards the attainment of a balanced physical, mental/intellectual, and spiritual self. These verses include supernatural, physical and spiritual subjects, through which truth and reality are manifested.

Those who sing and listen to verses of other saints are awakened by devotion and their eyes automatically close by going for a momentary or long 'bhavsamadhi' (primary stage of deep meditation). But by reading or singing these innovative verses written by Guru Parnerkar, man realizes the aim of his existence and truly moves towards the state of awakening. He gains a positive outlook towards life.

Only the Guru can dispel the ignorance of his disciple. Each subject in His Holiness Dr Parnerkar's book can be the subject of a dissertation. The book teaches that struggle is the study of time, and constant renewal is its special quality. The innovative verses help to teach the philosophy of perfectionism in a material way through spirituality. These verses teach the meaning of our struggle for existence in a material environment. Problems of individual life and their solutions are also found in these verses. The verses also touch upon issues in social life, national and global issues and their solutions. By embracing the virtue of surrendering to God through worship, one should experience happiness in this life.

Guru-Shishya Tradition

Let us briefly discuss the special relationship in the Indian tradition—the guru-shishya parampara (the mentor-disciple tradition) with reference to the subject of philosophy. One such great mentor-disciple pair was Ramakrishna Paramahansa and Swami Vivekananda. The British had designed a system of education for Indians with the intention of enslaving their minds and intellects. Those Indians who sought government jobs, started adopting the system without paying much heed; they saw only the pros and not the cons.

But, when the self is forgotten, a state of confusion is created, and religion and Dharma lose their position. God incarnates when Dharma is afflicted, so says the Bhagavad Gita. In this context, Ramakrishna Paramahansa is also called 'Yugavatar', an incarnation of God sent down for a particular epoch. Ramakrishna Paramahansa himself was an avid devotee of Devi Jagdamba or Goddess Durga and Kali. Through devotion, he became one with the Goddess such that he did not want to feel his duality. Such a devotee received sannyasa initiation from a Vedanti Guru.

It was very difficult for a worshipper of form, a 'sagunabhakta' of the Goddess to practice Vedanta that was the path of knowledge. But it was only by her grace that he was able to do that sadhana. Though his Guru was a man of knowledge and never emphasized religious sense of devotion in his teaching, disciple Ramakrishna Paramahansa used to share his beliefs and experiences without arguing with his Guru.

In order to understand both forms of beliefs, Ramakrishna studied the path of devotion and the path of knowledge, i.e. Vedanta. Thereafter, he consciously nurtured his disciple Swami Vivekananda, because it was through Vivekananda that he wanted to take ahead his intended work for the welfare of all mankind. Swami Vivekananda, being a physician of intellect, would not do anything without being fully convinced himself. Before accepting Ramakrishna Paramahansa as a Guru, Vivekananda tested his Guru in various ways. His Holiness Dr Parnerkar always used to say that just as it is better to filter water before drinking, likewise make someone your mentor only after proper testing.

At the age of eighteen, Vivekananda made a comparative study of Eastern and Western philosophy. It was Vedanta itself. He did not believe in idol worship. He even did not believe Ramakrishna's God's manifestations. But he got the opportunity to stay for five years in the presence of his Guru, who was the iconic symbol of devotion. Due to the Guru's companionship and the hard work done by the Guru, a radical change took place in Vivekananda's life and he became a perfect disciple as expected by his Guru. Going through a dedicated, disciplined period of hardship is necessary to realize meaningfulness of one's existence. Also, life cannot develop without knowing both joy and sorrow.

At the World's Parliament of Religions held in 1893 in Chicago, Swami Vivekananda was present as the representative of Indian Sanatan Vedic Dharma. Any great work can be achieved through unity and organization. This was acutely felt by Swami Vivekananda. Influenced by the organizational power of the Western world he started the Ramakrishna Mission by bringing together ascetics and householders to expand the work of nation-building. The progress of any country depends on the progress of the common man. Therefore, the organization works to lead them towards progress by educating them in this regard.

Ramakrishna Paramahansa himself was driven by devotion, while his guru was a Vedanti or follower of knowledge and later his disciple, Swami Vivekananda, too, was a Vedanti or a knowledge-seeker. Without any clash of opinions, these Gurus and Shishyas dedicated their lives for the betterment of society. These two great personalities from Indian history— Ramakrishna Paramahansa and Swami Vivekananda—became the best example of Guru-Shishya relationship in the modern age.

Concluding Lines

Our universe is a three-dimensional universe and in line with that, we must also approach life through a three-dimensional manner. Only two dimensions of life—the metaphysical and the material—are prioritized generally. Poornavad philosophy defines the importance of the third dimension, in addition to meta—the divine aspect of life, and brings to attention the importance of balancing all three dimensions of life: Metaphysical, Material and Divine. These three are the Trinity of our life, and those who manage to balance all three, are said to have mastered the Trinity of life.

However, in this modern and dynamic world, it is difficult to spare too much time for devotion or *bhakti* or longer forms of achieving this balance. To combat that, Poornavad philosophy developed the Upasna method, as discussed earlier, through careful experimentation, and has suggested other practical ways to achieve a harmonic and holistic balance for one living in the 21st century, based on the Indian vedic system.

Through this Poornavad philosophy—a modern approach to the traditional Indian vedic system—the universe can be in one's grasp, and can align to help people achieve their dream, goals and wishes.

Acknowledgements

THREE GREAT authors inspired me to write this book. Two were authors of books given to me by my Master, Dr Vishnu Ramchandra Parnerkar: *The Tao of Physics* by Fritjof Capra, and Roger Penrose's *A Road to Reality*. The third was *Being Different* by Rajiv Malhotra, that I gave to my Master.

Authorities of the Poornavad school of thought—Adv. Gunesh Parnerkar, and Dr P. Kant.

My academic ideals—Prof. S. Panneerselvam of Madras University, Prof. R.C. Sinha, Chairman Indian Council of Philosophical Research; H.R. Kulkarni (rtd I.A.S.); Prof. Ambika Datt Sharma, Sagar University; Prof. S.G. Ingle, Sir Vishweshwaraiya Engineering College, Nagpur.

My colleagues in India—Mr S.S. Aboti, Prof. Sharad Paralkar, Prof. Guljar Singh Rajpur, Prof. P.H. Dharamsi, Prof. R.V. Wattamwar, Mr Shrikant Rangnekar, Mr Vinayakrao Joshi, Mr Pushkar Agashe, Mr Avinash Diwalkar.

My colleagues in USA—Mr Madhav Apte, Mr Arun Koparkar, Ms Geetanjali and Mr Milind, Mantry, Ms Revati, Ms Arna, Mr Prasad and Ms Deepti Inamdar, Mr Rajat Dashrath and Mr Shantanu Mantry. All of them have given their heartiest cooperation and rendered their services.

My close family members—Gangadhar Deshpande, Geeta and Hemant Dashrath, Yogesh Dashrath, Shampa and Tushar Joshi, Adv. Uttamrao and Pramilatai Dashrath, Padmakarrao and Mandatai

Joshi, Dr Anand and Mandvi, Mahima, Ishita, Trisha, Riya, Rajat, Onkar, S.P. Jamkar and Manisha Jamkar, and Rangnath Jamkar. A special mention to my grandchildren—Rajat Dashrath and Riya Dashrath—who have helped me tremendously to add final touches to this book.

I thank you all.